Your Britain

YOUR BRITAIN

*Media and the Making of the
Labour Party*

LAURA BEERS

Harvard University Press
Cambridge, Massachusetts, and London, England   *2010*

Library of Congress Cataloging-in-Publication Data

Beers, Laura, 1978–
    Your Britain : media and the making of the Labour Party / Laura Beers.
        p.   cm.
    Includes bibliographical references and index.
    ISBN 978-0-674-05002-0 (alk. paper)
1. Labour Party (Great Britain)—History—20th century.   2. Mass media—
Political aspects—Great Britain.   3. Mass media—Great Britain—History—20th
century.   4. Great Britain—Politics and government—History—20th century.
I. Title.
    JN1129.L32B48 2010
    324.24107—dc22   2009044458

To DMB, DOB, and LB

Contents

Acknowledgments   *ix*

Introduction   *1*

1   The Rise of a Mass Media Culture   *11*

2   Speaking to the People   *27*

3   The Anti-Labour Turn   *50*

4   Changing Attitudes in the 1920s   *68*

5   The Labour Alternative   *83*

6   Battling for Public Opinion   *99*

7   Rapprochement with the Media   *116*

8   Experimenting in the 1930s   *139*

9   Election Victory   *165*

10   Impacts and Influences   *186*

Conclusion   *199*

Archives Consulted   *207*
Notes   *209*
Index   *255*

Acknowledgments

This book was written (and rewritten) over several years in two Cambridges and the one and only London, and over the course of its writing I've incurred many debts on both sides of the Atlantic. First and foremost, Susan Pedersen and Charles Maier were present at the creation, and gave me invaluable advice and support at every step of the way. Jon Lawrence and Niall Ferguson have also proved unfailing as both advisors and editors. Versions of the manuscript were also read, in whole or in part, by David Cannadine, Nina Fishman, Peter Mandler, Ross McKibbin, and Philip Williamson, by my editor at Harvard University Press, Kathleen McDermott, and by Harvard University Press's two peer reviewers, and the final product has benefited substantially from their input.

I would like to thank the Center for European Studies at Harvard, the trustees of the John Clive Memorial Fund, the History Department of Warwick University, the Institute of Historical Research (IHR) in London, the Economic and Social Research Council of Great Britain, and the Fellows of Newnham College, Cambridge, for providing me with research funding without which this project could not have been completed. Grants from these institutions gave me time to devote to writing, and allowed me to spend countless months at the National Archives, the British Newspaper Library at Colindale, the BBC Written Archive Centre, the Labour and Conservative Party archives, the Trades Union Congress Library, the Modern Records Centre (MRC), and the London School of Economics archives. The archive staff at all of these institutions, and particularly Richard Temple, then at the MRC, proved invariably helpful. Further, Warwick University, the IHR, Newnham College, and in particular the

Center for European Studies, all went beyond simply funding my research. Each institution provided an intellectual and collegial environment in which this project was able to thrive.

I had the opportunity to present portions of this project at several conferences and seminars, and I appreciate the valuable feedback that I received from my colleagues at these fora, including Ed Baring, David Blackbourn, Jim Cronin, James Curran, Steve Fielding, Margot Finn, Fred Leventhal, Mary Lewis, Kris Manjapra, Sian Nicholas, Sharrona Pearl, Jean Seaton, Caroline Shaw, Penny Sinanoglu, Judith Surkis, Duncan Tanner, Pat Thane, James Thompson, Andrew Thorpe, Daniel Ussishkin, James Vernon, and Juliet Wagner. Chris Hilliard, Helen McCarthy, and Glen O'Hara, in particular, combined the roles of friend and colleague in ways which have earned them my eternal gratitude.

Finally, the process of producing a book is not just about research and writing, and I would like to thank Rebecca Green, Will Phelan, Katie Pickett, Leah Platt, Tristan Snell, and Annie Stilz, who were all then in Cambridge, Massachusetts, Branwyn Polykett in London, and Barbara Koenczoel in Cambridge, England, for their friendship and their comparative lack of interest in British political history. My deepest gratitude is reserved for the three people to whom this book is dedicated. Firstly, to my parents, whose love and unshakeable faith in me has sustained me through the course of this project. And, finally, to Lawrence, who is literally and metaphorically the last footnote of this book.

Your Britain

Introduction

I N 1906, the Labour Representation Committee (LRC), the forerunner of the modern Labour Party, ran fifty candidates in an election campaign that was not only local, but localized—fifteen of the candidates ran in Lancashire, fourteen in Yorkshire and the northeast, and another four in Scotland. While the fifty candidates all ran under the Labour banner, their campaigns were essentially small affairs, run principally by local trade union branches and trades councils. The Labour candidates received just over 250,000 votes out of a total of 5.2 million cast nationally, and successfully elected twenty-nine members to Parliament. The main contribution of the national Labour leadership was the distribution of posters such as "His Own," which depicted a Labour dog guarding the bone of "industrial constituencies" from his fellow hounds, and of party leaflets appealing to electors "in the name of a million trade unionists."[1]

In 1945, in contrast, the Labour Party fielded a nearly full slate of candidates throughout Britain, received almost half of all votes cast, and elected 393 members to the House of Commons, giving it an absolute majority in that Parliament. The party's supporters included not only male trade unionists, but also millions of women, enfranchised as a result of the 1918 and 1928 electoral reforms, and a significant proportion of members of the lower-middle and professional classes.[2] The victory was the culmination of an election campaign that had reflected a degree of professionalization hitherto unknown to British politics.[3] Labour's 1945 campaign was distinguished by the large number of "experts" that the party brought in. An army of commercial illustrators, printers, journalists, and campaign strategists were recruited to advise on a campaign which included the distribution of fifty-five thousand large-scale color posters, two million pictorial magazines, and over a million copies of the *British Elector,* the "election special" newssheet produced by party headquarters. Furthermore, more than thirteen million civilians heard Labour's leaders broadcast their party's message over the British Broadcasting Corporation (BBC).[4]

The story of British politics in the twentieth century is the story of mass parties and their relationship to the democratic public. In the forty-five years following its formation, the Labour Party evolved from a working-class interest group into an organization that claimed to be "the one party which most nearly reflects in its representation and composition all the main streams which flow into the great river of our national life."[5] By 1945, the party was also at ease with mass communication and the role of the mass media in modern politics. Its leadership accepted that the popular press, the BBC, and cinema newsreels were increasingly central to political communication, and that publicists and commercial advisors could play a valuable role in crafting a political party's appeal through these and other media. These two developments—of the Labour Party's evolution into a national party, and a party comfortable with new modes of mass communication—were intimately related. Historians have emphasized the changes within the Conservative Party's political culture in the interwar period, and in particular that party's use of the press, broadcast media, and film to refashion itself, not as the party of privilege, but as the embodiment of "English" values and the guardian of the British people.[6] The 1920s and 1930s also witnessed equally, if not more, dramatic changes to the Labour Party's self-conception and self-presentation, changes that were crucial to its political success in 1945, but which have hitherto received little attention.[7]

Labour's rise to power has traditionally been explained either in terms of the advent of a self-conscious working-class politics, or in terms of the decline (or implosion) of the Liberal Party, which opened a space on the left of the political spectrum.[8] Several scholars have stressed the transformative social experience of the Second World War in creating a national constituency around social reform and regeneration and thus laying the groundwork for the 1945 Labour victory.[9] Still others have focused on the work of local activists, implying, if not explicitly stating, that Labour's national rise should be best understood as an amalgamation of myriad local efforts.[10] While these factors may have provided an opportunity for Labour, they are ultimately insufficient to explain the party's rapid rise between 1900 and 1945. Any comprehensive explanation must take into account how the national party organization capitalized on the structural

Figure I.1. Labour Party appeal to working-class voters, 1903. (© Labour Party. Courtesy of People's History Museum, Manchester)

Figure I.2.   Labour Party election poster by Philip Zec personifying Labour's appeal as the party of the nation and the troops, 1945. (© Labour Party. Courtesy of the People's History Museum, Manchester)

and cultural changes wrought by the First World War. Labour's use of the mass media to project an image slated to win over a broad, diverse coalition of supporters was crucial to the party's rise to power. Here, the national leadership played a pivotal role in shaping public perceptions of Labour at both the local and national level.

The New Left political scientist Ralph Miliband and others have argued that the influence of the national party leadership was at best negligible and at worst malign.[11] However, the interaction between the national party and the democratic public in the interwar period was often productive. This book shines a spotlight on the efforts of the national Labour leadership to communicate with the mass electorate of the post-1918 era and to persuade those men and women of the merits of voting Labour, underscoring the importance of the national media of political communication to our understanding of modern political history. While some will doubtless read its focus on national publicity and the national media as dismissive of the role played by social forces, local activists, or contingent moments such as the two world wars, this is certainly not the case; rather, such explanations *alone* are inadequate to explain Labour's rise.

The shift in Labour's conception of British politics and society and its implications for the party's attitude toward the mass media were intimately tied up with changes to British political and cultural life in the early twentieth century. The franchise expansions of 1918 and 1928 more than quadrupled the electorate, and introduced mass democracy to Britain. This process of democratization occurred at the same time that changes in technology and the social organization of culture meant that Britons were increasingly united around a common culture of sports, newspapers, radio, cinema, and consumer goods—a culture that increasingly took its cues from London, and from America. While common cultural pursuits did not break down existing barriers of class and place, they did tend to blur these distinctions, and to create what could be considered a mass public.[12]

It is impossible to identify the Labour Party attitude toward this new democratic public, as the Labour Party was an uneasy coalition of socialists, trade unionists, and Fabian planners whose views of the British public were all inflected by their personal and ideological understandings of British society. Certain leaders of the party, such as Herbert Morrison, Sidney Webb, and Ellen Wilkinson, harbored an instinctive appreciation for the varied interests of the British electorate and the need to appeal to voters, not solely on the basis of class solidarity or social conscience, but through a concrete engagement with issues such as employment, home-ownership, and consumption that impacted voters' daily lives. Such men and women were early advocates for embracing mediated politics, viewing the mass media as a crucial vehicle of political communication in an era of mass democracy.

Other party leaders, however, held significant reservations both about the legitimacy of using so-called capitalist commercial methods to convert voters to socialism and about the moral and intellectual capacities of the new electorate—particularly the female electorate. Many men and women had entered Labour politics with the ambition of patiently educating citizens in the merits of socialism and winning converts to the cause. For them, that the party should (as they perceived it) privilege winning votes over changing minds, and that it should make use of the supposedly cheap expedients of headline journalism and sound-bite politics to do so, seemed a betrayal. So too did certain leaders' emphasis on the need to appeal to voters outside of the party's traditional base and to present Labour not as a class, but as a national party.[13]

In the decade after the First World War these two tendencies vied for ascendancy within the party leadership, and, for a brief period in the mid-1920s, those who opposed making use of the mass media to broaden

Labour's appeal won the upper hand. However, experiences such as the 1924 Red Scare election campaign and especially the defeat of the 1926 general strike pushed many within the party leadership to reassess the risks of failing to engage their political opponents with all available weapons. Over the final years of the 1920s, the Labour Party came to embrace both the perceived wisdom of a national political appeal and the imperative to make use of the new mass media to popularize that appeal. This acceptance did not reflect a cynical rejection of the need properly to educate voters on the benefits of socialism. Nor did it reflect a decision by the Labour leadership merely to mimic the "capitalist" commercial techniques of their Conservative opponents. Instead, the Labour Party pioneered a new form of mediated politics that continued to emphasize political education while simultaneously showing a sophisticated appreciation for new developments in mass communication and in advertising and marketing psychology. This strategy was epitomized in the overhaul of the party-owned mass circulation newspaper the *Daily Herald,* and was also visible in the party literature produced in the 1930s and in the targeted appeals of the party's election broadcasts from 1929 onwards.

The 1930s were a crucial period in Labour's political development, throughout which the party laid the national groundwork on which it would successfully build during the war. Labour's shift toward a more broad-based and inclusive politics in the 1920s has been interpreted as the triumph of "MacDonaldism," with the implication that when Ramsay MacDonald abandoned the Labour Party in 1931, the party abandoned its commitment to a national political strategy.[14] It is true that MacDonald, the leader of the Labour Party from 1922 to 1931 and the country's first Labour prime minister, embraced an expansive vision for the party long before many of his colleagues. But, while many on the left of the Labour movement, and many more within the Communist party, saw the 1930s in terms of class politics, the post-1931 party leadership remained broadly united in a determination to win over the center ground and gain power as a majority government elected by a broad coalition of the British voters.[15] The party also remained committed to the use of the mass media to communicate this agenda to the public.

This book integrates political and cultural history to revise our understanding of interwar Britain. In its focus on the importance of political language and presentation in forging Labour's public identity and broadening the party's constituency, it contributes to the growing body of "new political history" that has highlighted the role of language and rhetoric in building a bridge between high and popular politics.[16] Party literature, political journalism, public speeches, and radio broadcasts all illuminate the Labour Party's efforts to reframe the political discourse around the importance of social welfare, community, and equal opportunity.

The historian Ross McKibbin has described the Conservative Party's predominance in the 1920s as based "not on economic self-interest but on ideologically determined class-stereotypes and conventional wisdoms." Britain's "constitutional classes," he contends, rallied around Conservatism despite the adverse impact on many of its supporters of the deflationary economic policies that the party advocated because they saw Labour as the party of the manual working classes and held deep-rooted prejudices against manual labourers as "sectional, collectivist, and masculine," "greedy," and "full of malevolence."[17] Over the past two decades, McKibbin's argument, or at least his conclusion that interwar voters came to identify Conservatism with the "public" or "national" interest, has become a kind of conventional wisdom of its own, seemingly substantiated by studies which have emphasized Conservative prime minister Stanley Baldwin's rhetorical appeal and his sophisticated use of the media to project that appeal to the nation.[18] But Conservative rhetoric was not constructed in a vacuum. The interwar Labour Party actively sought to turn the rhetorical tables on the Conservatives, and to make the rhetoric of the nation its own.[19]

In the late 1920s and the 1930s, the Labour Party made sophisticated use of the popular press, radio, cinema, and political advertising to project an image of itself as a truly national party representing all of the productive elements of British society. Just as the Conservatives had articulated a vision of the nation as a community of consumers, the Labour Party made use of new methods of mediated propaganda to present its own counter-vision of a nation of producers, of "workers by hand or brain." It has been suggested that, while the Conservatives embraced the more inclusive rhetoric of "the nation," Labour tended to employ the comparatively demotic and class-conscious rhetoric of "the people."[20] While this generalization may hold for the post–World War II period, in the 1920s and 1930s, at least, Labour was more likely to speak in national terms.

The Labour Party's efforts to translate its socialist program into an appeal that would resonate with the democratic public tell us much about both the party's political agenda and the way in which it perceived its public. Such insights are particularly valuable in expanding our understanding of Labour's relationship with the female electorate. Although historians have devoted significant attention to the role of women in

British politics before female enfranchisement, they have had comparatively little to say about the impact of female enfranchisement on the
conduct of politics post-1918.[21] A close analysis both of Labour's evolving rhetorical appeal to female voters and of the way in which the party
made use of the media to appeal to this new constituency reveals the central role of gender in shaping Labour's politics. From an early period, the
party developed an appeal to women as mothers and heads of households,
which presupposed a feminine sympathy with social welfare concerns
and sought to counter Conservative appeals to the financial prudence of
the "domestic chancellor of the exchequer." Such appeals had considerable success, particularly during the 1929 election. These efforts, however,
were counterbalanced by a focus, in both propaganda and policy, on the
interests of producers at the expense of consumers, a focus that served
to alienate female voters who remained largely outside of the productive
sphere.[22]

Much of the scholarship on the development of Labour politics has
focused on politics from below—the growth of Labour's grassroots.[23] In
this narrative, Labour politics developed organically, first taking hold in
Labour's "heartlands" in northeast England and Scotland, then spread-
ing to Wales, east London, and other working-class constituencies, and
finally tentatively branching out into constituencies in the West Midlands
and the southeast once perceived to be irredeemably hostile to Labour.
Such studies have highlighted the role of publicity and propaganda in
Labour's expansion, but their emphasis has been on locally produced
literature such as the *Bermondsey Labour Magazine,* identified as a crucial component of efforts to create a vibrant Labour community in South
London.[24]

Although locally produced publications undeniably formed an important aspect of Labour's publicity strategy, they were only one arm of a
policy that showed a growing reliance on the national media. While Bermondsey voters may have developed an appreciation for the achievements
of the Labour-controlled council through reading the *Bermondsey Labour Magazine,* their views about the parliamentary Labour Party, and
even to an extent their attitudes toward their local councillors, were increasingly formed through the national news media. As with council elections today, though local circumstances mattered, the fate of interwar
Labour councillors was not independent of national political developments.[25] However, instead of emphasizing the reciprocal relationship between the national and the local, studies of the national party's role in
popular politics in the interwar period have suggested either that the
party leadership at Transport House in London took its lead from local

developments, or that the leadership hindered Labour's growth by attempting to subvert activist enthusiasm and by keeping the party on a narrowly parliamentary path.[26] We need to appreciate the degree to which the national leadership offered a lead to local parties both through its construction of a positive national discourse of Labour politics and through its exploitation of the mass media to project that discourse into homes that remained inaccessible through traditional methods of local political activism.

A focus on the centrality of national media policy in forming and sustaining public opinion on politics in the interwar period is not meant to discount the importance of other forces of opinion formation. Traditional modes of political education persisted, and the interwar period has been described as the "heyday of political literature" with party leaflets outnumbering registered voters by a considerable margin.[27] Despite contemporary concerns about the decline of the platform, speechmaking remained an important component of interwar politics.[28] Both the Left and the Right ran their own subscription-based book clubs in the interwar period; organizations such as the Young Conservative Union or the Co-operative Youth League and local Labour clubs combined political education with dancing, whist drives, and "Irish Sweeps"; and ostensibly apolitical sources, such as civic organizations, novels, and children's fiction, arguably worked to reinforce political stereotypes and prejudices.[29] Although these influences on political opinion should not be discounted, it is difficult to escape the conclusion of the interwar social commentator, Norman Angell, that the popular newspapers were "the witnesses upon whose evidence, mainly, the daily judgments of civilised mankind today are based."[30]

For better or worse, the Labour Party in the interwar period came to the conclusion that the road to power ran through Westminster; that the pursuit of a parliamentary majority entailed the establishment of a broad cross-class and cross-gender base of support; and that such a base of support could not be laid on the foundations of radical revolutionary or class rhetoric. As a consequence, the party leadership committed themselves to a policy of "selling socialism," not in terms of socialist revolution or class government, but in terms of gradual social democratic reform.[31] While they refused merely to mimic the methods of their competitors, Labour's leaders embraced the mass media and the techniques of commercial advertising to put over its moderate, reforming appeal to the nation. A commitment to consensual "one nation" politics and the embrace of the mass media have continued to go hand in hand throughout Labour's history. It is not coincidental that the party leaders who have been most successful at appealing to a broad cross-section of the electorate have also been those who showed the greatest attention to the role of the mass media in democratic politics.[32] By taking seriously sources such as popular newspapers, BBC broadcasts, cinema newsreels, posters, and party magazines, we can gain a better understanding of the central importance of Labour's relationship with the mass media and the democratic public, not only in the interwar period, but throughout its history.

CHAPTER ONE

The Rise of a Mass Media Culture

O N 6 NOVEMBER 1935, Herbert Morrison, the leader of the London County Council (LCC) and former minister of transport, delivered the Labour Party's final radio broadcast before the general election on 14 November. Born in Brixton in 1888, the son of a police constable and a domestic servant, he had risen through the ranks of the Independent Labour Party to become one of the most prominent men not only in London, but in national politics.[1] Though a skilled politician, Morrison, like his grandson Peter Mandelson, was fundamentally a political strategist, and Labour's victory in the 1934 LCC elections owed much to his organizational capabilities. The broad mix of peoples and socioeconomic classes in London meant that he had had to design an electoral campaign that would appeal across economic, professional, cultural, and gender divides. A year and a half later, he was keen to apply the same strategy in the national arena, and the National Executive Committee (NEC) had such faith in his appeal that they allotted him one of Labour's four broadcasts, despite the fact that he had lost his parliamentary seat in 1931 and had not been a member of the 1931–1935 Parliament.

Morrison's speech was broadcast on the BBC's national and regional programs and was heard by an estimated 40 percent of the population, including nearly a third of middle-class electors.[2] He used the occasion to stress the achievements of the London Labour government and the potential for Labour to make similar strides on a national level. "The nation," he claimed, "must now decide between Tory negation and the positive and constructive policy of the modern Labour Party." He concluded with an appeal to all Britons, regardless of class or gender: "The working and middle classes love their country with love that is real and enduring. Their patriotism is the patriotism of service and not that of possession. . . . That is the patriotism of the Labour Party."[3]

The broadcast exemplifies the changes that had taken place in British politics over the previous half century. In less than fifty years, British politics had been transformed from an elite club composed of and representative of a narrow stratum of property-owning men into a mass democracy. By 1935, nearly all men and women over the age of twenty-one were eligible to elect a parliament that, while still dominated by middle-class men, included a growing contingent of working-class and female representatives. Nine women were elected to Parliament in 1935, and, by the end of the 1935 parliament, there were 90 Labour members of Parliament (MPs) classified as either trade union or ex-trade union secretaries, or members of the manual working class.[4] The rapid expansion of the electorate—the number of Britons eligible to vote quadrupled between 1884 and 1928—had occasioned a profound shift in the issues and emphases of party politics. The two traditional parties, the Liberals and the Conservatives, responded to working-class enfranchisement with an increased emphasis on social legislation.[5] This political reorientation was encouraged by the creation of the Labour Representation Committee (LRC) in February 1900, which proclaimed itself the defender of working-class interests in Parliament. The partial enfranchisement of women in 1918 and the subsequent granting of the vote to women on equal terms with men in 1928 put pressure on all three parties to adapt their politics to appeal to these new electors, who outnumbered men in four out of five interwar constituencies.[6]

The arrival of mass democracy altered not only the content, but also the conduct of British politics. Whereas Victorian politics had relied much more heavily on public participatory encounters, twentieth-century politics was an increasingly impersonal affair, with electors "meeting" their representatives via the pages of their morning paper, ministerial and party political broadcasts, and cinema newsreels. Traditional methods of political communication—public meetings, rallies, and educational propaganda—did not disappear from British politics after the First World War, but they were increasingly inadequate in a political world where the average number of electors in a constituency had risen from around ten thousand to fifty thousand. In such a context, the outcome of election contests, particularly the three-cornered contests that characterized the 1920s, might be determined by a small number of *floating voters* (a term first coined in the 1930s) who could not be guaranteed to engage with traditional forms of public political debate.[7]

National newspaper circulations grew rapidly in the first decades of the twentieth century; by 1939, the circulation of the major London daily papers was over 10.5 million, and the average Londoner read 1.25 morning papers.[8] The expansion of national newspaper readership was coupled with a consolidation of ownership and a decline of readership of the regional and local press, with the result that voters from Yorkshire to the Midlands increasingly took their news from London. Radio ownership also grew exponentially in the two decades after the formation of the BBC in October 1922. Cinema attendance similarly boomed. The growing importance of marketing and advertising changed the way in which consumers (and increasingly voters) were conceptualized, understood, and addressed.[9]

These changes were, of course, not limited to Britain. What became known as the "Northcliffe Revolution" in the style and content of the daily press was similar to developments within the Hearst and Pulitzer newspaper chains in the United States, or the French evening paper *Paris-Soir,* or *L'Ami du Peuple,* which Orwell famously described as seeking, "by hook or by crook," to outsell its competition and "strangle free speech in France," and not worth the cut-rate cost of ten centimes which its proprietors charged for it.[10] But while part of a wider international cultural revolution, the consequences of these changes were more acutely felt in Britain due to the unparalleled importance of London in the nation's cultural and political life. The development of the mass media helped drive a renegotiation of the relationship between political parties and the public after the First World War, with the media playing a significantly larger role in political communication.

Morrison was particularly well suited to this new style of mass politics. He instinctively conceptualized the British public in terms of demographics—trade unionists, clerks, secretaries and other "black-coated" workers, housewives, middle-class suburbanites—and his political appeals were constructed to reach across social and cultural divides and unite these disparate interests.[11] Morrison's speeches, propaganda literature, and broadcasts were littered with words such as "nation," "patriotism," "constructive," and "modern." The London leader was comfortable with the new modes of political communication, and particularly with visual propaganda and broadcasting. He appreciated the value of well-produced publicity, and would, according to one BBC producer, go to "any amount of trouble" to get his broadcasts just right.[12] In this sense, he differed profoundly from other politicians, and particularly many members of the Labour Party, who were initially less inclined to embrace the potentialities of the new mass media culture.

While new media technologies allowed for new methods of political communication, such changes to the practice of politics could not have occurred without the simultaneous democratization of British cultural consumption in the first decades of the twentieth century. The extent of culture democratization in this period has been debated by historians; nonetheless, it is clear that, to an unprecedented degree, interwar Britons shared in a national media culture.[13] Even before the emergence of the new mass media, the rise of display advertising had reshaped the visual landscape of urban Britain. Commercial advertisements on sandwich boards, billboards, and omnibuses bombarded the eyes of urban men and women from the mid-Victorian period onwards. In 1902, John Dewar & Sons (makers of the world-renowned Scotch whiskey) constructed a multistory illuminated tower depicting the company's mascot on the north bank of the Thames River between the Blackfriars and Waterloo bridges—the largest illuminated sign in Europe.[14] The cultural historian Lynda Nead has described display advertising as an "extreme instanc[e] of the visual presentation and consumption of London. . . . Modernity was understood to be a visual phenomenon and its most characteristic forms were those which spoke to the eye."[15] These beacons of modernity spoke to the working-class as well as the middle-class observer and worked to "evoke an imaginary 'community of spenders' . . . [and] forge new kinds of allegiance which often cut across the boundaries of both class and locality."[16] Commercial advertising also had a profound effect on the presentation of politics, as political parties adapted modes of commercial communication to the needs of modern politics.[17]

The "community of spenders" was given further coherence from the rise of the film industry in the early 1900s. In the decades between the wars, men and women from all classes and all regions of Britain went to the cinema in record numbers.[18] By 1939, an average of twenty-three million Britons, out of a population of just under fifty million, attended the cinema each week. Women, young people, and members of the working class went to the cinema more frequently than the older, wealthier, and better educated; nonetheless, the middle classes were frequent cinemagoers throughout the period as well.[19] Price differentials between theatres and between seating sections within the metropolitan picture palaces meant that mistresses and maids rarely sat side by side at the cinema—a circumstance that Evelyn Waugh parodies in his novel *Put*

Out More Flags. Waugh's upper-class heroine Angela drunkenly insists on sitting in the cheap seats at the front of the theatre on the grounds that she "want[s] to be *near*, in the three and sixpennies," not decorously far away in the "5 and 9s"—a demand that upsets the composure of the cinema staff.[20] Nonetheless, the explosion in cinema attendance led inevitably to a certain cultural homogenization as moviegoers came to admire the same stars and mimic the same styles.

This "star culture" had a visible impact on women's fashion. Hollywood starlets—with a few exceptions such as the British actress Vivien Leigh, most interwar movie stars were American[21]— became fashion icons for both middle- and working-class British women. And while the typical working-class woman could not afford the Hollywood-inspired fashions on display in department store windows, she was usually able to approximate the look with a sewing machine and a dress pattern ordered through the pages of the women's press. The feminist historian Sally Alexander has argued: "In this way, via the high street or the sewing-machine, the mantle of glamour passed from the aristocrat and courtesan to the shop, office or factory girl via the film star."[22] Similarities in dress were augmented by similarities in makeup and hairstyle, as lipstick, nail varnish, and salon permanents became regular features of both working-class and middle-class life.[23] The result, as J. B. Priestley famously put it, was that "for the first time in history Jack and Jill are nearly as good as their master and mistress . . . Jill beautifies herself exactly as her mistress does."[24] The perception of collapsing cultural differences between young women in this period was evident in political appeals to women voters after 1928—while parties differentiated such appeals between old and young, there was little attempt to disaggregate the "flapper" electorate on the basis of class.

This cultural homogenization was similarly evident in newspaper readership as national mass-market dailies replaced the smaller, more market-differentiated publications of the nineteenth century. Though publications such as the *Daily Mail* and the *Daily Express* have since shifted down-market, in the interwar period these papers were middle-brow publications with a much broader cross-class appeal. The interwar popular press did not cater only to "the working-class political culture where opinions lent more to patriotism, empire and monarchism and where the mood favoured sport, gambling drink and sex."[25] Mass-market newspapers were not only read by the likes of Mrs. Maggs and Betty, the archetypal working-class women of 1920s Conservative Party literature. Middle-class men like Agatha Christie's Hercule Poirot and Captain Hastings were also avid consumers of the popular press,[26] as were upper-class readers like Evelyn Waugh's Mrs. Stitch, an addict of the crossword puzzle in the parodic *Daily Beast*.[27] In 1939, two-thirds of the middle class read one of the four popular broadsheets discussed below. In comparison, less than 15 percent of the upper middle class and less than 4 percent of the lower middle class read either the *Times* or the *Manchester Guardian*.[28] The contents of the popular dailies reflected and reinforced the shared leisure preoccupations of the papers' readership. In addition to extensive cricket, football, boxing, and racing coverage,[29] newspapers also devoted substantial attention to film reviews, movie star gossip, and photographs of actors and actresses.

Finally, the interwar period saw the birth and rapid expansion of radio. The BBC was initially owned by a consortium of six wireless manufacturers—Marconi, Metropolitan Vickers, General Electric, Western Electric, Radio Communication Company, and Hotpoint Electric Appliance. From the manufacturers' point of the view, the purpose of the BBC was to spur the purchase of wireless radio sets by providing broadcast content to which wireless owners could listen. During the first years of its existence, the BBC's broadcast content remained fairly limited— orchestral music, radio plays, educational talks, religious broadcasts, and an evening news bulletin. Timely news and sports coverage were initially severely limited in deference to the newspaper proprietors' association and the wire agencies, which lobbied hard to constrain what they saw as a dangerous source of competition.[30] With time, however, the BBC's production repertoire expanded. Further, continental broadcast stations such as the commercially owned Radio Luxembourg and Radio Normandie could be picked up by most British listeners. These stations provided a lighter alternative to the BBC's broadcasts, with schedules dominated by dance music and variety programs. The popularity of such stations in turn put pressure on the BBC to expand its repertoire, with the result that, by the 1930s, the BBC had developed a broad program of news, discussion, and entertainment which attracted listeners across class and geographical boundaries, and which most Britons professed to prefer to the commercial alternatives.[31]

As a consequence, in part, of the growing centrality of the BBC in national life, radio ownership rose throughout the interwar period and in particular from the late-1920s onward. Between 1922 and 1939 licensed radio ownership increased from 1 percent to 71 percent of British households.[32] And while ownership was more concentrated in the south than the north, and in urban than rural areas, a 1938 survey found that even in rural Oxfordshire and Gloustershire three out of four households had a radio set.[33]

D. L. LeMahieu has argued that these new media took off so spectacularly in the interwar period because they managed to provide "a culture for democracy"—a cultural product that appealed across class and regional divides to a democratic mass audience. The appeal of such media lay primarily in their entertainment value, not in their provision of news content. When surveyed, listeners professed to prefer variety programs, music, and comedy to talks and discussions.[34] Moviegoers obviously went to the cinema to see the latest Mary Pickford feature, not the *Pathé Gazette* newsreel. And the 1938 Political and Economic Planning (PEP) *Report on the Press* noted that, when surveyed about their interest in particular sections of the paper, readers rated the picture page highest.[35] However, while interwar Britons might have initially turned to (or tuned into) the new mass media for their entertainment value, those media quickly became their primary source of political news and analysis.

Of course, the interwar public's knowledge and views about political issues were informed by many sources in addition to the media. Personal encounters with political activists at the local level obviously played an important role. Similarly, organizations such as the Left Book Club and civic groups such as the National Federation of Women's Institutes, the Rotary Club, and the League of Nations Union functioned as alternative sources of political information.[36] Yet it is hard to imagine certain members of the interwar electorate actively seeking to join such organizations. Young women such as Rosemary, the materially minded heroine of George Orwell's *Keep the Aspidistra Flying,* were more concerned with cocktail dresses than with Molotov cocktails, and unlikely to own too many Gollancz paperbacks, or to spend their weekends at Rotary meetings. As Paul Addison noted in his study of wartime social change, there were limits to the Left Book Club's usefulness for preaching to any but the already converted: "As Muriel Spark's heroine Miss Jean Brodie remarked, on the subject of Brownies and Girl Guides, 'For those who like that sort of thing, that is the sort of thing they like.'"[37]

The vast majority who did not go in for that sort of thing were most likely to take their political news from the popular press. A survey by the social anthropology organization Mass-Observation, conducted in 1940, identified the print press as Britons' most important source of political and international information, and the authors of that report speculated that the importance accorded to the press in opinion formation actually represented a decline from interwar levels, as the misleadingly pacifist reports of the major papers in the years before the war had led to a spike in skepticism about press reporting. After the press, the BBC was cited by most respondents, rating well above public talk or even "reason" as a molder of public opinion.[38] The authors of the 1938 PEP survey of press readership appreciated the implications of such media-dependence on the newspapers' ability to shape the news agenda. "Most subjects," they argued, "remain on the margins of public awareness, with more or less frequent excursions into the limelight. The strategic position of the Press is largely due to the limited human capacity for opinion-expressing, which makes it, in practice, necessary for someone to choose which subjects shall have the limelight, and when."[39]

In the first three decades of the twentieth century, the London-based national press grew from a circulation of a few hundred thousand, largely limited to the middle-classes in the south of England, to a broad national circulation of 5.5 million in 1920, to over 10 million in the 1930s. By 1939, nearly 80 percent of families read one of the popular London dailies—a figure that becomes even higher if one subtracts families in Scotland and the industrial north who were disproportionately likely to read a Scottish paper. Newspaper readership in 1930s Britain was higher than election turnout. And though readership was slightly skewed by income status, the only demographic group in which less than half read a national morning paper was working-class women. A study of working-class budgets published by the Fabian Society revealed that between 1913–1914 and 1937–1938 the average working-class consumption of newspapers and periodicals had doubled. Daily newspaper readership was taken to be such a key component of British life that in 1936 Joseph Rowntree allocated seven pence for newspapers in his calculation of a minimum budget to cover the "necessities of a healthy life."[40]

The lion's share of this enormous newspaper circulation was comprised of popular national morning papers—principally the *Daily Express,* the *Daily Herald,* the *Daily Mail,* the *Daily Mirror,* and the *News Chronicle*—whose readership exceeded that of the "quality" press—the *Times,* the *Manchester Guardian,* the *Morning Post,* and the *Daily Telegraph*—by a factor of ten.[41] While the opinions of the largely middle-class readership of the quality press arguably influenced party policy more strongly than those of the black-coated readers of the *Daily Mail,* the opinions of the latter determined the outcome of elections. Even as the circulation of the national morning press exploded after the First World War—nearly doubling between 1920 and 1939—the circulations of the metropolitan evening press, and of the provincial morning and evening papers, either declined or at best remained stationary. Further, the absolute number of provincial publications sank from forty-one morning and eighty-nine evening papers in 1921 to twenty-five morning and seventy-seven evening dailies in 1939. While certain organs of the regional press retained significant circulations in the interwar period, particularly in Northumberland, Durham, and Scotland, in no area did more than half of the population read the provincial morning press, and only in Scotland did readership of the local press approach readership of the national dailies.[42] In his study of provincial newspapers in the southwest of England, Michael Dawson argued that "the growth of the London press had both extended the market for newspapers and eroded the preeminence of local papers among their established clientele," with the result that the London dailies left provincial publications such as the *Western Morning News* and the *Western Daily Mercury* "trailing in their wake" in the circulation race.[43]

The provincial papers that remained were more likely to be owned by national trusts controlled by London-based press barons and to reflect the same political biases as the London press.[44] The *Northern Echo,* one of the largest and most profitable of the regional dailies, was owned by the North of England Newspaper Company, a holding company whose directors overlapped substantially with the board of the Westminster Press, publishers of the London-based *Daily News.* The *Western Morning News* was owned by the Harmsworth press.[45] The situation was the same with the London evening press. By the mid-1920s, the only three London evening papers that remained were the *Star,* the *Evening Standard,* and the *Evening News,* and their political views closely mirrored those expressed in the pages of their respective stablemates, the *Daily News,* the *Daily Express,* and the *Daily Mail.*

The new national dailies that dominated the interwar marketplace differed from their Victorian predecessors not only in the size of their circulations, but also in the style and content of their political coverage. Victorian newspapers had been densely printed affairs, designed for the leisured reader who had time to pore through verbatim reports of political speeches made both inside and outside of Parliament. By the interwar period, this style of reporting had almost completely disappeared, even from the columns of publications such as the *Times* and the *Morning Post.*[46] The reduction of political coverage in the new mass-circulation dailies arguably conferred a greater political power on their editors and publishers, as the imperative to pick and choose between competing news items gave the producers of modern dailies a formidable agenda-setting power.[47]

The selective coverage of news also limited readers' ability to draw their own unbiased conclusions about political and industrial events. For example, while the *Daily Express* made much of the threat of Labour during the 1922 general election, the paper rarely reprinted speeches by any of the Labour leaders, excepting occasionally Ramsay MacDonald, on its "Election News" page. As a result, *Express* readers were given little opportunity to gauge the accuracy of such allegedly objective reports in the paper's news columns as, "a vote for Labour is a vote for wasting your savings on a Palestinian war."[48] The divergent political agendas of the rival papers meant that "the retired businessman in Bournemouth relying for his news on the *Daily Mail* or the *Sunday Dispatch*" was likely to have a very different perception of national politics and world events than "the South Wales miner subsisting on the *Daily Herald* and the *News of the World*."[49]

The most widely read and arguably most influential publication from the 1900s through the 1920s was the *Daily Mail*, launched by Alfred Harmsworth, later Lord Northcliffe, on 4 May 1896. In addition to his leading role in forging a new brand of popular journalism, Lord Northcliffe was also a pioneer in the field of mass production and distribution.[50] By 1910 the paper's circulation had reached nearly one million at a time when the circulations of all other national dailies still measured in the tens of thousands. After the *Mail*, the second most popular daily was the *Mirror*, also owned by Northcliffe. While the *Mail* was a broadsheet and the *Mirror* was a tabloid picture paper, the two shared a similar political outlook, and both had a broad national readership, though in the 1920s the *Mirror* was more strikingly a women's paper than the *Mail*.[51]

The politics of the two Harmsworth publications changed considerably over the postwar decades. In 1916, Northcliffe had been integral in the successful campaign to replace the Liberal prime minister, Herbert

Table 1.1 Circulations of Principal London Dailies, 1921–1945

	1921	1930	1935	1940	1945
Daily Mail	1,533,000	1,845,000	1,719,000	1,533,000	1,700,000
Daily Mirror	1,003,000	1,072,000	950,000	1,571,000	2,400,000
Daily Express	579,000	1,693,000	1,911,000	2,546,000	3,300,000
Daily Chronicle	661,000				
*Daily News/ News Chronicle**	300,000	1,452,000	1,345,000	1,299,000	1,550,000
Daily Herald	211,000	1,119,000	2,000,000	1,850,000	1,850,000

* In 1930 the *Daily News* and the *Daily Chronicle* merged to form the *News Chronicle*.
Figures from Colin Seymour-Ure, "The Press and the Party System between the Wars," in *The Politics of Reappraisal, 1918–1939,* ed. Gillian Peele and Chris Cooke (London, 1975), 237, and James Thomas, *Popular Newspapers, the Labour Party and British Politics* (London, 2005), 15.

Asquith, with the then secretary of state for munitions, David Lloyd George. Two years later, the *Mail* and *Mirror* backed the Conservative and Liberal supporters of Lloyd George's coalition government against the independent Liberal and Labour candidates in the general election. From 1920, however, Northcliffe and his brother Lord Rothermere, who by then controlled the *Mirror,* became increasingly concerned with what they perceived to be the dangerously inflationary policies of the coalition.[52] Northcliffe died just before the general election of 1922, and control of the *Mail* reverted to Rothermere. The two papers supported the newly independent Conservatives in the election, though they maintained a loyal appreciation for Lloyd George's six years of leadership. Over the course of the 1920s the Harmsworth press became increasingly hostile to political and industrial Labour, and the *Mail* was the most virulent of the anti-Labour press in this period.[53]

While Lord Northcliffe led the popular revolution in journalism in 1896, other press proprietors quickly followed his lead and sought to challenge the Harmsworth papers on their own terms. After the *Mail,* the two most successful broadsheet dailies in the 1920s were the *Express* and the *Chronicle.* The *Express* was owned by Max Aitken, later Lord Beaverbrook, a Canadian who assumed control of the paper from Lord Pearson in 1916. In 1948, Beaverbrook told the Royal Commission on the Press that he "ran the [*Express*] purely for the purpose of making propaganda and with no other object.... [Empire free trade] and an Empire Customs Union, Empire unity for the purpose of securing peace, and if necessary for making war. I look at it as a purely propagandist project."[54]

Beaverbrook's commitment to British imperialism generally led him to support the Conservative Party in the 1920s, though his belief that Conservative leader Stanley Baldwin was not going far enough in the direction of protectionism explains his at best half-hearted support in the years between 1924 and 1929. At the end of that decade, Beaverbrook and Rothermere paired up to launch the Empire Crusade, running candidates first in the general election of 1929 and then in a series of by-elections in 1930. The Empire Free Trade campaign was an audacious attempt by the two men to translate their indirect influence over politics through the pages of their newspapers into direct political influence in Westminster.[55] The gambit, which ultimately failed miserably, led Baldwin to issue his famous jibe that the two press barons were "aiming at power without responsibility ... the prerogative of the harlot throughout the ages."[56]

The deep personal animosity between the press lords and Baldwin notwithstanding, it would be wrong to overstate the schism between the

Conservative Party and Lords Beaverbrook and Rothermere, particularly the latter. The two men supported the Conservatives at each of the general elections between 1922 and 1935, as well as at each municipal election. The proprietors and editors of the *Mail* and the *Express* maintained close contact with the leading figures in the Conservative Party, and the *Mail* made a practice of running Conservative Party election posters on its picture page. The Zinoviev letter, the forged document insinuating that Soviet operatives had been allowed to gain a foothold in British politics during Ramsay MacDonald's brief term as prime minister in 1924, was leaked to the *Mail* editor Thomas Marlowe by the Conservative Central Office.[57] As *News Chronicle* journalist A. J. Cummings wrote in the 1930s: "It may be taken for granted that when a government of the Right is faced with a real crisis, or is in the actual throes of a General Election, the recalcitrant Conservative newspapers will shed their differences in a single revolution of the globe and re-form themselves on a united front."[58]

Some scholars have suggested that it was the uncertain loyalties of the press barons that drove the Conservative Party to aggressively explore alternative media in the interwar period.[59] The Conservative Party chairman J. C. C. Davidson, however, was quick to recognize the publicity advantage that the party received from the print press.[60] The Conservatives, unlike Lloyd George or the Labour Party, did not feel the need for direct ownership of a national daily because they essentially received the benefits of a kept press without the burdens of ownership. As press historian Stephen Koss wryly noted, "there is a name, too, for those who live off the earnings of harlots."[61]

The broadsheet paper with the third largest circulation was the *Daily Chronicle,* which in fact outsold the *Express* until the mid-1920s. From 1918 through 1928, the *Chronicle* was essentially the personal property of Lloyd George. The paper was owned by United Newspapers Ltd., a syndicate whose major investors included the prime minister himself and Henry Dalziel, a Liberal MP who has been described as "Lloyd George's creature."[62] The paper was run by a series of Lloyd George-ites, and the prime minister's son, Gwilym Lloyd George, acted as his father's direct representative on the Board of Directors. The *Chronicle*'s editorial line swung back and forth with the erratic inconsistency of its patron throughout the 1920s, but in the years after the First World War it is most remarkable for its fierce hostility to organized labor. Over the period from 1918 to 1922 the Lloyd George coalition grew progressively conservative and reactionary, and the *Daily Chronicle* served as the mouthpiece of reaction. When the "Welsh Wizard" swung back toward progressive politics in the mid-1920s, the *Chronicle* swung with him. The paper continued to espouse a pro–Lloyd George position until its amalgamation with the *Daily News* in 1930.[63]

The Liberal *Daily News* was a Victorian daily which had been bought by George Cadbury in 1901 and relaunched along more popular lines. The paper was never able to compete successfully with its more popular rivals, and its circulation, though respectable, remained shy of the coveted one million mark. While detailed statistics on the demographics of readership do not exist for this period, it is fair to make certain assumptions about the *News'* readership from an analysis of its news coverage (it carried significantly more industrial news than its rivals) and advertising (comparatively more ads for tobacco, OXO cubes, patent medicines, and other products believed to appeal to a working-class market). Like the *Manchester Guardian,* the paper's politics were "Wee Free," or supportive of Asquith and those Liberals who remained independent of the Lloyd George coalition. Despite its support for Asquith, it remained exceptionally tolerant of the Labour Party and took a generous view of the rights of trade unions during the period of industrial conflict in 1918–1919. It is tempting to rationalize that the measured attitude of the *Daily News* toward Labour indicated an unwillingness to antagonize the paper's working-class readership. However, to do so would be in part to confuse causation and correlation. The paper likely had a greater proportion of working-class readers because of its more progressive approach to labor issues.[64] The gradual estrangement of the *News* from the Labour movement was as much the result of Labour's growing antagonism toward the Asquithians as of Liberal anxieties about Labour policy, and reflected the limits of the impact of commercial considerations on editorial policy.

Finally, there was the Labour-owned national paper, the *Daily Herald.* Labour's strategic approach to press publicity—from the nineteenth century through the post–World War II period—centered on ownership and control of its own press. As early as 1869, two different delegates to the second annual Trades Union Congress (TUC) presented papers on "The Necessity of Working-Class Newspapers, and the best means for their establishment." At the end of these presentations, it was voted by acclamation "That this Congress sympathises with those who have made and are making efforts to establish newspapers for the political and social advancement of the working classes, and to advocate the cause of labour, and earnestly recommends the members of trade unions to give in future a more general support to newspapers started on their behalf."[65] The successful creation of a movement-owned daily paper would, however, have to await the formation of the Labour Representation Committee (LRC) on 27 February 1900.

The alliance of the TUC with the Independent Labour Party (ILP), the Fabian Socialists, and (briefly) the Social Democratic Federation to form the LRC brought the unions into contact with a group of men who had both the will and the determination to launch a paper "to which the workers might . . . look for a fair and unprejudiced report of matters affecting their daily life."[66] Amongst the ranks of organized labor, C. W. Bowerman, secretary of the TUC from 1911 to 1921, and T. E. Naylor, both of whom served as secretaries of the London society of compositors, particularly appreciated the importance of the press. Outside of organized labor, several of the men who joined the LRC in 1900 were particularly well suited to push forward with the scheme to start a Labour paper. Keir Hardie, the father of the Labour Party, was the founder, editor, reporter, and columnist of the weekly *Labour Leader*. Ramsay Mac-Donald, the first secretary of the LRC and first Labour prime minister, wrote for a series of publications, including F. W. Pethick-Lawrence's short-lived evening paper *The Echo,* for which he was a weekly columnist; the London *Star;* and the *New Liberal Review.* John Bruce Glasier, one of the founders of the ILP, edited the *ILP News* and later took over control of the *Labour Leader* from Hardie. In addition to those with journalistic backgrounds, the push for a Labour daily benefited from the enthusiasm of socialist activists such as the ILP member Clifford Allen, the journalist Norman Angell, and the east London politician George Lansbury.

Together, the parliamentary committee of the TUC and the NEC began to consider plans for a Labour-owned paper almost immediately after delegates to the party's annual conference, held in Newcastle in 1903, agreed to impose a one penny levy on all members to build up a central fund for the party. The need to "draft a scheme with the object of the combined forces of Labour owning and controlling a daily Labour paper" was endorsed at the TUC at Leicester that fall.[67] Over the next several years, progress toward the creation of a Labour daily was slow, but steady. A special meeting of representatives of political and organized labor was convened at Caxton Hall in London on 26 February 1908, at which the representatives endorsed the proposal to establish a limited liability company with a capital of £100,000 in £1 shares, and to invite trade unions to buy up the shares, and "if not enough money was raised that way, to invite individual friends of Labour to buy them."[68] However, in 1909 the Osborne judgment intervened. W. V. Osborne, a railwayman and Liberal Party supporter, sued his union for its attempt to levy union members in support of the Labour Party. The case reached the law lords, who in December 1909 issued a judgment in the plaintiff's favor, and thus rendered the subscription of trade union funds in support of a Labour paper legally dubious.[69]

By 1910 the NEC was becoming so irritated with the perennial resolutions that "immediate" steps be taken to produce a Labour daily that the party treasurer, Arthur Henderson, lashed out at that year's sponsor (W. H. Taylor of the compositors) by proclaiming that "[h]e liked those delegates who came forward and moved this hardy annual, who took up the time of the Conference in talking on points upon which there was general agreement. . . . [but] they must possess their souls in patience a little longer. . . . When [the NEC] could see its way through the Osborne Judgment, and when it could be supported by some of the Compositors' funds and those of other societies, they would have a paper."[70] Yet Henderson's terseness belied the fact that the leadership was by that time firmly committed to the establishment of a Labour daily. Within a year a provisional board of directors had been appointed and legal negotiations were begun to prepare a prospectus for Labour Newspapers Ltd., the publishing company established to produce the *Daily Citizen*.

The *Daily Citizen* represented a bold move by the Labour and trade union movement. Fifty thousand pounds sterling of trade union and private funds were secured on 8 October 1912 to launch the paper.[71] The new daily sought to be both a party organ and a general interest paper, which included such popular staples as sport news and betting tips. Politically, the paper was staunchly centrist and reflected the views of its trade union backers; its staff included both Herbert Morrison and the future Labour Party press and publicity director, Will Henderson. In this respect it was markedly distinct from the unofficial Labour paper, the *Daily Herald*, which began publication earlier the same year.

The *Daily Herald* was launched on 15 April 1912 as the successor to the strike sheet *cum* labor paper of the same name issued by the London Society of Compositors from 25 January to 28 April 1911. The *Herald* was edited by the radical Labour politician George Lansbury, and it gave frequent support to shop steward and Minority Movement campaigns.[72] Aside from its political and industrial coverage, its content reflected the moral prerogatives of its owner, and the paper did not carry a racing tips column or report on society gossip or Paris fashion—subjects of particular interest to women readers. Neither the *Herald* nor the *Citizen* was a commercial success, but both managed to retain an average weekly circulation of between 100,000 and 150,000. And while the directors of the *Citizen* voiced considerable resentment of the competition posed by the

Herald, the existence of the latter paper was to prove a blessing in disguise when paper rationing and rising costs of publication drove the *Citizen* into bankruptcy less than a year after the outbreak of the First World War.[73]

The *Herald* managed to survive the war by converting itself from a daily to a weekly publication in October 1914. After the war, the *Daily Herald,* which resumed regular publication on 31 March 1919, was the only Labour daily left in circulation. Certain leaders of the party and the TUC may well have wished that the paper had gone under alongside the *Citizen.* The paper that emerged from the war was as politically radical as its predecessor, and its continued advocacy of revolutionary syndicalism, shop steward socialism, and international communism under the banner of the "only Labour daily" nearly drove men like Arthur Henderson and the railwaymen's leader, Jimmy Thomas, to distraction.[74] However, financial exigency ultimately forced Lansbury to turn to these very men for support, and the TUC and the Labour Party assumed financial and editorial control of the paper in 1922 and proceeded to transform it from a voice of radical dissent into an organ of trade union orthodoxy.[75]

Although the process of "taming" the *Herald* was essentially complete, the future of the newspaper was still very much open to debate. Would the movement-owned *Herald* remain a staunch educational publication with a nominal circulation like its predecessor? Or would Labour leadership seek to transform the newspaper into a popular advocate of socialist politics and industrial reform that would be both accessible and attractive to a broad democratic audience? The debate over the future of the *Herald* drew into focus the differing prejudices and priorities of the various members of the Labour Party toward commercialism, political education, and propaganda.

CHAPTER TWO

Speaking to the People

F ROM ITS INCEPTION, the Labour Party's leaders, in particular Ramsay MacDonald and Arthur Henderson, had big visions for its future. The two men were the principal architects of the inter-war party. The Scotsman, a professional politician and journalist who began his career in the ILP, was the more romantic and visionary of the two.[1] Henderson, an ironmonger, Methodist lay preacher, and founder of St. Paul's Football Club (a forerunner of Newcastle United), was brought to the project of independent working-class politics through his union. Temperamentally more pragmatic than MacDonald, Henderson was a skilled political organizer. In 1912, he took over the secretaryship of the party from MacDonald and held that position nearly until his death in 1935.[2] Despite their legendary personal antipathy, the two men worked together remarkably effectively for nearly thirty years. Labour's rapid transformation from a sectional interest group to a national party which received over 20 percent of the vote in the 1918 election owed much to their dedication and leadership.[3]

Both men, for different reasons, had reservations about the changing political culture of British politics. At the same time, both appreciated the potential of new modes of political communication for a young party seeking to establish itself in the national arena. Together with other members of the party's national leadership, including most notably the Fabian and London politician Sidney Webb, these two men expanded Labour's publicity machinery with the aim of broadening the party's appeal. While domestic and international political developments, changes in the ownership and structure of the mass media, and internal tensions within the

Labour movement would all combine to drive a wedge between it and the commercial media in the mid-1920s, in the period before and immediately after World War I, the Labour leadership showed a remarkable aptitude for facing the new challenges of mediated democracy.

Pictorial Politics

After the 1906 general election, R. P. Houston, Unionist MP for West Toxteth, identified his Labour opponent James Sexton of the Dockers' Union as being "intelligent and advanced" in his use of publicity and "up to date in the matter of advertisements." Sexton apparently made use of emotive pictorial posters, processions, and imaginative publicity stunts to associate his Unionist opponent with the alleged evils of "Chinese slavery," or the controversial practice of importing indentured Chinese laborers to work in the gold mines of Britain's Transvaal colony in South Africa.[4] Pictorial posters were one of the primary contributions that the NEC made to the campaigns of Labour candidates in 1906, as the economies of scale in design and production of such posters made it more practical for local parties to buy nationally mass-produced posters than to produce them locally. This contributed to a nationalization of political campaigns in the Edwardian era, though, as James Thompson has emphasized in his recent research on posters and political communication, headquarters sold several different posters on a range of issues, and the selection of posters by local committees underscored regional variations.[5]

According to one scholar, the frequent exploitation of emotive imagery as well as the crude appeals to class solidarity and trade union loyalty in such early Labour propaganda belied the party's claims to be "morally superior in its propaganda techniques." In this view, MacDonald is a hypocrite for professing to believe that "the sole way leading to Socialism is the way of education," and arguing that "too much Socialist propaganda has been upon . . . insubstantial lines," only to turn around and advocate the employment of "insubstantial" tactics to win votes.[6] Yet, rather than viewing MacDonald as a hypocrite, it is perhaps more useful to consider him—like Winston Churchill or Tony Blair—as a man exceptionally skilled at squaring a contradiction. MacDonald believed that political education was the end goal of socialist politics, but he also accepted that conversion was more easily accomplished from a position of power, and power could most quickly be obtained through the practical expedient of securing votes. In this respect, his political outlook was similar to that of Herbert Morrison, though MacDonald arguably held a more

cynical view of the intelligence of the British electorate.[7] As a consequence, MacDonald (and many of his NEC colleagues) often frankly accepted the use of irrational or simplistic appeals to encourage electors to
vote Labour. In his 1904 NEC report to the annual party conference, for
example, MacDonald noted that the Executive had "prepared a few co-
loured posters which will put our case in a striking and dramatic way.
These posters will . . . no doubt, by simplifying the issues to the man in the
street, considerably influence polling results."[8]

MacDonald's interest in visual imagery is similarly evident in his approach to leaflet production in the 1900s. In a period when most candidates' election addresses did not contain photographs or other pictorial
imagery, from his first general election campaign in 1895, MacDonald's
election leaflets all featured prominent photographs of the Scotsman. This
probably owed something to his vanity, but his commitment to the visual
was not limited to the reproduction of his own profile. In mid-1903, the
NEC, in the mistaken belief that another general election was imminent,
appointed an election subcommittee which included MacDonald to consider the production and distribution of propaganda material. Whereas
in 1900 the NEC had produced a single election leaflet, the 1903 committee planned to produce more than ten, each with an initial print run
of two hundred thousand. Unlike the 1900 leaflet and its successor, "Why
We Are Independent," both of which were ponderous and text-heavy, the
new run of leaflets would make use of "striking sentences" and cartoons.
MacDonald even ventured a possible theme for a cartoon on Old Age
Pensions which would "show Mr. Chamberlain consoling a rather starved
workman by telling him that if he goes on starving for another 30 years
he will receive 5/- a week when he reaches the age of 65."[9] Thompson has
noted the exceptionalism of Edwardian Labour propaganda, arguing
that, unlike Liberal and Conservative posters, Labour propaganda often
made use of a positive appeal.[10] Yet even Labour's leaders apparently
could not resist the occasional cheap shot.

MacDonald's Chamberlain cartoon proposal was not ultimately adopted, though the Chinese slavery posters offered a similarly negative
and reductionist interpretation of Conservative policies. The NEC also
commissioned several more inspirational cartoons to be printed as both
handbills and full-size posters, including the "His Own" poster; one with
the caption "Clear the Line," which depicted the LRC as the engine of
progress steaming down a track obstructed by the fat cow of privilege
and protection; and another with the caption "Labour at the Gate" featuring a determined young man wielding an axe labeled "LRC" hacking away

at the gates of Parliament, whose planks were marked "Landlordism," "Prejudice," "Low Wages," "Rents & Royalties," and "Misgovernment." Though the expected general election did not come that year, or the next, the posters were used, "with, we are told, excellent effect," at by-elections in Lanark and West Monmouth in 1904.[11] These were the posters that MacDonald had prophesied would play particularly well with the man in the street. The large demand for the posters from local party organizations in 1906—the NEC had to order an additional print run—corroborates the assessment that they played an important role in constituency campaigns.[12]

Subsequent NEC leaflets and posters continued to show a concern for visual impact. The bulk of these leaflets (at least until Webb's addition to the NEC in 1916) were written by MacDonald, and their content is relatively predictable. However, their layout suggests an eye toward readability and an emphasis on variety—as of February 1910 the party had in circulation five different leaflets on the need for independent Labour representation and another six on tariff reform.[13] The party also continued to expend considerable time and money on poster production. While responsibility for commissioning new posters was delegated to MacDonald, poster designs were presented to and considered by the full NEC, and occasionally sent back to the artists to be reworked.[14] And, whereas in 1903 the NEC had hired an unknown cartoonist to produce their first series of pen and ink posters and handbill images at a relatively low cost, in 1909 they commissioned the illustrator Gerald Spencer Pryse at much greater expense to produce a group of evocative painted posters, including the famous "Forward! The Day Is Breaking!"[15] The posters that Pryse designed for the Labour Party in the 1910s and 1920s are still considered among the best political artwork of the period.

The dramatic impact of these posters in the January 1910 election was, admittedly, hampered by their comparatively small size. Despite their striking appearance, the majority of Labour posters were not as large as those of their opponents—a disadvantage attributable to cost considerations. The NEC sold its posters to the local party organizations in two sizes—40" by 30" and 60" by 80." The smaller and less dramatic posters, which were significantly cheaper both to purchase and to display, outsold their grander counterparts by more than six to one.[16] The Labour candidates' comparatively limited supply of these larger posters was especially conspicuous in the 1910 elections, when this "expensive, and in other senses extravagant, method [of propagandizing]" reached an unprecedented pitch.[17] A decade earlier, it would have been common to see the

"FORWARD! THE DAY IS BREAKING!"

Figure 2.1.   Labour Party election poster by Gerald Spenser Pryse, 1910.
(© Labour Party. Courtesy of the Cambridge University Library)

smaller posters on billboards and in shop windows, but by 1910 the situation had changed dramatically.[18] The *Pall Mall Magazine* referred to the January contest as "The Poster Election," and noted that "it is being fought by posters as never an election has been fought before."[19] In commenting on the new emphasis on poster-electioneering, the *Manchester Guardian* asserted that "[a]rgument by poster depends as much as anything else on size, and one large and effective poster has a more arresting appeal in it than four small ones put together."[20]

Whereas local Labour parties often found the cost of both purchasing and displaying large posters prohibitive, their Conservative and Liberal rivals had appreciably deeper pockets, and were able to cover billboards for the full month between the dissolution of Parliament and election with large display posters.[21] In Northeastern Manchester, the sitting Labour MP, J. R. Clynes, had to contend with a bevy of Conservative posters that depicted such images as "a gang of unemployed men manacled by Free Trade chains and driven by a man who carries a whip labeled

'Free Imports' " and "John Bull fighting desperately with a scarlet monster inscribed 'Socialism.' " While Clynes's agent had a stock of the larger NEC display posters, he could not afford to hang them for the full campaign period, and held off displaying them until the fortnight before the election.[22] It is arguable, however, that Labour's size disadvantage was partially, if not largely, offset by its emphasis on quality. As the *Pall Mall Magazine* observed, the quality of the artwork made a large difference to the impact of the poster and by most accounts, the Labour posters were notable for their artwork.[23] Even the unsympathetic *Times* described the Pryse posters as "striking" and "of exceptional merit as artistic productions," and admitted that they were "of such a character as to arrest the eye and rivet the attention of the passer-by."[24]

Neither the Labour Party nor its more well-funded rivals produced many posters during the 1918 election campaign, as the wartime paper restrictions were still in effect. The posters that the party did produce were characterized by the *Times* as "very bold."[25] Herbert Morrison's election to the NEC in 1920 brought a new poster enthusiast to headquarters. Morrison quickly became a member of the literature committee and took an active interest in poster production.[26] He was most likely influential in the decision to again retain Pryse to design a new series of posters in 1921 and to order reprints of "Forward the Day Is Breaking," as well as in the decision to engage several other poster artists, including A. S. Merritt.[27] Merritt's poster "Greet the Dawn—Give Labour It's [*sic*] Chance" was a striking evocation of the future promise represented by Labour, and was used at multiple elections in the 1920s. Morrison was also involved in number of other campaigns: he commissioned posters for Labour's Fighting Fund campaign in the 1928; he headed a special subcommittee on election posters during his chairmanship of the NEC in 1928–1929; and he engaged an advertising firm to design the posters for Labour's 1937 LCC campaign. The magazine artist Emile Verpilleux did at least one of the posters for the Fighting Funding campaign; and the party engaged Merritt, the London tramways artist V. L. Danvers, the cartoonist and comic book illustrator Ernest "Ern" Shaw, and several others to design posters for the 1929 election.[28] Morrison's interest in visual media was not limited to poster art. It extended to a concern with the layout and design of party literature, which, in the 1930s, became increasingly pictorial. After MacDonald's expulsion from the party in 1931, Morrison's involvement guaranteed that Labour did not abandon its former leader's commitment to visual propaganda.

Figure 2.2. Labour election poster by A. S. Merritt, 1923. (© Labour Party. Courtesy of the People's History Museum, Manchester)

The Press and Publicity Department

While poster art and party leaflets played an important role in popularizing the young party, they were increasingly insufficient to combat the subtler and more ubiquitous propaganda being served in the pages of the *Chronicle*, the *Mail*, and other anti-Labour papers. The party leadership viewed the anti-Labour bias of the national press as particularly injurious to its political prospects, and, as press circulations continued to soar in the 1900s and 1910s, they sought to improve press coverage of the movement. One strategy was to create an alternative pro-Labour paper, a project in which the NEC and the TUC General Council invested considerable time and money throughout the interwar period.[29] An equally crucial strategy was to improve Labour's coverage in the news and leader columns of the existing "capitalist" press. Although Arthur Henderson personally disapproved of the low gimmickry of popular journalism to the extent of opposing the publication of racing tips in Labour journals, as party secretary he was hard-nosed enough to realize that the party could not rise to national prominence without support from the national press.

Thus, in September 1917, Henderson proposed the creation of a Labour press and publicity department to improve the party's public relations. The proposal was part of his larger scheme to reorganize the NEC through a formal system of standing committees, including a Committee on Literature, Research, and Publicity, and to form several full-time departments under the auspices of the NEC.[30] In advocating the need for the new departments, Henderson argued that "[a]t present the distribution of Labour Press News is anything but satisfactory; such news items are often picked up at random from various people who are supposed to be in close touch with the Movement, and the information so obtained is often inaccurate, sometimes biased, and not infrequently wilfully misleading." In his view, "in the absence of our own Daily Paper," the party needed a full-time publicity bureau to put over its case to the national and provincial press.[31] The NEC endorsed the secretary's proposals and agreed to hire his chosen candidate, the former *Christian Commonwealth* reporter Herbert Tracey, to head the new department. Three years later, Tracey moved from the political to the industrial side of the movement and took up the new position as head of the TUC press department. Henderson's nepotistic nomination of his son William, the press department's parliamentary correspondent, to replace Tracey ensured that the relationship between the party secretary and the press department remained extraordinarily close.

Before his departure to the TUC, Tracey made significant progress in normalizing relations between the party and the popular press. By 1920 he was able to report that "communications with the press through the Press and Publicity Department have become quite regular and systematic. . . . In addition . . . , the Department has been at the constant call of the newspapers and of press correspondents, both at home and abroad, for information regarding the Party's general activities and details of its programme and organization, and interviews for the British and foreign press."[32]

The department's stated goal was "not merely to send [Labour information] round the press but to get press publicity."[33] As such, Tracey and Will Henderson sought to introduce a degree of strategic nous to Labour's press relations. As Henderson wrote in October 1921:

> It is well known as a rule that the Prime Minister chooses an afternoon for making a speech in order to catch both the evening and the following morning papers. . . . If Parliament is sitting and the Prime Minister is delivering either in the House or in the country an important speech on policy, it is useless to issue a long document to the Press for the following morning, since practically all newspapers will devote great space both to Parliament and to the Prime Minister. These are considerations which ought to be taken into account . . . and it often pays to hold up a document for one day or two days or even more.[34]

While recognizing that Labour news would not be accorded priority by most of the popular dailies, Tracey, Will Henderson, and the publicity department staff attempted to secure the best coverage possible for the movement.

In addition to publicizing official statements, the department also developed a scheme to provide the national and provincial press with pro-Labour editorial content and features. In early 1918, Sidney Webb, a member of the NEC's Literature Committee as well as a founding member of the Labour Research Department (LRD), proposed a scheme for a joint LRD–press department "Labour News Service" to be run along the lines of the commercial wire services. The LRD was an outgrowth of the Fabian Research Department (FRD) established by Sidney and Beatrice Webb, and Douglas Cole in 1912. The FRD was essentially a research and lobbying firm that trade unions, cooperative societies, trades councils, and local Labour parties could hire to produce books, reports, and pamphlets on their behalf. While it retained its ties to Fabianism and, through Cole, held sympathies with guild socialism, the links between the FRD and the Labour Party became increasingly close, and in 1919 the FRD changed its name to the LRD and moved its offices to the party and

TUC headquarters building in Westminster, Transport House. In his study of the early Labour Party, Ross McKibbin noted that, although the organization was tainted by left-wing sympathies, even conservative unions continued to affiliate to it because, "although it was often not admitted . . . the LRD was very successful at the task it had contracted to do."[35] As such, it was probably the best qualified institution within the movement to run a publicity scheme.

As Webb and Tracey argued in a co-authored memorandum advocating the creation of a Labour press service: "The Press generally has shown a marked interest in the party's activities, and it has become the practice for some of the news-agencies . . . to keep in close touch with the press department; their representatives call almost every day for information, all of them want special (and excessive) interviews, some of them come in only to pick up news." They emphasized that, despite the systematization of press releases, the distribution of Labour news was still "hap-hazard" at best. What was needed was a department that would offer "a regular supply of Labour news, including perhaps something in the nature of a London letter, news paragraphs, and even . . . occasional memoranda on Labour policy (not necessarily for publication but for editorial guidance)." If such information was made readily available, its effects might well be widely felt, "as newspapers are essentially competitive, [and] if only one or two begin to print the Labour news the others will have to follow their example." The two men were quick to emphasize that such a service ought to be as free as possible from explicit propaganda, though propagandizing was of course the ultimate objective.[36]

Plans for the venture were finalized on 1 September 1918, and the Labour News Service was up and running by the end of the war in November. Labour was to cooperate more closely with, and to receive much better treatment from, the commercial press in the immediate aftermath of the war than it would once the party had established itself as a more formidable force in British political life. In part this discrepancy reflects changes in press attitudes toward the political and industrial wings of the Labour movement, but it also reflects the movement's efforts to use the news and editorial columns of the major dailies to communicate with an audience who may not have bothered to attend political meetings or read party literature.

Webb's commitment to press publicity was part of his larger strategy for expanding Labour support by appealing to demographic groups outside of the party's traditional base. In part, this stemmed from his Fabian commitment to a policy of gradual social change through the permeation of existing institutions and the attendant necessity to court the professional classes. Further, as a member of the London Labour Party, which covered an exceptionally socioeconomically diverse geographic region, Webb was more intimately attuned than some members of the NEC to the importance of wooing middle-class voters.[37] In a 1922 article, Webb argued: "We should, as far as possible, 'stratify' our electioneering; appealing to each section of the electorate in the language which that section understands; emphasizing just the points in which that section is interested; subordinating the question that each section finds dull or unpleasant; addressing to each section the literature most appropriate to it."[38] This policy would become known within the party as "stratified electioneering." Though Webb did not coin the term until 1922, the theory behind stratified engineering was in evidence during the 1918 general election campaign, as it would be the following autumn during the national railway strike.

Though separated by less than a year, the 1918 general election and the national railway strike of September-October 1919 played out in very different political environments. The election was held on 14 December 1918, just one month after the end of the First World War. Although the Labour Party fought against pledged supporters of a continued Lloyd George–led coalition government in the election, Henderson had been a member of the Asquith and Lloyd George war cabinets before resigning from the latter over the issue of support for the Russian revolution. J. R. Clynes had briefly served as Food Controller in 1918. Despite division among members over support for the war, the party held together between 1914 and 1918. Moreover, the participation of certain party leaders in the wartime governments gave Labour prominence and legitimacy, while their colleagues' proven commitment to international peace contrasted with the bellicosity of the coalition's election campaign. Meanwhile, the changed social conditions brought on by the war combined with the 1918 franchise reform to provide a political opening that the party was quick to exploit.

During the 1919 railway strike, in contrast, Labour was fighting on much less stable ground. The resurrection of the Triple Alliance (miners, transport workers, and railwaymen) and its threatened use of direct action to force the government to abandon its support for the White Army in Russia caused uneasiness amongst both the government and the public. The actions of the Triple Alliance combined with a series of high profile strikes over the summer, including the so-called lightening strike of the Liverpool policemen in August, to fuel growing anxieties about the resurgent strength of organized labor. The persistence of high levels of inflation—initially encouraged by government policy—led to fears among consumers that continued industrial wage rises would lead to spiraling prices. Many in government shared these concerns, and, in the preceding months, ministers had made several public pronouncements of the government's intention to take a stand against the unions.[39] While the odds were more favorable in 1918, in both instances the Labour movement was fighting an uphill battle to get its side heard.

The 1918 General Election

One of the most remarkable aspects of Labour's publicity campaign during the 1918 general election was the NEC's innovative use of daily columns in the pages of the *Daily Mail,* the *Continental Daily Mail,* the soldiers' edition of the *Mail,* and the *Evening Standard.* The provenance of this arrangement, in which Lord Northcliffe allowed the party to address the public through his newspaper columns, is uncertain. The proposal likely originated with *Mail* journalist Hamilton Fyfe. While Northcliffe's papers did not support Labour's withdrawal from the coalition government, the press baron allowed Fyfe, then one of his star reporters, to publish a signed editorial in the *Daily Mail* on "Why I Shall Vote Labour," in which Fyfe emphasized his belief that "changes are necessary" and that the Labour Party was the only force committed to making those changes "by evolution, along parliamentary lines." A Labour government, he argued, would act as a safeguard against revolution.[40] In his correspondence with Northcliffe over the editorial, Fyfe suggested to "the Chief" that he meet with Arthur Henderson so that the two men could discuss promoting what Fyfe alleged to be their mutual goal of incorporating the Labour Party safely within the constitutional structure.[41] It is not clear whether the arrangements between the Northcliffe press and the party resulted from a personal meeting between the press baron and Henderson; however, the decision to give column space to Labour was made at some point after Northcliffe's receipt of Fyfe's letter. In a signed contribution to the first issue of the *Daily Citizen* six years earlier, Northcliffe had argued, "We have the only representative Parliament in the world, and I should like to see a really representative Press"; and it is not unreasonable to attribute his decision, at least in part, to a genuine sense of civic responsibility.[42]

Two days after the publication of Fyfe's column, the *Mail* ran an (unsigned) riposte, "Why I Shall *Not* Vote Labour."[43] However, the issue also included what was to be the first of eight daily columns given over to the Labour Party, the last of which was run on the morning of the election. Labour's press and publicity department worked together with the NEC's

Literature and Information Subcommittee, the party's information bureau, and the LRD—a high-powered group that included Webb, Cole, Arthur Greenwood, and Susan Lawrence, among others—to devise a series of "stratified" appeals.[44] Each *Mail* column included a testimonial from a representative of a different social group explaining why all the component members of the British nation should support the party.

The first column was written under Arthur Henderson's byline. It began by announcing the party's gratitude to Northcliffe and noting that "the Labour Party has always believed that if it could obtain full publicity for its propaganda it need never fear hostile criticism from the orthodox parties. All that we have asked from the Press is a 'square deal.'" The remainder of the article was taken up with the constitutional argument in favor of Labour's leaving the coalition—more or less a direct refutation of the arguments put forth in the *Mail* over the previous weeks. According to the Henderson column, the persistence of the coalition "would have the effect of making the new Parliament the docile servant of the government." Thus it was that the Labour Party, not from opportunism or a lack of patriotism, but "[h]aving *the national interest solely in view*," decided to run an independent campaign.[45]

Labour's second column appealed to the working-class vote, though from two widely different angles. It contained two testimonials, the first from a World War I officer arguing that soldiers should vote Labour because the party supported the abolition of conscription, opposed the invasion of Russia, supported free trade, and was "for the working-man; against unemployment; and for the abolition of want." The second was from an Oxford tutor and argued that Labour supported an "ideal of new rights," including the right to employment and the "right of access of knowledge, a right not guaranteed at present to thousands capable of profiting by its enjoyment."[46]

The following day saw a piece by the Bishop of Oxford, who contended that in a democratic society, the working class needed to be represented and that their representation was "the only hope of averting revolution."[47] Both the tone of the bishop's article and the character and position of the man who wrote it suggest a conscious appeal to a middle-class audience, as did further testimonials by the Dean of Worcester, the author J. D. Beresford, and Brigadier-General W. H. H. Waters. Waters stressed the party's support for open diplomacy and the League of Nations, and argued that Labour was best situated to lead the reorganization of industrial society in pursuit of "ordered social progress by constitutional methods." The Dean of Worcester's column was titled "A Christian Programme: New and Sounder Foundations: Honest Effort to Apply Sound Principles."

Beresford's "Why a Brain Worker Supports Labour" focused on pacifism and Labour's support for the employed over the rentier classes.[48]

Other aspects of Labour's pitch appealed more directly to middle-class pocketbooks, such as the bold-type headline, "The Labour Party is genuinely determined to introduce a fair system of taxation and to relieve the burden on the middle and working classes,"[49] or their response to a letter from a "small tradesman" who had been reading the Labour columns in the *Mail* and wanted to know Labour's attitude toward "small capitalists" like himself: "You are a Taxpayer. The traders' party is the Labour Party. Your interest is to vote Labour because the Labour Party means to lighten the burden of taxation you have to bear and to put it upon the big incomes and large private fortunes."[50]

In its columns, the party presented itself as the representative of nearly every group other than those with "big incomes and large private fortunes," including, and perhaps especially, women. The emphasis on clerical support for the Labour Party was probably intended to appeal not just to a middle-class audience, but also to the new female electorate. The 5 December column was peppered with boldface rhetorical quotations, such as "Who equaled the food supply?" and "Who first demanded equal political rights for women?" The following day saw a piece by Lady Henry Somerset on "Why a Woman Will Vote Labour," which notably focused not on gender policy, but on Labour's determination "to help the average man and woman."[51] Furthermore, the party ran a single advertisement in the *Mail* during the election campaign. Part of the press and publicity department's "carefully devised scheme" of advertisements to "counterac[t] the efforts of our opponents," it focused on Clynes's service as food controller in the coalition government.[52] It was run on the women's page and titled "Mr. Clynes Says 'Good-bye' and 'Thank you' to the Housewives of Britain." In it the outgoing food controller paid homage to "the work of the housewife who through the sad and anxious years of war worked on cheerfully, uncomplainingly, patriotically, making the best of it— 'making do.' "[53]

Labour's strategy of appealing to a broad national audience was made explicit in the announcement that the party ran in their column on 3 December: "Don't be fooled by those who tell you that the Labour Party is a sectional party, which only looks after the interest of the men and women who work with their hands. The Labour Party is the only true National party. It is the party of all who work for their living. It will look after the interest of the people as a whole." The press and publicity department was satisfied with its attempt to address this broader public through the *Daily Mail* columns, and was generally pleased with its coverage in most organs of the national press during the election.[54] In fact, the only mass-circulation papers to take an unequivocally hostile attitude to Labour were the pro-coalition *Daily Chronicle* and *Daily Express.*

The *Daily Express* began the election campaign with a leading article championing the rights of organized labor and the need for a new era of industrial cooperation.[55] The road to this new era was, in the view of the *Express,* decidedly not through independent Labour representation outside of the coalition. After Labour committed the "Colossal Blunder" of leaving the government, the paper turned its full weight against the party. During the three weeks prior to the election, its editorial columns denounced the Labour Party as a cabal of extremists unrepresentative of "real Labour"; described the transport leader, Robert Williams, as "a young man of violent, almost Bolshevist opinions, who threatened this country with insurrection and revolution"; and mocked trade unionists for allowing themselves to fall under the spell of "that representative workman, Mr. Bernard Shaw." It ventured the prediction that "a large proportion of the rank and file of the trade unions will certainly not vote for the Socialist Falstaff, the pacifist Bardolph, or the anarchist Pistol."[56] Any overtures that the party may have made to the paper were evidently ill-received. Yet Labour did make its voice heard in the *Express*—in the advertising columns. Two pro-Labour advertisements, paid for by the *Herald,* were run. The first, titled "The Labour Party Is Fighting for You," was a specific appeal to the soldiers' vote. The second, which focused on the Defense of the Realm Act and civil liberties, appealed to a more general and presumably more educated audience. While the impact of these advertisements is unknowable, the *Express* was concerned enough about their possible effect to run an accompanying disclaimer: "the *Daily Express* takes no responsibility for opinions that appear in its advertising columns. . . . Our own views are well known to our readers."[57] Notably, while the *Herald* ran two advertisements in the *Express,* it ran four in the *Times,* suggesting an appeal to middle-class electors. The first focused on Labour's support for the League of Nations, the second on the soldiers' and sailors' vote, the third on the women's vote, and the final one on housing.[58]

Altogether, Labour had a good election from a publicity point of view. Their coverage in the press combined well with a generally successful poster and leaflet campaign. Despite winning only 57 seats out of 361 contested, they succeeded in polling 20.8 percent of the votes cast, and their candidates, on average, did better than the Asquithian Liberals. After the election, even the more unsympathetic organs of the press appeared willing to give Labour a chance to play its role in the "national tasks of Peace and reconstruction."[59] In the industrial realm, union demands were still receiving considerable support from the press, and the prime minister had been returned to power in part on the promise of a land fit for heroes to live in. The Speaker of the House of Commons had granted press credentials to a Labour lobby correspondent, and the NEC had appointed Will Henderson to the position. In March 1919, the press and publicity department was able to report that, over the past fifteen months, "the Party's relations with the press have become closer and more systematic."[60] The events of the following summer would strain these relations considerably.

The 1919 Railway Strike

On the afternoon of Friday, 26 September 1919, J. H. Thomas, secretary of the National Union of Railwaymen (NUR), issued a press statement announcing that the negotiations between his union and the government had irrevocably collapsed and that the union would go out on strike at midnight that night. A few hours later, John Bromley, secretary of the Associated Society of Locomotive Engineers and Firemen, declared that his union would support the NUR. The points at issue between the railwaymen and the government were the right of the men to retain the bonus (33 shillings) granted to them during the war regardless of future deflation, and the principle of standardization upwards, which argued that all men performing a certain job should receive the highest wage then being paid for that job within the industry. Negotiations broke down when the government stated its "definitive" refusal to concede to either demand.

All of the Saturday morning papers emphasized the importance of public opinion to the outcome of the strike, and nearly all sought to depict public opinion as naturally and implacably hostile to the strikers. The *Daily Express* and the *Daily Mail* respectively branded the strike as an "act of tyranny and oppression" and an attempt to terrorize the British public through a "starvation strike." Other journals took broadly similar lines. Only the *Manchester Guardian* withheld judgment, on the grounds that "there has not been a sufficient body of admitted fact" to reach a conclusion about the strike's merits. The prime minister understood the importance of public opinion to the struggle and immediately set about mobilizing "the whole of its vast publicity machinery to get it own case rather than the men's before the public."[61]

The railwaymen were understandably anxious to change the tenor of press discourse on the strike, and on Saturday, Thomas, who as a prominent Labour MP had close associations with the party organization, authorized the LRD and the Labour Party's press and publicity department to work with the union to "secure[e] publicity for the Railwaymen's case."[62] In doing so, they faced an uphill battle. The railwaymen could at least count on the support of the *Daily Herald,* which had resumed daily publication on 31 March 1919 after four and a half years as a weekly journal. They also received a fair hearing in the *Manchester Guardian,* as well as some muted sympathy from the *Daily News,* which, despite its view that "the men have struck unfairly [and] unreasonably," conceded that, "the misuse of the right to strike does not mean that the right to strike does not exist," and accused the government of "provocative folly" inflaming opinion against the strikers. Still, the *News* accepted the government's conclusion that the strike was "a strike against the community," only differing in its belief that the strike's goal was industrial, not revolutionary.[63]

The Labour publicity team's strategy was, first, to obtain an opening "for statements of the Railwaymen's case and articles in their favour" and, second, "by some means or other," to induce the press "to abandon their unqualified support of the Government." They pursued these goals through a combination of moral suasion and veiled threats. Two days after the strike was called they issued a statement under Thomas's name, making it clear that "if the Press continued to accept Government propaganda as true statements and did not show the Railwaymen's side, the country's condition might rapidly become full of danger."[64]

While fears of the impact on sales and journalistic prestige doubtless went some way toward persuading the major dailies to open their columns to the strikers and their sympathizers, another equally if not more important factor at work was the unofficial threat of a printers' strike. On the same day as the publicity team's statement, Thomas granted an interview to one of the press agencies in which he revealed that "a deputation of compositors . . . voluntarily went to his office to intimate that they themselves, recognizing the issues involved, were not disposed to be the medium of issuing 'poison gas' to their fellow Trade Unionists." He went on to say that the head of the National Society of Operative Printers and Assistants, George Isaacs, had reported to him that he was having trouble keeping his men at work. "Both he and myself recognize the absolute necessity of a free Press," Thomas averred, "but when war is being waged against Trade Unionists as this is being waged, then Trade Unionists must not be blamed for accepting the challenge." He ended on a distinctly threatening note: "I give this clear intimation, inasmuch as newspaper proprietors will know what value to attach to it . . . The railwaymen's case is too sacred to the Labour movement as a whole to have it prejudiced. . . . This fight is going to be seen through and the railwaymen's case is not going to suffer. That is my final statement."[65]

Whether the press's greater receptiveness to pro-NUR copy was more the result of the publicists' carrot or Thomas's stick, the end result was the same. Over the next week, the Labour team successfully placed several articles in both popular and quality dailies. Commencing on 1 October, the *News* ran a daily article under Thomas's signature (albeit with the caveat, "The *Daily News* is not responsible for the views expressed."). The tabloid paper the *Daily Sketch* similarly gave over a daily column to the presentation of the railwaymen's case, and the *Express* ran a piece by Cole in which he sought to explain the financial issues at stake and the pressures that had led Thomas to call the strike. The objectiveness of the *Express* in running the article was somewhat undermined by their explanation as to why they were printing it: "Because the *Daily Express* has been, is, and will always be, anxious to discover the reasons which lead any large body of citizens of this country to courses of action instinct with peril for us all."[66] However, Cole's article did have the effect of encouraging the editors to attack his claims on their merits, and to switch from branding the railwaymen as revolutionary anarchists to criticizing them for striking in an overly precipitate manner. The *Mail*'s "Special Labour Correspondent" Alexander Thompson had been covering the strike from the men's point of view even before Thomas issued his threatening statement. The *Guardian* ran an exclusive interview with Thomas.[67] Gradually, the contents of these special articles started to be reflected in the editorial lines of the daily papers.

What the railwaymen could not achieve through well-placed articles they sought to achieve through paid advertising. The NUR ultimately guaranteed a daily budget of £1,500 per day—and actually spent over £10,000 during the course of the strike—for advertising alone.[68] These funds went to pay for advertisements in all the major London dailies and the *Manchester Guardian,* as well as in various evening and Sunday papers, and to the production and distribution of several hundred thousand posters.[69] Like the campaign during the 1918 general election, the railway publicity campaign was a sophisticated attempt at audience differentiation and persuasion.

One series of advertisements run in the *Times* and the *Manchester Guardian* was targeted to the editorial leadership of those papers, on the one hand, and to their middle-class readership, on the other, to persuade both groups of the industrial nature of the dispute and of the legitimacy of the railwaymen's specific claims.[70] Another set, run predominantly in the *Herald* and the popular Liberal press, emphasized the threat posed to the entire trade union movement by the railwaymen's defeat and attempted to encourage donations to the NUR strike fund and to bolster the determination of the railwaymen's colleagues in the Triple Alliance in the event that strike action might spread outside the railway sector.[71] Finally, a group of hybrid advertisements appeared in the *Daily Express* and the *Daily Mail,* targeting such disparate groups as housewives, shop clerks, and manual workers. Many of these were similar to advertisements run in the quality and Liberal press, though they tended to have less text and to be more emotive. They attempted to appeal—without recourse to specific facts or figures—to the readers' instinctive sense of justice and empathy. Though there was some overlap between these three categories, the attention to audience was clear. Each day saw new advertisements unveiled, often in direct response to advertisements run by the government on the previous day. In at least one instance the Labour group even managed to get advance information on the advertisements that the government was preparing, with the consequence that the government's "Is the strike justified?" and the NUR's rebuttal "Who is speaking the truth?" ran side by side in the pages of most major papers. The two advertisements, which put forth competing figures on the cost to the state of the NUR wage demands and the inflation-adjusted value of the government's offer, were both reproduced as wall posters.[72]

"Is this man an anarchist?," indisputably the most brilliant advertisement run during the strike, was the railwaymen's response to the prime minister's claim that the strike was an anarchist conspiracy.[73] The display space was largely taken up by a drawing of a railwayman and his family by the celebrated *Herald* cartoonist Will Dyson. The quiet dignity of the man and his wife and the wretched appearance of their four children and elderly dependent grandmother are heartrending, and underscored the absurdity of Lloyd George's claims about the railwaymen's revolutionary intentions. The advertisement, like "Who is speaking the truth?," was reproduced as a wall poster.[74] The *Railway Review* referred to the use of persuasive posters during the conflict as "a new feature of strike publicity," and while posters had previously been used during strikes to announce the time and location of mass meetings and to appeal for relief funds for strikers' families, the railway strike appears to have been the first occasion in which posters were designed for a general audience.[75]

Figure 2.3. Advertisement issued by the National Union of Railwaymen, with artwork by Will Dyson, October 1919. (Courtesy of the Cambridge University Library)

While the poster campaign must have had a striking visual impact, its novelty paled in comparison to the use of the cinema by both sides in the dispute. Newsreels had been a feature in British film-going life since the introduction of the *Pathé Gazette* in 1910; hence, movie viewers were not unused to a mild dose of politics at the cinema. However, the 1919 strike represented the first instance in which filmgoers were subjected to a direct pre-recorded message from the government at the beginning of their program. On Thursday evening, 2 October, Lloyd George compelled all cinemas to run a still-frame photo of a message, typed on plain office paper and signed by the prime minister, which showed the degree to which the balance of power had shifted from the government to the strikers by that point in the conflict. Whereas Lloyd George's earlier statements had been bellicose, the cinema statement had a strong ring of defensiveness: "The Government is NOT fighting Trade Unionism. Trade Unionism is a recognized factor in the industrial life of the Country. What the Government is fighting for is to prevent the extremists of any industrial body from attempting to gain their ends by attacking the life of the community, and so bringing untold misery upon thousands of innocent people."[76]

Labour's publicity team was quick to fashion a response, arranging through Pathé for Thomas to be filmed and for a message signed by the railway leader to be displayed along with the footage on the evening after the Government's announcement was shown.[77] Thomas's message was typed on NUR letterhead, and read:

> Railwaymen are not fighting the country. I have always done my best to avoid strikes. I did on this occasion, but those who wanted to fight Labour rendered my efforts ineffectual.
>
> We are fighting for the lowest paid wage-earners against a conspiracy to lower wages. If the wages of railwaymen are reduced other trades will follow.
>
> This is only the first battle in the campaign and the Government has thrown all its weight against the men.
>
> We fought to free England. Railwaymen played their part in the struggle. We were promised an England worthy of our sacrifices."[78]

Unlike Lloyd George, Thomas did not have the clout to force theatres to run his message, and the *Times* noted that, "whether it received the same publicity is a doubtful matter."[79] However, it is noteworthy that the *Pathé Gazette* segment on the strike included thirteen seconds of footage displaying the NUR statement, and only two seconds of the government's notice, a discrepancy that seems exceptional even in light of the greater length of the NUR statement. The message and the film footage of

Thomas may well represent the first publicity stunt specifically engineered by Labour to ensure coverage in the new medium—the *Railway Review* proudly referred to it as Thomas's "cinema trick."[80]

It is always difficult to make definitive pronouncements about the impact of the media on public opinion. However, in the case of the NUR campaign, its success seems hard to dispute. Between the first day of the strike and its conclusion, the major metropolitan dailies radically changed their tune. By Friday, 3 October, even the *Express* was plumping for a fair negotiated settlement. The paper argued that the public (and the press) had, over the past week, come to "recognis[e] some clear facts." These they listed in "order of importance" as:

1. The railwaymen have a case;
2. There was no excuse for the strike;
3. The revolutionary and anti-social forces in this country are negligible;
4. We can carry on the national life, railways or no.

Though fact 2 may have rankled with many of the NUR rank and file, the primacy given to fact 1 and the presence of fact 3 provided a sharp contrast to the paper's earlier characterization of the strike as "a challenge by a few conspirators to the liberties, the rights, and the honour of Great Britain."[81] Within a week of the strike's start, every paper, with the exception of Lloyd George's *Daily Chronicle,* was bending over backwards to appear objective. The *Daily Herald* reported that "[a]fter four days of the most bitter calumny we find in the Press, suddenly, a fairly general desire for 'peace and fair play.' "[82] As Robert Page Arnot of the LRD proudly reported, "By the end of the week most of the papers were hampering the Government if they were not helping the Railwaymen."[83]

To a certain degree this change in rhetoric reflected the profoundly unrevolutionary character of the strike. As the *Times* wrote at the end of the strike, "Except for a few isolated cases of intimidation and assault by individuals, and certain attempts at sabotage on the railways, which were also the work of violent extremists, the strike has been without disorder."[84] The lack of violent activity on the streets doubtless contributed to the diminution of violent rhetoric in the press. However, the lack of violence was not necessarily evidence that the strike was a legitimate industrial grievance and not an anti-constitutional action; the altered tone of the press did owe a considerable amount to the efforts of Labour's publicity team in putting over the railwaymen's case. That the language of the popular press by week's end so closely mirrored the arguments put forth in the NUR advertisements placed in their pages was not coincidental.

Through skillful publicizing of their case, the railwaymen managed to win a relatively fair hearing from the press.

The extent to which this change in press opinion reflected a change in public opinion is harder to gauge. At least one commentator saw the success of the campaign, both among the working and middle classes, as impressive. According to C. F. G. Masterman:

> Towards the end it was evident that railwaymen were having it all their own way. They were winning because they got the question away from the question of the strike to the question of wages. . . . It is not too much to say that before the strike had ended the railwaymen had rallied nine-tenths of the industrial workers to their side; that—partly, indeed, through the strongest provocation—they were increasing sympathizers from the middle classes by hundreds of thousands a day.[85]

Although the actual impact of the campaign is impossible to quantify, perceptions as to its role had a significant impact on future debates over publicity within the Labour movement. The campaign had "showed for the first time how skillfully handled publicity could be a weapon of prime importance in a great Labour struggle," and many were determined to take better advantage of that weapon.[86] But while certain techniques pioneered in the year after the war were incorporated into Labour's publicity arsenal in the 1920s, the early 1920s were notable for the lack of engagement between the Labour Party and the popular press. The experiments in press advertising in the immediate postwar period were not replicated on the national level in the 1920s, and less and less energy was expended on press relations. The period of industrial militancy after the war, combined with the continued improvement of Labour at the polls in the early 1920s, further stoked the fears of the publishers and editors of the national press. Their hostility, in turn, disillusioned many in the party who had previously held with a policy of cooperation with what they now came to refer to as "the poison gas press."[87]

CHAPTER THREE

The Anti-Labour Turn

CCORDING TO A *Daily Mail* article published in November 1923, "[t]he choice before the country is between Conservatism and a Labour Ministry. . . . The public views with the utmost a l a r m the programme of the Labour Party. The main planks in the Labour platform are Nationalisation and the Capital Levy, both of which involve *terrific taxation and probable disaster to the national industries.*"[1] The violence of Conservative propaganda and press attacks on Labour in the early 1920s is difficult to appreciate, especially in light of the two parties' respectful relationship within Parliament. While quotes such as this actually made reference to the substance of Labour policy, much of the anti-Labour press coverage in the 1920s simply dealt in stereotypes and scaremongering. Conservative Party propaganda unsubtly insinuated that British socialism was a front for rapacious Soviet greed, and articles in the daily press followed a similar line. At the time, both Conservative and Labour leaders believed that the Conservative Party benefited significantly from the press's anti-Labour bias.[2]

The relationships among the political parties, the popular press, and the electorate in this period are still only vaguely understood.[3] Why was the press so uniquely hostile to Labour in the 1920s? And why was Labour, which had proved so effectual at grassroots campaigning and political organization, so markedly ineffectual at managing its press publicity in this period?

The change in the tone of the popular press was driven primarily by genuine concern on the part of press proprietors about Labour's growing popularity and seeming radicalization. While the press's emphasis on the alleged Bolshevist threat can be viewed as a cynical scare tactic, their initial turn away from Labour stemmed from genuine anxiety over the party's policy proposals. And the press rhetoric was at times effective in shaking public confidence in Labour. Unsurprisingly, anti-Labour propaganda was most powerful when it successfully resonated with and amplified existing anxieties held by the public.

The Conservatives capitalized on negative stereotypes about the working classes, fears of Bolshevism, and positive associations between the Conservative Party and an organic vision of the British or, more accurately, English nation.[4] Yet, there was nothing inevitable about this process, and the mechanism by which so-called class wisdoms were translated into conventional wisdoms accepted by a broad coalition of interwar voters merits exploration. In terms of its performance in government, and in terms of its public presentation, Ramsay MacDonald's Labour Party was about as far from Bolshevist as a self-proclaimed left-wing political party could be. And although Ross McKibbin has emphasized the importance of the trade unions to Labour Party organization in the 1920s, the party sought to portray itself not solely as the political voice of organized labor, but as the second party of the state, representative of national as opposed to sectional interests.[5] Why then was Labour so vulnerable to accusations of sectionalism and political extremism in this period?

Scholars of the Labour movement have tended to assume that the hostile relationship that existed between Labour and the mass media in the 1920s was characteristic of the time periods that preceded and succeeded this decade.[6] However, as discussed in Chapter 2, Labour's relationship with the popular press was not uniformly hostile in the immediate postwar period. Further, the break between Labour and the popular press was far from clear cut. Though the conservative *Daily Mail* discontinued its "Labour Notes" column in early 1920, the column's principal author, A. M. Thompson, continued to contribute frequent articles under the byline, "Daily Mail Labour Correspondent." Many Labour leaders in the early part of the decade continued to encourage liaison between Labour activists and the "capitalist" press.[7] The breakdown was gradual, yet by the mid-1920s the relationship between Labour and the press had deteriorated to its lowest level in the interwar period.

Coverage of the 1918 general election and of the 1919 railway strike seemed to indicate that the national press could be persuaded to give Labour a fair run. When a disgruntled reader wrote to the *Newspaper World* in February 1919 lamenting that "[t]he way in which newspapers, dominated as most of them are by financial speculators, write down and misrepresent the claims of the workers is infamous," the editor responded: "We have rather been under the impression that lately the so-called 'capitalistic Press' had rather gone out of its way to accentuate the claims of Labour to a fair hearing."[8] Three years later, the correspondent's charges of infamy were harder to dispute. The *Daily Express* called the November 1922 municipal elections, in which Labour lost control of all but four borough councils, a "sweeping victory for . . . sanity."[9] On the day of the elections, the *Express* ran a cartoon by Sidney Strube showing John Bull tearing the false beard off a kindly looking old man labeled "Labour Programme" to reveal his "RED" bowtie underneath.[10] And the *Mail* warned its readers, "[*Labour*] *threaten every man's house and furniture, and every woman's clothes and jewellery,* as was done in Russia. . . . If the Labour Bolshevists once get control *we shall all be irrevocably dragged along the Russian Road to Ruin.*"[11] The *Mail* and *Express*'s coverage of the 1922 general election was little different in tone, though the *Mail* was more strident than the *Express*. The paper ran an election-day leader headlined: "DON'T FORGET TO VOTE TODAY: AGAINST SOCIALISM"; and, just in case its readers were not frightened off by the prospect of communist Armageddon, the paper reminded them that the Labour Party "*stands for dear beer and very little of it.*"[12]

Labour did catch a comparative break from the Liberal press in 1922. While Lloyd George's *Daily Chronicle* was if anything even more hostile to Labour than the Conservative press, the Independent Liberal *Daily News* and its evening and regional stable mates were initially friendly toward Labour. The Independent Liberal press's venomous treatment of the former prime minister was such that Sidney Webb hypothesized that a postelection reunion of the party under Lloyd George might drive many of the Liberal papers into the Labour camp.[13] However, Labour's heightened hostility toward the Liberals in the postwar period combined with its increasingly radical rhetoric to antagonize the Liberal press, and by the fall of the Labour government in October 1924, the press's process of "simplif[ying] major issues into the two main elements of socialism and anti-socialism" was essentially complete.[14]

The hysterical tone of the *Daily Mail*'s anti-Labour coverage from 1922 onwards is partially attributable Northcliffe's death in August of that year and the assumption of control of the paper by his brother, Viscount Rothermere. Northcliffe, despite his personal antipathy to socialism, maintained a comparatively philosophical attitude about the rise of Labour. Though his views hardened in his later years, in 1921 he was still discouraging the staff of the *Mail* from attacking Labour outright.[15]

Rothermere, in contrast, was an ardent anti-socialist, who allegedly paid an unexpected visit to his brother in 1921, driving an old Ford car, and "explained that Bolshevism was coming, that they would all be reduced to beggary, that he was trying to get used to it in advance, and had therefore sold his Rolls-Royce, dismissed his valet, and reduced his expenses to the lowest limit."[16] His replacement of Northcliffe meant that *Mail* editors Thomas Marlowe and Herbert Wilson no longer faced any attempts to curb their anti-Labour tendencies.

But the personal eccentricities of press barons are insufficient to explain the broader shift that took place across the popular press in this period. To be sure, the major press proprietors—with the exception of George Cadbury of the *Daily News* and C. P. Scott of the *Manchester Guardian*—had little active sympathy for the Labour Party. Northcliffe's limited support for Labour between 1918 and 1922 stemmed largely from an anxiety not to antagonize his pro-Labour readership, while Beaverbrook's lifelong imperial obsession made him naturally hostile to a party wedded to free trade and internationalism.[17] The sympathies of the *Daily Chronicle* syndicate perforce lay with Lloyd George. Nonetheless, the personal prejudices of the press proprietors did not translate into consistently hostile coverage of the Labour movement until the early 1920s, when Labour's political successes, changes in party policy, and developments in the industrial sphere both at home and abroad combined to make the possibility of a Labour government a more ominous threat.

Labour's by-election gains, its successes in the March 1919 LCC elections, and its spectacular advance in the municipal elections that autumn made the party appear a more serious political contender than it had in 1918. In 1919, Labour won by-election victories at Bothwell, Widnes, and Spen Valley, and nearly edged out the coalition candidate in Bromley and St. Albans.[18] At the LCC elections, the London Labour Party (LLP) raised its representation on the council from one to fifteen, and went on to secure fantastic gains in the borough council elections eight months later.[19] By January 1920, the *Times* was reporting that "the lowest estimate of skilled political organisers puts the Labour strength in the next Parliament at 150; the highest at a clear majority in the House."[20] On the eve of the 1922 election, underwriters at Lloyd's were selling insurance policies against the possibility of either a Labour majority or a hung parliament leading to the formation of a Labour government.[21]

Not only more popular at the polls, Labour also began to appear more revolutionary. The 1918 party constitution has in retrospect been described as moderate.[22] However, the inclusion of Clause IV, calling for the nationalization of major industries, suggested a swing to the left.

Combined with the LLP's inclusion of municipal ownership of public utilities in its 1919 election platform and the Miners' Federation's insistence on the need for nationalization in their ongoing negotiations with the mine owners, Clause IV apparently belied the more moderate pronouncements of men like Arthur Henderson and Labour MP J. R. Clynes. In 1920, when several Labour-controlled London boroughs offered outdoor relief to the unemployed at levels well above what the Minister of Health was willing to sanction, radicalization of the party seemed assured. The following year, the Poplar council refused to divert scarce resources from its poor relief funds to pay its annual contribution to the LCC operating budget, in contravention of regulations prioritizing a borough's payment of the contribution over any local budget expenditure. In the decade to come, "Poplarism" remained a bogey that the popular press would trot out at successive local elections.[23]

The adoption of the capital levy in the 1922 party platform, committing a Labour government to levy a one-off tax on wealth to help alleviate war debt, similarly intensified the growing suspicions of revolutionary intent in the minds of the press and Labour's political opponents. In addition, the assertive attitude of member unions of the Triple Alliance and the three-month miners' strike of April–June 1921 suggested that while the larger unions might act as a bulwark against shop steward militancy, they were not willing to set aside what they felt to be their legitimate grievances.[24] Though the decision of the Transport Workers and the National Union of Railwaymen not to come out in support of the miners on Black Friday, 15 April 1921, suggested that the Triple Alliance had more bark than bite, the high-profile coordination of industrial leaders reinforced a we-they vision of labor versus capital or, as the press increasingly depicted it, labor versus "the community."

Specific incidents that precipitated the press's turn against Labour varied from paper to paper, but the rates rebellion in Poplar was critical in that it triggered the break between the movement and the country's largest circulating paper, the *Daily Mail*. The *Mail* initially reported that the London unemployed who came out to demonstrate in favor of higher relief were seeking "not a penny too much for a family."[25] However, the paper quickly lost sympathy for the Labour councillors' attempts to ameliorate the plight of the unemployed through direct action, denouncing Islington's proposed relief scales as most probably illegal and likely to lead to workers shirking available employment in favor of the dole—a theme hammered home in several vicious cartoons by the paper's cartoonist "Poy" (Percy Fearon). While Islington's relief schemes were ill-advised and irresponsible, Poplar's actions in refusing to pay its LCC contribution were "anti-social" and the clear work of "Reds" and "Communists."[26]

For the *Daily Chronicle,* the moment of disenchantment with Labour came significantly earlier. As noted, the *Chronicle* took a uniquely inflexible stance against the legitimacy of the 1919 railway strike. The paper was frankly hostile to the miners, and alone among the capitalist press denounced the creation of the TUC General Council on the grounds that it was likely to "make the bigger Labour conflicts even bigger than they have hitherto been."[27] It was similarly incautious in its support for Woodrow Wilson's use of wartime emergency powers to break the 1919 U.S. Steel Corporation strike, and approved Alexandre Millerand's use of military conscripts as scab labor to break the French railway strike the same year.[28] The *Chronicle,* like the premier whom it slavishly supported, had become "a deliberately counter-revolutionary force," and it is unsurprising that it denounced the "unconstitutional" behavior of the Poplar "Communists" as an "abuse of their powers . . . actuated by extreme political motives."[29]

Other than the *Daily Herald,* the only organ of the popular press that refused to vilify the Poplar councillors was the *Daily News,* which evinced a strong sympathy for London's unemployed and reserved its blame for the situation for the perfidious coalition.[30] In part, the *News*'s support for the Poplar councillors, like the Asquithian Liberals' support for them in the House, was a strategic move aimed at discrediting Lloyd George's administration, yet it also represented the paper's fast-fading belief that the prewar Progressive coalition in London politics could be reconstituted. The *News* had welcomed Labour's successes in the borough elections with the hope that "the responsibilities of power may do something to temper the intolerance" that the LLP had shown toward their Progressive colleagues, and many Liberal press proprietors clearly desired a revival of Liberalism through what Lloyd George termed the "fusion of Limehouse into the Liberal Party blood."[31] However, Labour's continued hostility toward their Liberal colleagues gradually extinguished this hope. By March 1922, the *News*'s sister paper, the London evening *Star,* was blaming the Poplar rates rebellion for the success of the Municipal Reformers in the LCC elections.[32] The Liberal press was willing to support Labour when it believed that the party could be kept within respectable boundaries, but by 1922 many within the Liberal camp shared Lloyd George's anxiety that "the violence of Labour is frightening moderate men away" and driving them into "the camp of the Conservative party."[33]

According to Beatrice Webb: "To read the capitalist press [in November 1923], whether Tory or Liberal, the Labour Party barely exists as a political party: it is a mere group of disorderly extremists without brains or money—of course they don't say this in so many words, they only imply it by refusing steadfastly to report anything about the Labour Party."[34] Her observation leaves one wondering how often she actually read the "capitalist press," since, by 1923, the Conservative press—like the Conservative Party—had clearly focused its attention on Labour as its principal target.[35] The *Mail* commenced its campaign coverage that year with a headline that declared, "The choice before the country is between Conservatism and a Labour Ministry."[36] While the two Liberal papers focused their wrath on the Conservative leader Stanley Baldwin, the *Mail* devoted substantial column space to attacks on Labour, and the *Chronicle* denounced the "Robin Hood policy" that the party's "fanatics" had foisted on its more moderate members.[37] Even the *Daily News*, despite its comparative objectivity, joined in the denunciations of Labour's support for the capital levy and its proposals for the nationalization of industry.

The principal anti-Labour strategy in the 1920s was to present the party as a cabal of foreign-influenced extremists. The *Daily Mail* first began referring to the Labour Party as the "Socialist Party" (or, initially, the "Labour-Socialists") in November 1922. This involuntary rechristening was picked up by the *Express* a few months later, and by 1924 the terms *Labour Party* and *Socialist Party* were being used interchangeably in all of the major newspapers, despite the fact that, as the historian Matthew Worley has pointed out, the party itself actively "refrained from using the 'S' word. . . . Indeed, the term was not used in any of Labour's general election manifestos between 1918 and 1923, and was used just once in 1924 (in the final paragraph) and twice in 1929 (including a negative reference to Tory 'misrepresentations' of the word)."[38] Conservative literature similarly rejected Labour's rhetorical claim to represent manual workers. The party journal, *Gleanings and Memoranda,* consistently referred to the Labour Party in inverted commas, and the journal's monthly digest of Labour Party news was printed under the heading "Socialist Politics," a catch-all category that also contained reports on the activities of the Communist Party of Great Britain, known as the British Bolsheviks, and ongoing news of atrocities in Soviet Russia.[39]

By calling Labour "Socialist," the Conservative Party and press were seeking to evoke a set of analogies and stereotypes associated with the socialist-dominated coalition governments in Germany and (from 1924) France, with all of their connotations of economic instability and large-scale labor unrest.[40] The Catholic Cardinal Bourne, who had little sympathy for Labour, "publicly deprecated its being called Socialist" on the grounds that the "label" conveyed an "anti-Catholic connotation" that the party's principles did not embody.[41] Rather than dangerously revolutionary, in the 1920s the Labour Party was perceived by many within the Catholic Church to be a bulwark against communism.[42] While the *Times* did not begin to use the epithet "Socialist Party" until April 1923, in November 1922 the paper argued that "[e]xception . . . might justly be taken to the name 'Labour,' since the Labour Party has by no means a monopoly on the wage earning vote, and many of its tenets are frankly Socialist. Indeed, the name 'Socialist' might be more adequate than the name 'Labour.' "[43]

The language used by the press during the 1923 election campaign was even more alarmist. In November, press reports on Labour focused on the party's "Bolshevist" proposal of instituting a capital levy. While the capital levy had been a part of Labour's program since 1918, in previous elections it had attracted much less attention, notwithstanding several articles run in the *Daily Mail* during the 1922 campaign with headlines such as "Goblin Gold: The A.B.C. of the Capital Levy."[44] Two weeks before polling day, the *Mail* launched a creative smear campaign that played up the party's membership of the Second International, which the paper referred to as the "Sozialistische Arbeiter Internationale," and suggested that a Labour government would merely be a front for "[d]ictation from Socialists of Germany and Russia."[45] The stunt inspired a series of brilliant cartoons by Poy, in which a supine Ramsay MacDonald is manipulated and abused by a militaristic German officer and a fat-cat Russian apparatchik. The cartoons played to stereotypes and jingoism in a foreshadowing of the Zinoviev letter scare ten months later.

Blatantly biased propaganda alone was not enough to turn voters against the party—as the 1922 and 1923 general election results illustrated. But when political events raised doubts in the minds of undecided voters over Labour's competence to govern or the party's commitment to representing national—as opposed to sectional—interests, the popular press played a central role in reinforcing those doubts and convincing wavering electors to abstain or vote against the party. In particular, the anti-Labour rhetoric of the popular press during the Red Scare campaign of October 1924 intentionally appealed to groups such as the middle classes, women, and, to a lesser extent, the unemployed. The conservative press harnessed the specter of Bolshevism to tap into existing fears on the part of the middle classes about the sanctity of property, on the part of the working classes about rising unemployment, and on the part of women about the protection of family life and the autonomy of the home. The Red Scare campaign was so successful not simply because it managed to convince the electorate that the government was under Moscow's thumb, but because it used the rhetoric of communism to reinforce more general misgivings about Labour rule.

The Red Scare campaign became notorious as the Zinoviev letter campaign, a reference to the *Daily Mail*'s eve-of-election publication of an alleged communication from Comintern chairman Grigory Zinoviev to the Communist Party of Great Britain, in which Moscow offered the party financial support to carry out revolutionary political activity. The Foreign Office had had a copy of the letter for a month, and it had been seen by the prime minister, but the government had not taken any action against the Russians. The *Mail*'s editors claimed that MacDonald's failure to act "prove[d] that the Socialist Ministry is under the control of the Communist Party."[46] The letter's publication, though admittedly the most scandalous journalistic scoop of the election (and arguably of the century), was merely the capstone of a month-long campaign which began with the parliamentary uproar surrounding Attorney General Patrick Hastings's withdrawal of the Crown's case against J. R. Campbell, the acting editor of the communist publication *Workers' Weekly*.[47] The attorney general had initially brought a case against the editor for publishing an article that urged soldiers, if necessary, to disobey government orders to fire on striking workers. The case was subsequently withdrawn at the instigation of the Cabinet, many of whom feared that a public trial would draw unwanted attention to the communist cause. Ironically, press and parliamentary critics accused the government of squashing the prosecution in response to pressure from influential communists. It is arguable that the scandal itself did not lead to the fall of the government, but that MacDonald was actively looking for a pretext to dissolve Parliament and seized on the Campbell affair to force an election.[48] Either way, the result was the resignation of the government on October 9, 1924.

Between October 9 and the publication of the Zinoviev letter on October 25, the issue of the Labour Party's ties with communism was never far from the front pages, particularly of the *Daily Mail,* which at this point had the largest circulation of any of the broadsheet papers, selling nearly as many copies as its two closest competitors combined.[49] The press made much of the Labour ministry's decision to formally recognize the Soviet Union, and of trade agreement negotiated between to two governments, which included a £30 million commercial loan from London to Moscow. The question of whether or not to ratify the Russian treaty became the central issue of the October campaign, despite Labour's attempts to focus discussion on domestic issues. But while the conservative press devoted significant column space to a head-on attack against the proposed Russian loan, the Red Scare campaign was less about concrete issues of international trade than about the perceived Socialist menace. As the historian of the Conservative Party, Ewen Green, argued, the conservative press worked in step with the Conservative Central Office to portray the Tories as representing "sound finance, low taxation, economic stability, Christian duty, and national unity. The Socialist Labour party was, in contrast, portrayed as an economically irresponsible tax-and-spend party, concerned only with the sectional interests of trade unions, and also atheistic."[50]

The main pillar of the Conservative attack on Labour focused on the party's economic policies, or lack thereof. The *Daily Mail* ran a stark five-column photo of a seemingly endless Labour Exchange queue with the caption "The Socialists' Contribution towards the Alleviation of Unemployment," which presaged Saatchi and Saatchi's "Labour Isn't Working" campaign sixty-five years later.[51] Given that Labour, hamstrung by its position as a minority government, had not actually managed to implement any remotely socialistic policies during its ten months in government, the campaign concentrated not on the party's record but on its alleged intentions. The Conservatives issued dire warnings of what Labour would do if it were given free rein to act—warnings designed in part to undermine Labour's claims that things would be better if only the party were returned with a clear majority.[52]

In a signed editorial in the *Daily Mail*, the Conservative politician Lord Birkenhead described the Labour Party as "Our Kerenskys"—seemingly "moderate men" who were nonetheless merely fronts for the "avowed extremists" from which the Labour movement "derives its vitality and driving power."[53] Much was made of the party's commitment to the "Bolshevist" platform of nationalization and the capital levy, a proposal whose dire effects, when carried out in other countries, the press had consistently highlighted in articles such as "Savings Levy: Even the Threat Upsetting Swiss Trade," and "The Capital Levy Bubble: How It Burst in Czechoslovakia."[54] This occurred despite the fact that these aspects of the party platform were deemphasized, if not outright excluded, in many candidates' campaigns.[55] While the Red Scare campaign was ostensibly centered on the Labour Party's plot to "[unleash] in Britain all the horrors from which Russia has suffered," its emphasis on concrete policy proposals—proposals which had in fact been carried out by socialist governments in other European countries—was intended to remind middle-class voters of Labour's links, not with Russian Bolshevism, but with continental socialism.[56]

At the same time, the Conservatives targeted working-class voters by emphasizing the link between Labour's support for free trade and loans to Russia, and rising British unemployment. The government's domestic failings were depicted as the product of its preoccupation with bolstering international communism, as in the headline "Another Jump in Unemployment: 16,284 More in a Week: Socialists' 'Positive Remedy' Fraud: Premier Salutes Red Flags All Day."[57] The Russian loan was equated with the Labour Party's advocacy of increased trade with Germany to help rebuild its economy, and the two policies were presented as squeezing the British worker at the expense of the foreigner. The equation of Labour with foreigners and foreignness was as much a part of Conservative electoral strategy as the equation of Baldwin with Englishness, and John Ramsden has pointed to Baldwin's references to "Monsieur Zinoviev" during the 1924 campaign as a conscious attempt to make the Comintern leader "sound that much more alien than a mere 'Mister.'"[58]

The alleged foreign influence on Labour was made visually explicit in the Conservative Party's election posters. The party produced a series of simple text posters explaining the evils of Labour's "Bolshie loan" proposals. One poster read: "The Socialists say the Bolshie loan means jobs. It does—For Russians and Germans."[59] These text posters were supplemented by a series of pictorial posters, including one by the illustrator Alfred Leete, most famous for his 1914 recruitment poster in which Kitchener points to the viewer above the caption "Your Country Needs You." Leete's 1924 poster depicted a greedy figure clad in a Russian fur hat clutching at a pile of gold coins, evidently plundered from the hapless John Bull standing with his pockets emptied in the back left corner of the poster. The poster's caption, "It's Your Money He Wants," is a reference to the Moderates' famous 1907 LCC poster "It's Your Money We Want," which sought to associate Progressive council members with embezzlement and fraud. The 1907 poster was reworked and reissued at successive election campaigns throughout the Edwardian period, and the 1924 poster would doubtless have evoked memories of the earlier image, creating a further subconscious association between the Labour Party and corruption.[60]

This iconography of the sinister foreigner was similarly on display in the Poy cartoon "Motor Show Marvels," published in the *Daily Mail*. The cartoon was a reference to the annual motor exhibition at Olympia, which had opened the preceding day. It also, doubtless, reminded many of the Grant affair of the previous month, in which the prime minister injudiciously accepted a £30,000 "endowment" to support his ownership and upkeep of a Daimler town car from his friend Sir Alexander Grant, to whom he had recently offered a knighthood. While the scandal ultimately subsided, at the time several members of the cabinet had believed that the government would fall over the issue.[61] The Russian passenger in MacDonald's "Red Car" shares many of the physical attributes of the money grubber in the Conservative poster. The German, in contrast, is an overfed businessman, fat off the riches of German dumping facilitated by MacDonald's free trade policies. While both poster and cartoon may initially appear too ridiculous to be efficacious, such humorous portrayals sought less to rationally persuade viewers than simply to trigger subconscious associations between Labour's Russian loan and free trade policies, and graft, foreign greed, and British impoverishment. And as their humorousness made them more memorable, it arguably increased their impact.[62]

Finally, the Conservative campaign sought to influence the electorate, and in particular female voters, through an equation of the Labour Party with Bolshevik lawlessness and disrespect for the family. Given the contemporary belief that women were more religious than men, Conservative attacks on Bolshevism's professed and Labour's alleged atheism should also be read as an appeal to female voters. Though the *Mail* did seek to appeal to women on the level of rational political discourse through a series of "Talks with Women" on "Why You Should Vote Conservative," the column space devoted specifically to so-called women's issues was comparatively slim in 1924.[63] However, the lack of explicit coverage of women's issues masks the degree to which much of the rhetoric of the 1924 campaign was clearly targeted at frightening women voters. The relationship between the Labour Party, the Bolsheviks, and atheism was stressed in articles such as "Torturers of Christians: Bolshevik Comrades of Mr. MacDonald" and "Cabinet's Moscow Friends," which outlined the "horrors a 'loan' would support," including a "malignant war on the church." Labour's Russian cronies were also said to support the "torture of women" in a country where "[m]arriage is easier than the purchase of a broadcasting licence, and can be dissolved by a 'husband' taking his 'wife' before a local official and there discarding her, as a buyer returns

Figure 3.1. Conservative Party election poster by Alfred Leete, 1924.
(Courtesy of the Cambridge University Library)

damaged goods to a shop."[64] Over the previous two decades the Conservative Party had developed a political language that emphasized the defense of the family and made conscious appeals to "the sanctity of 'hearth and home' and the 'domestic idyll.'"[65] In 1924 this discourse of family was yoked to the campaign against socialism to a greater degree than in any previous election.

In addition to being a threat to family and religion, the so-called Labour-Bolshevists were also presented as a threat to law and order, an attack which again could be expected to resonate in particular with the new female electorate.[66] On 24 October, the day before the publication of the Zinoviev letter, the *Mail* ran an article on "Angry Socialist Hooligans," reporting that "Candidates, as well as women supporters, have been attacked or threatened. There is no mean trick to which the Socialist mobs have not stooped. . . . There does not seem to be much doubt that Bolsheviks with Bolshevik money are at work stirring up riots and attacks on all opponents of Socialism." The same day, the *Express* warned readers that campaign violence, carried out on behalf of the socialists by

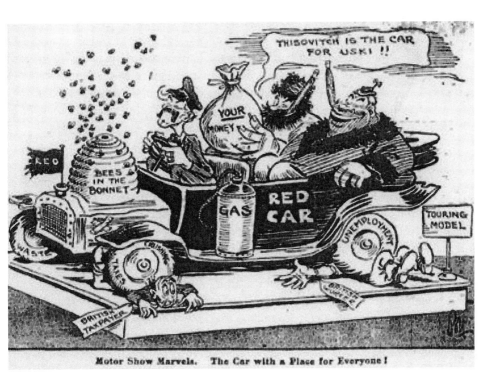

Figure 3.2. Cartoon by "Poy" (Percy Fearon), insinuating Labour's subservience to German and Russian interests. (© *Daily Mail*, 18 October 1924)

rowdies who were "often of alien origin . . . goes far beyond the limits of legitimate excitement. It is a familiar form of terrorism, and marks a well-defined stage on the road to the strangulation of liberty. . . . London is a day's march closer to Moscow and the people of this country are moving towards a supine enslavement."[67] The accompanying cartoons by Strube and Poy illustrated the threat posed by these rowdies. The following day, the *Mail* ended its leader on the implications of the Zinoviev letter by suggesting that "the organized violence at the elections is part of the Bolshevik plan" of "armed insurrection."[68] In emphasizing alleged Labour rowdyism, the conservative press was following the lead set by Conservative Central Office.[69] As with pictorial imagery, press reporting during the campaign both complimented and amplified the election propaganda put out by Conservative headquarters.[70]

Though it is impossible to quantify the impact of the Red Scare campaign on the outcome of the election, few contemporaries or historians have doubted that its impact was in fact significant, particularly in increasing turnout among middle-class and female voters. The day after the election, Beaverbrook cabled Rothermere: "I congratulate you most heartily on your magnificent victory STOP You have made the new Baldwin ministry STOP Now control it if you can."[71] Herbert Morrison later recorded that he sensed a cooling toward Labour among women voters over the course of the campaign.[72] The interwar social chroniclers Robert Graves and Alan Hodge credited the surge in middle-class votes for the Conservatives largely to the publication of the Zinoviev letter, a view endorsed by the journalist and social commentator Kingsley Martin.[73] Fifty years later, media scholars James Curran and Jean Seaton put forth the same view, arguing that "the effect of the sustained red scare in the press was to polarize the election between left and right. . . . The hysteria whipped up by the press also contributed to a massive increase in turnout. . . . The combined effect . . . increased the Conservative vote and resulted in a landslide Tory victory."[74]

The campaign's attempt to scare working-class supporters of Labour away from the party appears to have been less successful, as the party's total vote not only held, but increased by 2.6 percent. But while the Labour vote increased by just over a million, the number of Conservative voters shot up from under 5.3 million to over 7.4 million—a surge in support that cannot merely be attributed to the collapse of the Liberal vote.[75] The 1924 election saw the highest turnout of the interwar period, and a large number of these first-time voters were doubtless women, casting their votes against socialism.

In assessing the impact of the Red Scare campaign, we need to consider how press coverage interacted with other types of information in forming public opinion. The press served an important and arguably dominant role in shaping interwar opinion about politics; however, readers did not blindly follow the voting advice of their daily paper.[76] While the popular press, on balance, served a conservative function throughout the interwar period, voters seemingly heeded its advice more closely at certain moments.[77] Only by considering the interaction between Bolshevist rhetoric and existing political realities can we appreciate why this form of propaganda was so effective in tarring the Labour Party in the early 1920s.

Curran and Seaton have argued that the main function of the interwar press was to reinforce conservative values and opposition to progressive change through a process of agenda-setting and selective interpretation that "helped to sustain the dominant culture by stigmatizing radical opponents of the political order."[78] But even with this disadvantage, the Labour Party made considerable progress in the early 1920s. In part the explanations for this are obvious. Electors' information about politicians and political parties is not solely gained from the media or from political propaganda. Personal encounters with Labour politicians in voters' communities and experiences with Labour in local government obviously informed opinions about the party. The same was true in industrial relations, and, as in the case of the 1919 railway strike, there were limits to the capacity of anti-Labour propaganda to convince Britons that organized, nonviolent strike activity was an assault on the community. Additionally, Labour's lack of political power, at least at the national level, from 1918 to 1923 worked to the party's advantage. As an opposition party, it could criticize the inadequacy of government attempts to combat rising unemployment or the persistent housing shortage without the responsibility of actually attempting to solve these problems themselves. A vote for Labour in the general election of 1922 or 1923 was, in many cases, as much a protest vote against politics as usual as a vote for socialism, or even for greater social redistribution. Of course, the flip side was that, in 1924 (or during the municipal elections in 1922), Labour's opponents could tar the party with the same claims of incompetence that Labour had previously thrown at them.

Conservative propaganda and the almost universally hostile press coverage were not without effect on the party's fortunes. But that impact was felt most forcibly at moments when conservative accusations that the Labour movement was an anti-social, anti-constitutional, anti-British, crypto-communist political force had the most resonance. Thus, the public was more responsive to the anti-Labour critique in the wake of the avowedly unconstitutional action of the Poplar councillors in 1921, or after ten months under a Labour government that failed to produce any substantive cure for unemployment (or any substantive legislation at all, save the Russian treaty and the Wheatley housing act, which provided public subsidies for rental housing), or during the chaos of the general strike, than it was during the 1918, 1922, and 1923 general elections in which Labour candidates, many of them ex-soldiers, fought on a platform of patriotism, moderation, and gradual reform, or during the 1919 railway strike in which the supposedly anarchist strikers both abjured violence and persuasively argued for the legitimacy of their grievances and the constitutionality of their action.[79]

Even at those moments when voters were most likely to be open to anti-Labour propaganda, certain sectors of the electorate were more susceptible to Conservative discourses about the threat of Labour than others. Labour's vote not only held but increased in 1924, and it is clear that many members of the organized working class especially were unwilling to attribute the economic downtown to the premier's preoccupation with saluting red flags all day. Gareth Stedman Jones has rightfully emphasized that "there are no simple rules of translation from the social to the political"; but while political language may be relatively autonomous from social experience, it cannot be completely divorced from it. Propagandistic arguments cannot be cut from whole cloth, but must be "forged" from the "raw material" of actual experience.[80] Throughout the 1920s, the Conservative Party and its allies in the press consistently painted Labour and its interests as separate from "the public," to the detriment of the Labour movement politically and industrially.[81] However, there were limits to the success of such propaganda and those limits became most apparent at moments when Labour's actions accorded least with Conservative depictions of them. The Conservative argument lost purchase at those moments when "a gulf opened up between its premises and the perceptions of its constituency."[82]

While the impact of Conservative propaganda and press coverage may have been limited by the essential reasonableness of the British voter, the hostility of the popular press toward the Labour movement is significant not only for its effect on public opinion but also for its effect on Labour attitudes toward the mass media. The growing hostility of the popular press strengthened the position of those who argued that the "poison gas press" could not be trusted to give fair and unbiased news, and that any attempt to work through the mass media was foredoomed to failure. This attitude combined with the instinctive antagonism of many within the Labour movement toward commercial culture to undermine support for efforts to engage with the mass media in the wake of the First World War.

CHAPTER FOUR

Changing Attitudes in the 1920s

I N APRIL 1922, Will Henderson warned his colleagues in the Labour press department against complacency: "It would be a grave mistake to assume that, because Labour has made headway in the past, despite the lack of press and publicity media of its own," it could continue to advance in the face of this new wave of press hostility.[1] Even the general election success in 1923 did not assuage anxieties about the impact of anti-Socialist press coverage. Writing immediately after the formation of the first Labour ministry, the editor of the *Daily Herald* argued that Labour could never hope to form a majority government with "the Press so steadily against us," an opinion shared by Beatrice Webb.[2] The conviction that the anti-Labour attitude of the popular press was undermining the party's political fortunes was accompanied by a newfound fatalism about the role of the press in British politics. Prominent party members in the 1920s increasingly argued that any attempt to permeate the capitalist press was foredoomed to failure.[3] This attitude was encouraged by social theorists who argued that the commercial nature of the modern press dictated that it would act as a socially, and by extension politically, conservative force. Their belief in the structural relationship between commercial ownership and anti-Labour bias in the press led Labour's leaders to ignore potential avenues for rapprochement with individual newspapers—most obviously the *Daily News*, but also the *Daily Express*—which might have offered them opportunities to reverse some of the damage done.

Similar suspicions poisoned the relationship between the movement and the BBC in the first decade of its existence. Even after the BBC was re-chartered as a publicly owned corporation, many on the left continued to harbor suspicions that the corporation was too inherently politically and socially conservative to give Labour a fair run. As a result, Labour arguably missed a valuable opportunity by not supporting the expansion of "controversial" broadcasting in the 1920s, as the mere fact of holding broadcast debates on political and social issues was likely to redound to the party's advantage by drawing into question the status quo.[4]

The party made huge political strides in this decade, but it did so largely through an emphasis on grassroots politics at the expense of national publicity. The press in the early 1920s responded to the growth of Labour with a determined campaign of vilification; the Labour movement in turn responded to the hostility of the press first by misunderstanding its significance and then by failing to combat its effects successfully. While in the late 1920s and the 1930s such suspicions of the "capitalist" media spurred Labour's leaders to work that much harder to make their voices heard, in the decade after the war, hostility and paranoia widened the breach between the Labour movement and the new mass media.

Political and industrial reformers had long held that the "capitalist" press was out to distort their message and subvert their interests. As far back as the second Trades Union Congress in 1869, a delegate had argued for the creation of a working-class press on the grounds that the "newspapers were dependent on and enlisted in the interests of capital," and thus were reliably anti-Labour, as "it did not 'pay' a newspaper to devote itself to the advocacy of Labour's rights."[5] Furthermore, as press readership soared in the first decades of the twentieth century, a body of literature emerged which argued that the very nature of the capitalist ownership of the media dictated that the press must *necessarily* work against working-class interests, and against the interests of political progressives, a threatening prospect for Labour's political future.

The first two serious considerations of press bias came from the American author Upton Sinclair and the Roman Catholic conservative writer Hilaire Belloc. In *The Brass Check: A Study of American Journalism,* Sinclair argued that the conservative bias of the popular press was a direct result of its ownership by capitalist interests. "A capitalist newspaper," he asserted, "lives by the capitalist system, it fights for that system, and in the nature of the case cannot do otherwise. . . . to expect justice and truthtelling of a capitalist newspaper is to expect asceticism at a cannibal feast." With equal vividness, he denounced the influence that commercial advertisers had over press content, writing of the "extent to which the bait used in the game of journalistic angling is selected and treated by the business fisherman. . . . Not merely is there general control of the spirit and tone of the paper; there is control in minute details, sometime grotesque."[6]

Belloc, a frequent contributor to Lansbury's *Herald,* put forth a similar argument in his work, *The Free Press.* Belloc emphasized the general congruence of interest between press proprietor and advertiser: "They were of the same kind and breed. The fellow that got rich quick in a newspaper speculation . . . was exactly the same kind of man as he who bought a peerage out of a 'combine' in music halls or cut his throat when his bluff in Indian silver was called."[7] Six years later, Kingsley Martin offered a less colorfully articulated but no less serious assessment of the impact of capitalist ownership of the press on news content and public opinion:

> The real education of the masses to-day is the Press, which, with the exception of one or two struggling Labour papers, is owned by a few well-known capitalists, and is completely unscrupulous in misrepresenting the Socialist case, in inventing scares to influence a timid electorate, and in using every device known to the skilled propagandist for keeping the worker ignorant, amused and docile. . . . *Capitalists have all become democrats since the discovery that, in the twentieth century, it is, after all, possible to fool almost all the people all the time.*[8]

While these authors focused on the role of press proprietors and advertisers in determining press content, American journalist and social theorist Walter Lippmann argued that the imperative of newspaper proprietors to explain the world in simple, easy to digest stereotypes would lead to their adopting a conservative slant. In his seminal work, *Public Opinion,* Lippmann offered a wide-ranging analysis of the way in which information is disseminated, public opinion is formed, and political decisions are made in modern societies. He argued that the distinctive characteristic of modernity was the complexity and volume of information that decision makers—be they voters, politicians, or civil servants—are asked to assimilate on a daily basis. While certain decision makers might have the benefit of specialist knowledge, the majority take their views, particularly on complex issues, from their daily newspaper. These newspapers "acting upon everybody for thirty minutes in twenty-four hours, [are] asked to create a mystical force called Public Opinion," a task which they are ill-suited to perform with any objectivity as "the facts of modern life do not spontaneously take a shape in which they can be known. . . . the facts are not simple, and not at all obvious, but subject to choice and opinion."[9] Ultimately, newspapers make choices about which facts are most important, and put their own gloss or spin on those facts.

While theoretically this system of distortion has the potential to undermine capitalist or conservative interests as effectively as labor or progressive interests, Lippmann argued that in practice the press would tend to reinforce conservative biases. Unlike Sinclair and Belloc, he did not attribute this tendency to the political prerogatives of capitalist press magnates or the coercive power wielded by commercial advertisers, so much as to the plain fact that it is easier to pander to conventional wisdom than to convince readers of the merits of a complex issue. Industrial disputes were complex issues par excellence, which is why, he argued,

> if you study the way many a strike is reported in the press, you will find, very often, that the issues [over which the workers are striking] are rarely in the headlines, barely in the leading paragraphs, and sometimes not even mentioned anywhere. . . . It comes from the economic necessity of interesting the reader quickly, and the economic risk involved in not interesting him at all, or of offending him by unexpected news insufficiently or clumsily described. All these difficulties . . . cause him naturally to prefer the indisputable fact and a treatment more readily adaptable to the reader's interest. The indisputable fact and the easy interest are the strike itself and the reader's inconvenience.[10]

Thus, according to Lippmann, it was the readers' own prejudices, combined with a commercial imperative to sell papers, that led to the conservatism of the popular press.

Lippmann's most influential admirer in Britain was Norman Angell, who was in turn one of the most important influences on Labour's press policy in the 1920s. Angell, like many writers of the interwar Left, began his career as a commercial journalist. During his years as managing editor of the Paris-based *Continental Daily Mail* (1905 to 1912), he wrote his famous critique of the Edwardian arms race, *The Grand Illusion*. While in France, Angell attempted unsuccessfully to increase the coverage of social welfare issues in the paper, suggesting that Northcliffe run a weekly feature on "the record of social organisation the world over—old age pension schemes, insurance against sickness, unemployment, etc.—as necessarily what is done in each country interests and affects the forward parties of all the others."[11] His opposition to the war pushed him further to the political left, and his work in launching the Union for Democratic Control in 1915 was the beginning of a long relationship between Angell, Ramsay MacDonald, and the Labour Party.

After his return from the Paris Peace Conference, Angell wrote *The Press and the Organisation of Society*, a scathing analysis that was largely influenced by his observations of press coverage of the treaty negotiations. While the text quotes extensively from Lippmann's writings, it is, unlike *Public Opinion*, a distinctly leftist tract. It begins with an assertion of the near omnipotent power of the press over public opinion, arguing that "newspapers are practically the only means which the community has of informing itself of the facts which determine its collective decisions, social or political," and goes on to condemn these papers as "perhaps the worst of all menaces to modern democracy. . . . the main instrument by which any real movement towards a new social order is resisted." Like Lippmann, he largely rejected Sinclair and Belloc's arguments about the influence of capitalist advertisers, but he shared their belief that the direct stake of the proprietors of the commercial press in the capitalist system meant that they were unlikely to use their columns to champion social reform.[12] As the journalist A. J. Cummings would later point out, "the millionaire newspaper-proprietor" is "not prone to champion sincerely and consistently causes which do not appear to be in the selfish interest of great wealth."[13] Ultimately, Angell shared Lippmann's belief that commercial imperatives created a conservative bias within the popular press, as "it is both safer and more profitable to encourage the public in the falsehood with which it is familiar than to tell it the necessary but unpleasant truth that it does not like to hear."[14]

The views expressed by Sinclair, Belloc, Lippmann, and Angell were widely debated within the Labour movement in the early 1920s. An article in the *Labour Organiser* focused on the influence of advertising interests over press policy. In a review of Angell's book for *Labour Magazine,* the left-wing author and critic Gerald Gould took issue with Angell's conclusion that the press was conservative because it was itself a capitalist interest. Gould argued that capitalists sponsored newspapers as investments in propaganda, which was why a proprietor could *"go on losing gigantic sums every year and yet counting his business a success."* In the same issue, the secretary of the National Union of Journalists endorsed Gould's view. Herbert Tracey, at that point head of the TUC's press department, supported Angell's analyses, and further homed in on the concentration of media ownership in the hands of a small number of press barons. This theme, in turn, had been underscored in the 1923 ILP pamphlet, "The Capitalist Press: Who Owns It and Why," which attempted to illustrate the extent to which the popular press was effectively a "capitalist newspaper monopoly."[15]

This emphasis on the "trustification" of the popular press, or its consolidation in the hands of a very few proprietors, all of whom were antisocialist by both economic imperative and ideological conviction, remained a central theme of Left criticism throughout the interwar period. George Orwell, in writing about the French press in 1928, blamed the capitalist "press combine" for "strangl[ing] free speech in France" and undermining the progress of socialist politics.[16] Though critics continued to dispute the exact causes of press bias—with some emphasizing commercial and others ideological imperatives—all agreed that a commercially operated press was inherently inimical to Labour's interests.

In the immediate postwar period, such dire prognoses may have appeared exaggerated and unduly prejudiced. After all, Lord Northcliffe had allowed the party column space to put forward its case in November 1918, and though the press had been initially hostile toward the railwaymen during the strike, Labour's public relations campaign had shown that it was possible to obtain fair coverage by appealing to publishers' pocketbooks, if not to their consciences. Just three years later, however, the situation had begun to look very different, and charges of systemic anti-Labour bias increasingly led to the rejection of previous strategies of engagement.

In its reports to the Labour Party conference in 1919, 1920, and 1921, the press and publicity department had made much of its function as a liaison between the movement and the commercial press; from 1922 onwards, attempts to influence the commercial media were no longer discussed. Instead, the focus of the department's annual report shifted to its work in fostering local and national Labour media. The gradual abandonment of the previous policy of permeation was further visible in the attitudes of the rank and file. At the 1925 party conference, a resolution was placed on the agenda advocating that "our leaders should refrain from contributing articles to the Capitalist Press, which is avowedly antagonistic to the principles of the Party."[17] In a debate on a similar resolution the following year, the mover of the resolution argued that "it was a wrong principle altogether that their leaders should be writing in that way." Further, capitalist newspapers did not accept Labour articles because "they wanted to help the movement," but merely in hopes of attracting a working-class audience. Thus, in a situation where important Labour issues were at stake, these papers could not be counted on to support Labour's cause.[18] A few Labour politicians, most notably J. R. Clynes and Ellen Wilkinson, continued to write frequently for the "capitalist" press throughout the 1920s, and to encourage the party to make greater use of media such as film in appealing to the electorate. Wilkinson even secured a contract with the *Daily Express* to serialize her first novel, *Clash*, "a story about modern politics—and love [during the general strike]."[19] However, more radical Labourites, such as the head of the Clydeside group, James Maxton, made a point of repeatedly turning down lucrative contract offers from the London dailies.[20]

Figure 4.1. *Daily Herald* poster from the 1920s featuring the hand of monopoly: "Berry, Rothermere, Beaverbrook, Starmer, and Cowdray," the five press barons who owned the majority of Britain's newspapers. (Courtesy of the TUC archives, Modern Records Centre, Warwick University)

This growing antagonism was not directed solely at Conservative newspapers. The Liberal press, too, increasingly came under attack. Critics denounced Liberal papers which had formerly given publicity to Labour's cause as being "friendly in a lukewarm manner . . . when it suits [their interests]," or of "attempting to set groups of Trade Unionists against each other, by running campaigns in favour of some Trade Union demands and denouncing others."[21] Comments such as "the alleged 'sympathetic' newspapers are the most dangerous enemies of all" began to appear in Labour publications.[22] After the 1923 general election, the *Daily Herald* editor, Hamilton Fyfe, suggested a moral equivalency between the *Daily News* and the *Daily Mail,* claiming that the Liberal newspapers, no less than their Tory rivals, "were reckless as to what weapons and methods of attack they employed" and did not shrink "from employing Rothermerian tactics against Labour."[23]

Such criticisms reflected sincere resentment toward a press that had supported Labour when it was convenient for the forces of Liberalism, but had not hesitated to "blea[t] about the splitting of the Progressive vote" whenever Labour attempted to run candidates for seats formerly controlled by Liberals.[24] The Labour movement had long felt that "Liberal journals, without cherishing any ill-will towards working men, had failed to understand or sympathise with them."[25] The reception of such attacks on Liberal journals was bolstered by changes in the party's electoral strategy, which, from 1920 onwards, was increasingly focused on discrediting Liberalism as a political force. After its strong showing in the 1918 general election, Labour consistently represented itself as the "second party of the State, from which must come any alternative Government to that of Mr. Lloyd George."[26] This strategy entailed the displacement of the independent Liberals, and Labour not only made a point of running candidates against sitting Liberal MPs and councillors, but the party's propaganda became increasingly hostile toward its former allies. After Labour defeated Sir John Simon in the Spen Valley by-election of January 1920, the *Daily Herald* crowed that "we all know [the Liberal Party] is the corpse of a worn-out policy of make-believe. The election figures prove that there is no room in the world to-day for a camouflaged buffer party between the monopolists and the workers."[27] In the wake of the Progressives' poor showing in three-cornered contests against Moderates, as the Conservatives were known in London, and Labour opponents at the March 1922 LCC elections, the paper again emphasized that "this proves what has also been proven at Parliamentary elections—that London has no use for so-called 'Liberals' or 'Progressives.' "[28] Just as the anti-Labour papers took to calling the party the "Labour-Socialists" in an attempt to prejudice voters, the *Daily Herald* referred to the "Mod.-Progs" as the coalition of forces that together stand for "one class . . . the class whose name is Big Business."[29]

It is by no means certain that the policy of "permeation" of the capitalist press which the party pursued in the immediate postwar period would have succeeded in the heightened ideological environment of the 1920s, even had Labour's leaders been willing to follow such a course. However, several indicators suggest that it might have. As we have seen, the Liberal *Daily News* supported the Poplar councillors in 1920, and only gradually turned against the movement as a result of Labour's perceived radicalization and increased anti-Liberal rhetoric in the early 1920s. Even then, the Cadbury-owned London evening paper, the *Star,* endorsed the LLP in constituencies where no Progressive candidate was running.[30] The hostility of the *Daily Express* to Labour in the 1920s was occasionally tempered by Beaverbrook's desire to attract a wider working-class and lower middle-class readership. As Fyfe conceded in a backhanded compliment to the press lord, the *Express* had at least refrained from joining in the *Mail*'s cynical exploitation, during the 1923 election campaign, of Labour's participation a few months earlier in the Hamburg congress of the Labour and Socialist International. Throughout that campaign, the *Mail* had consistently referred to the organization as the "Sozialistische Arbeiter Internationale," in an effort to make it appear more foreign, sinister, and German-dominated.[31]

The *Express* made a point of advertising its alleged independence and lack of political bias throughout the 1920s. During the 1923 election campaign, the paper ran a leading article claiming that, "The great popular newspaper, independent of party, has come to stay. . . . It is the natural and inevitable development of the growth of an educated democracy with a stronger taste for wide reading and the expression of impartial opinions than for party hack leading articles on politics."[32] In a front page editorial during the 1924 campaign, the paper proclaimed that "the *Daily Express* is not obsessed by the idea that the Socialist Party is the equivalent of the 'Red Peril,' or that a Socialist Government means the destruction of society, the massacre and the barricade. Only those who do not read this newspaper impute such opinions to it. . . . Every side will have an absolutely fair hearing—and then it is for the people to decide."[33] In 1929, the paper ran a series of letters on their opinion page, including the following, from "A Socialist Reader": "Sir—As an enthusiastic supporter of the Labour party I am delighted to see that the *Daily Express* is giving fair play to all sides. . . . We have long been in need of a daily paper that will give all sides in an impartial way. I sincerely hope the *Daily Express* will continue to be impartial in its political matter."[34]

Though the paper's sincerity is at best questionable, the publication of such articles suggests Beaverbrook's desire, if only for commercial reasons, that his paper be perceived as objective. Labour writers could potentially have used this desire to their advantage, as they did during the 1919 railway strike, to secure column space in the *Express* to explain their position to the paper's readers. While the success of such a policy cannot be assumed, it is telling that the *Express* continued to serialize Wilkinson's novel *Clash* throughout the 1929 election campaign, in spite of its obvious political slant. Beaverbrook also hired the Australian cartoonist David Low in 1927, despite his Labour politics, and gave him relatively free rein to print cartoons injurious to the Conservative Party, and occasionally to Beaverbrook himself. While it begs credulity to suggest that either the *News* or the *Express* could have been won over to the Labour camp, it is possible that a more conciliatory attitude on the part of Labour could have won them a better showing in the Conservative and Liberal press.

With the party increasingly united in its determination to eschew the commercial press as an outlet for Labour news and propaganda, the leadership might have courted other potential mass media. However, the party took relatively little notice of the newsreels in the 1920s, and similarly ignored the potential of documentary and feature film. Labour's apparent disinterest in newsreel content in the 1920s put the party at a disadvantage, given the early attention devoted to the medium by their Conservative rivals, and is hard to account for in light of the party's active interest in print media. In the case of documentary and feature film, Labour's lack of initiative was largely attributable to its comparative penury. Whereas the trade unions could coerce and cajole their members into diverting two pence per annum to subsidize the *Herald,* there was less enthusiasm for the prospect of funding experiments with film. The NEC in the 1920s repeatedly rejected proposals to create films either of a "purely propaganda nature" or "not purely propaganda, but capable of being used to point a moral" which could be shown around the country in Labour halls and trade union buildings or outdoors through the use of traveling cinema vans.[35] But while penury may have prevented Labour from realizing these proposals, prejudice alone prevented them from exploiting the new medium of broadcasting.

Proponents of the expansion of political broadcasting in the 1920s could argue both that the government-regulated BBC presented a more

Figure 4.2. One of David Low's first cartoons for the *Evening Standard* (13 October 1927) mocking the pressures put on the artist by his employer Lord Beaverbrook to depict Conservative politicians in a favorable light. (© *Evening Standard*, 13 October 1927. Courtesy of the Cambridge University Library)

promising forum for unbiased political debate than the commercial press, and that the BBC's explicit educational mission meshed well with Labour's own agenda.[36] Certainly, there was a congruence between BBC director-general John Reith's desire for "a more informed and enlightened democracy" and Labour's own educationalist attitude.[37] Like many within the Labour leadership, Reith harbored anxieties about the interwar electorate. He believed that "the ignorance and indifference of electorates is proverbial" and that "it is admittedly a serious menace to the country that suffrage be exercised without first-hand personal knowledge." However, his conviction that "the extension of the scope of broadcasting" would provide "the essential basis on which reasoned and intelligent opinion can be formed" and lead to the creation of "a more intelligent and enlightened electorate" was treated with skepticism by men and women who feared lest political discussions on the airwaves would carry an anti-Labour bias.[38]

The first broadcast to call attention to the potential for bias in reporting controversial matters concerned not a political but an industrial dispute. In April 1923, the BBC broadcast a talk on the threatened builders' strike by the editor of *Building News*. The BBC deemed the broadcast to be an uncontroversial statement of fact, but the Builders' Union disagreed. The union took issue both with the speaker's statement that "building wages had increased to a rate higher than in any pre-War year," when "no mention was made of the fact that real wages were 17 per cent lower than pre-War," and with his concluding appeal to the two sides to submit to independent arbitration in order to avoid a strike.[39] While the BBC held that the broadcast was "entirely unexceptional and impartial," to the builders the broadcast was an attempt to influence public opinion to the detriment of their bargaining position. In the month after the broadcast, two Labour MPs spoke out in the House on the insufficient safeguards against the broadcasting of biased industrial and political news.[40] MP Charles Trevelyan, Labour representative to the 1923 Sykes Committee on the future of broadcasting, expressed similar anxieties.

The government appointed that committee, chaired by the Conservative MP and former commander of the Royal Flying Corps, Sir Frederick Sykes, to advise whether the government should assume control of the radio, or whether broadcasting should be left in private hands. Trevelyan used the committee's hearings to question the BBC's directors about controversial broadcast content. He pointed out to the directors that, legally, "there is nothing at all to prevent you as a Company issuing speeches or information which you think perfectly harmless," and indicated his view that the current situation was untenable. The directors responded that, given the risks involved, "it is better for the Broadcasting Company to keep away from controversial matter," adding, gratuitously, "Political matter is very controversial." Trevelyan pressed the issue, asking whether the directors could "not conceive a situation in which the public would rather like, not to have partial propaganda, but to have statements from both sides on great public questions; but would not feel safe in taking those statements if issued from a Company and not from some sort of body which represented the public." The directors reiterated their conviction that discretion in such cases should remain with the BBC.[41] The sole Labour witness before the committee, Herbert Morrison, shared Trevelyan's concerns. When asked his views on the future of the medium, Morrison stated, "instead of being in the hands of a partially controlled but otherwise irresponsible private monopoly, [broadcasting] should be publicly owned and controlled."[42]

The committee ultimately recommended that the company remain in private hands, but that a publicly appointed Board of Commissioners be established to oversee broadcast content. Their recommendation was adopted, and the government appointed Sykes to head the new advisory board. On the subject of controversial broadcasting, the committee merely suggested that "firm and consistent circumspection" be exercised by the BBC in selecting broadcast content. The committee's conclusions differed widely from those of its sole Labour representative, and, in a signed reservation, Trevelyan expressed the Labour view that the BBC should be reconstituted as a public institution, arguing that the public interest required a tighter degree of supervision of broadcast content than could be ensured by the appointment of an advisory board:

> The proposals of the committee show the necessity for regarding Broadcasting as a public service. It is agreed that the proposed Broadcasting Board will have to exercise a very effective general control over whatever system of operation is established. The operating authorities will have in the public interest to submit to a large amount of regulation as to the matter which they broadcast. The mere technical process of transmission is the only region in which public policy can permit the operating private company to have a free hand.[43]

The first Labour government came to power shortly after Baldwin implemented the Sykes Committee's recommendations. Given the continuance of the BBC as a privately owned company, the new government's policy during its nine months in office was to avoid creating any precedent for governmental support for the broadcasting of controversial matter, lest it be used by a future Conservative government less keen to safeguard the public against biased political and industrial broadcast reports. Postmaster General Vernon Hartshorn summarily dismissed a private member's question over the possibility of broadcasting parliamentary debates, stating that the two fifteen-minute nightly news bulletins, including as they did "any items of parliamentary news that are of special interest," could be presumed to "meet the requirements of the public in this respect."[44] A later request by Reith to broadcast a debate between the three party leaders on "some subject of political interest" was rejected on the grounds that "the potentialities of broadcasting for propaganda purposes [were] so considerable," and that, were one such broadcast allowed, "it would be found extremely difficult to draw the line between what should and should not be permitted." Reith's plea that "the utility of broadcasting as a medium of enlightenment is prejudiced owing to the ban upon such matter" produced no response.[45] The BBC's official historian, Asa Briggs, has stressed Reith's commitment to fostering political debate over the airwaves in this period, and laid the blame for the lack of "free discussion of public issues" at the steps of Westminster and Whitehall.[46] In the case of the first Labour ministry, he is certainly correct.

Hartshorn's one concession to the BBC was to authorize the broadcast of speeches by each of the three party leaders during the 1924 general election campaign, the first-ever party election broadcasts. MacDonald, however, signally failed to take advantage of this opportunity. Despite his noted success as an orator, he never became a talented broadcaster. The Labour leader, according to Briggs, affected a "Garbo pose" of disdain for the entire medium of broadcasting, made no special preparations for his first broadcast, and ended up giving what Reith considered to be a "hopeless speech" which might well have "do[ne] him harm" with the electorate.[47] Baldwin, in contrast, "took the opportunity seriously; came to [the BBC broadcasting studio at] Savoy Hill to see exactly what he had to do; asked many intelligent questions," and gave a well prepared broadcast which Reith thought would "win the election for him."[48] Unlike his two opponents (Asquith gave a similarly uninspired performance), Baldwin was quick to recognize that the new medium would become a powerful force in politics and took pains to learn how best to exploit its potential.[49]

Once out of power, Labour continued to argue that a privately owned monopoly should not have the prerogative to propagandize to the electorate at its own discretion. William Graham, MP, Labour's representative to the second committee on the future of broadcasting, convened in 1925, again pushed hard for the nationalization of the company. This time the advocates of nationalization prevailed, and the company was reconstituted as the British Broadcasting Corporation on 1 January 1927.

However, before the reconstitution went into effect, the nation was confronted with the drama of the general strike, in which the BBC was to play a starring role.

For the first four years of the BBC's existence, Labour had been preoccupied with the potential for political bias posed by the existence of a broadcast monopoly under capitalist control. The Baldwin government's willingness to exert pressure on the BBC during the strike, and the BBC director-general's apparent sympathy with Conservative interpretations of the "national interest," raised serious questions as to whether the reconstitution of the company as a public corporation would act as an insurance against abuses, or whether it would simply make the airwaves the tool of the party in power. The government's casual manipulation of the BBC during the strike also called in to question Labour's strategy of seeking to exclude broadcasting from the political sphere. The movement's policy of obstruction increasingly seemed likely to result, not in politics being excluded from the BBC altogether, but in Labour politics being excluded. Though the change was slow in coming, Labour eventually jettisoned its obstructionist stance in favor of a strategy of cooperation with the BBC, even though it meant accepting that Labour would not always receive the same access to the airwaves as their Conservative opponents. Limited access to the airwaves, party and industrial leaders came to feel, was better than no access. As Reith wrote in his diary after a meeting with MacDonald to discuss broadcast arrangements during the 1929 general election campaign, the Labour Party were "so dependent on the wireless . . . [that they] were ready to agree to almost anything."[50] This shift paralleled the shift in Labour's approach toward the popular press. Whereas previously the movement had refused to engage with a medium that it could not rely upon to give consistently unbiased coverage, in the late 1920s, Labour again sought to secure incremental improvements in its press coverage by courting "capitalist" editors and journalists. Labour leaders also reversed their policy toward the production and promotion of their own paper, the *Daily Herald,* restyling it as a gaudy commercial daily that could compete successfully with the anti-socialist organs of the press. In so doing, they overcame the deep-rooted prejudices that many of them held against commercial journalism and "irrational" political discourse.

CHAPTER FIVE

The Labour Alternative

As RAMSAY MACDONALD WROTE IN 1920, "[t]he Labour Party . . . recognizes public opinion as the only creator of social change which is to last."[1] The leaders of the interwar Labour Party recognized that to succeed in the "drastic readjustment" of society at which they aimed, they would need to convert the electorate to the socialist cause.[2] Yet their lack of support from the popular press posed serious challenges in terms of national publicity and propaganda, problems that were exacerbated by the deep-rooted prejudices of many in the Labour Party about the perils of mass democracy and the corrupting influence of the mass media. Labour activists believed the road to socialism to lie through the political education and enlightenment of the electorate, both working class and middle class; however, many suspected the newly enfranchised masses to be unprepared for the responsibilities of citizenship and overly susceptible to manipulation by unscrupulous propaganda.[3] This pessimism about the potentialities of mass democracy combined with a moral aversion to the new mass culture that emerged at the end of the nineteenth century to limit the willingness of many within the party leadership to engage with the anti-socialist media on its own terms.

Such anxieties were not, of course, limited to the Labour Party. The Liberals in particular held strong reservations about the impact of mass democracy on the British constitutional system. The constitutional theorist Walter Bagehot, writing in the wake of the second reform act, had already professed to see the seeds of Britain's political decline:

What I fear is that both our political parties will bid for the support of the working-man; that both of them will promise to do as he likes if he will only tell them what it is; that, as he now holds the casting vote in our affairs, both parties will beg and pray him to give that vote to them. I can conceive of nothing more corrupting or worse for a set of poor ignorant people.[4]

The Fabian-Liberal theorist Graham Wallas, writing nearly forty years later, believed that the principal risk of mass democracy lay not in politicians pandering to the untrained masses, but in the masses falling prey to the manipulation of cynical politicians. Wallas feared that a politician, having realized the limited reasoning power of his constituents, "may come to regard them as purely irrational creatures of feeling and opinion, and himself as the purely rational 'over-man' who controls them. It is at this point that a resolute and able statesman may become most efficient and most ruthless."[5] While these two Liberals approached their critique of mass politics from different perspectives, both were acutely aware of the threat of the irrational mind to Liberal ideals of representative government. This threat was felt so keenly that certain Edwardian Liberals, including Joseph Pease and Herbert Samuel, even contemplated raising the age of male suffrage to twenty-five.[6] The historian of nineteenth-century Liberalism Colin Matthew has argued that the party's decline in the early twentieth century can be partially attributed to the rise of irrationalist mass politics to which the party, with its long tradition of rationalism and self-improvement, was particularly ill-equipped to adapt.[7]

The Conservatives likewise had reservations about the irrationality of the British electorate. Stanley Baldwin believed the interwar electorate to be uneducated for universal suffrage and admitted that "I fear the mass mind."[8] But while anxieties about mass democracy extended across the political spectrum, they arguably played a particularly salient role in Labour politics. Liberals may have mourned the decline of rational political discourse, but they ultimately proved rather successful in adapting to mass politics in the Edwardian era.[9] Similarly, much has been written on the Conservative appeal to "working-class Toryism" from the late-Victorian era onwards.[10] And, while Liberal and Conservative political strategies for attracting new working-class voters after 1867 were not entirely centered around irrationalist appeals, the parties showed a willingness to exploit the new modes of mass communication—which tended to blur the line between politics and entertainment and to simplify and de-intellectualize political issues. Labour was, on occasion, willing to pursue the same tactics in order to bring its message to the broader public. Nonetheless, the party's publicity policy in the 1920s retained a strong educationalist ethos and its approach to the national press was notably impacted by its anxieties about mass democracy and mass culture.

The early Labour movement sought to educate the British population about the benefits of social reform, to "make socialists." Many of the early leaders of the socialist societies emerged out of a strongly autodidact working-class culture in which it was not altogether surprising to discover an engine tenter living in a Sheffield tenement reading "Tennyson, Pope, Masefield, the Bible, Shakespeare . . . and Plato's Republic" as well as the works of Dickens, Shaw, H. G. Wells, and Arnold Bennett.[11] The conversion to socialism of such men as Keir Hardie, Ramsay MacDonald, Philip Snowden, and Sidney Webb is well known. But the importance of socialist literature and ideology in the political development of many of the interwar leaders of the industrial movement is equally striking. Jimmy Thomas, the leader of the railwaymen's union, may not have read much socialist theory, but Walter Citrine, the Merseyside electrician who went on to serve as general secretary of the TUC from 1926 to 1946, could "quote whole sections of [Karl Marx's] *Value, Price and Profit*" at the age of twenty-five.[12] Ernest Bevin became involved with trade union organization through socialist politics, not the other way around. The largely self-taught lorry driver joined the Bristol Socialist Society in the early 1900s, acted as secretary of the Bristol Right-to-Work committee from 1908 to 1910, and ran as the Socialist candidate for the St. Paul's ward of the City Council in 1909 on a platform of "Down with poverty and slums."[13] Intellectual conviction as well as working-class consciousness spurred the allegiance of these men to the Labour Party, and many would have agreed with Bevin's belief that the role of a Labour press should be to "chang[e] the whole social conception of the people and give them a vision of purer, holier, civilization."[14]

One consequence of this belief in the power of political education through the Labour press was a suspicion of the corruptive influence of anti-Labour journalism. The Labour leadership's fear of the commercial press was augmented by the low estimation in which many of them came to hold the reasoning power of the democratic multitude. The Labour Party lobbied hard in support of the 1918 and 1928 franchise reforms, and was the one party to formally endorse the women's suffrage campaign.[15] Yet unalloyed optimism about mass democracy was quickly tempered by the newly enfranchised working classes' apparent inability to realize their economic self-interest and vote Labour. The uphill battle by Labour's pioneers to win over an apathetic and uneducated public is a frequent trope of early Labour memoirs and biographies. Rather than a working-class franchise paving the way for Labour government, the party is represented as coming to power *in spite of* the vote being given to these undeserving citizens.[16]

The failure of a class-conscious democracy to emerge in the wake of the 1884 and 1918 reform acts came as a surprise to all three political parties.[17] But whereas the Conservatives in the 1920s came to embrace a "less deterministic reading of class" and "gradually learned to distinguish the component elements of the working class, and to appeal to specific interest groups—trade-unionists undercut by foreign imports, housewives, co-operators and small savers," Labour was slow to recognize that members of the working class might rationally understand their interests to be different than those which the Labour Party believed they should possess.[18] Party activists remained convinced that the lack of political support for Labour was less the result of "apathy than bewilderment," and that the working classes were suffering from "mental poverty" as much as from physical deprivation.[19] Given their view that the working classes would not rationally choose to support their political rivals, Labour's leaders were forced to believe that the masses were "manifestly dim-witted," and hence easily hoodwinked "by the sensational poster on the hoarding or headline in the Press."[20]

A significant literature emerged at the beginning of the twentieth century emphasizing the irrationality of the group mentality and the suggestive power of propaganda on the mass mind, including most notably William Trotter's *Instincts of the Herd in Peace and War.*[21] The experience of mass jingoism during the Boer War and the First World War seemed to confirm the supposed capacity of the crowd to be influenced by propaganda and irrational argument.[22] MacDonald was particularly influenced by Trotter's analysis, which he referred to as "an important scientific discovery of the instincts and other mental and political forces which have to be considered by whomever is seriously concerned about the condition of Europe today both as to events and to frames of mind."[23] MacDonald's interest in Trotter reflected his own observed prejudices of the British "herd," which he believed to be composed of a "broad margin of electors who take no rational or abiding interest in politics or in their national affairs" and hence ran the risk of "their unawakened subordinate minds" being perverted by capitalist propaganda.[24] The New Liberal politician and theorist J. A. Hobson similarly feared that the "credulity" of the "mass of workers" left them susceptible to being "distracted and beguiled" by forces of conservatism; and Philip Snowden caustically dismissed the working classes as uneducated and less concerned with political reform than with wasting their money "in drink and gambling."[25]

These uneducated masses, it was feared, would simply "repeat th[e] promptings" of their daily newspapers.[26] Even Labour supporters who paid lip-service to the rationality of the democratic electorate, such as Norman Angell, believed in the capacity of the press to dupe would-be Labour voters:

> Though the waitress or typist may be . . . capable, inherently or potentially, of sound political judgment . . . modern conditions, both as they affect the readers and the newspaper industry itself, not only give native common sense and individual judgment less chance against mass suggestion than did conditions a generation or two ago, but the unwisdom of the million is politically much more serious and dangerous now than it was then.[27]

Angell's commentary is particularly telling of Labour anxieties about the female electorate—the waitresses and typists. MacDonald, luridly, blamed his 1918 defeat at Leicester on "the women—bloodthirsty, cursing their hate, issuing from the courts and alleys crowded with children, reeking with humanity—the sad flotsam and jetsam of wild emotion."[28]

Angell harbored a particular suspicion of the secret political agenda of the female-orientated pictorial press. Papers such as the *Daily Mirror* and the *Daily Sketch,* he argued, were targeted at an audience of mostly women readers, who were "not yet habituated to political discussion or judgment, or the consideration of political principles." The emphasis of these papers on the lives of the glamorous elite, and their serialization of romantic fantasies, "habituate these millions to the idea that a special class, a little tiny minority, should occupy a special position of power, of culture, of deference," and encourage the belief that "the lottery of life may one day take the avid reader of the society columns into the charmed circle." From here, "inevitably there grows up a bias against the idea of equality. The defenders of the old order have already won the battle."[29]

While the Labour leadership feared the impact of the popular press on the unformed mind of working men and women, reservations about the morality of the new commercial journalism prohibited them from producing a Labour alternative which might lure readers away from papers like the *Daily Mail,* and hence save them from its corrupting propaganda. As we have seen, MacDonald himself, despite his lofty rhetoric about educating democracy for socialism, was not above "simplifying the issues to the man in the street" in order to "influence polling results."[30] However, in the early 1920s, many of his colleagues, including Arthur Henderson, Ernest Bevin, and Ben Turner, refused to meet the anti-Labour press on its own turf. As a result, instead of attempting to produce a left-wing equivalent to the *Daily Mail*, Labour ultimately promoted an anti-commercial alternative to the popular press in the form of the *Daily Herald*.

The historian Stuart MacIntyre has suggested that "it occurred to no one [on the Left in the 1920s] that newspapers were commercial enterprises, competing against each other for a mass circulation and therefore bearing a close relationship to the tastes of their readers."[31] This is untrue. The wealth of sociological literature on the press that was produced in the wake of the First World War was not solely concerned with the social and political content of the new mass circulation dailies. Authors such as Angell and Lippmann offered not only a critique of the popular press but also a sophisticated analysis of what made newspapers sell, or why the popular press was popular. This analysis was absorbed and debated by the political Left in Britain. Labour's failure to adopt the commercial model of the popular press in the 1920s was not the result of ignorance as to what that model was, but the product of a profound dislike and distrust of the central tenants of commercial journalism.

Despite his preoccupation with the creation and dissemination of opinion on current events, Lippmann recognized that "[i]t is not primarily their political and social news which holds [newspapers'] circulation. The interest in that is intermittent, and few publishers can bank on it alone. The newspaper, therefore, takes to itself a variety of other features, all primarily designed to hold a body of readers together who, so far as big news is concerned, are not able to be critical."[32] Angell likewise understood that news was usually of secondary importance in selling newspapers. In his advice to the Labour movement on running the *Daily Herald*, he emphasized the importance of producing a paper "as palatable as its rival." If the *Herald* could not compete with the "the sporting page of their favourite trust paper" readers simply would not continue to read it, regardless of their political convictions—"the breakaway of Labour support might be gradual but it would certainly be sure."[33] Others gave similar advice. In 1923, the Printing and Kindred Trades Federation, whose members had launched the original *Daily Herald* as a strike sheet twelve years earlier, produced a memorandum for the joint TUC–Labour Party enquiry committee on the future of the *Herald*. In it, they argued that "the *Daily Herald* circulation will never be as large as is desirable until the paper gives more space and prominence to what may be called 'human emotion stories.' . . . We agreed that it is not to be expected that the unconverted will buy the *Herald* unless they find in it what they want in a newspaper. *Public taste may be low. If it is the fact has to be faced.* . . . The public wants these stories and will have them."[34]

The most scathing indictment of the *Herald* came two years later when the ILP journalist, Clifford Allen, produced a memo for his colleagues on the *Herald* Board of Directors in which he identified the weaknesses which he believed kept the paper from successfully competing with other organs of the daily press. Much of this memo was taken up with an assault on the political content of the paper, and the presence of supporters of the communist-led Minority Movement on the *Herald* staff. However, Allen also offered an incisive indictment of the paper's lack of commercial appeal. He began by asserting that "the general public from whom the circulation must be got (and the vast majority of even Labour voters must be included as 'general public')" refuse to buy the *Herald* because of their conviction that "it is not out to give them news, but to do them good." The paper would have to "live down" this "bad reputation . . . otherwise there is no hope of increasing our circulation." He pointed out that the "*Daily News* and the *Daily Mail* are not written for political agents and enthusiasts"; suggested "scrap[ping] like the plague eccentricities and propaganda in headlines and in the arrangement of matter"; and emphasized that, in pitching the paper, "[o]ur eyes should always be set on the general reader, who does not want 'doing good' but wants a bright general newspaper."[35]

Allen forwarded a copy of his memorandum to MacDonald, who wrote back to him intimating that Herbert Morrison shared Allen's view, as did Jimmy Thomas—who "is also on the war-path about it." As for himself, MacDonald felt that the paper "showed nothing but incapacity from beginning to end, and instead of being a great Party organ giving us spirit and uplift, it is a miserable, cantankerous, narrow-visioned and pettifogging propaganda sheet."[36] MacDonald's resentment of the paper largely stemmed from his bitterness at the *Herald*'s less than reverent treatment of him and quickly subsided into disinterest.[37] On the other hand, Morrison and Thomas's concerns persisted, and alongside Bevin, who underwent a profound conversion in his thinking about the popular press in the 1920s, these two would be integral in revamping Labour's press policy in the late 1920s. In 1925, however, the majority of Labour's leaders were not willing to accept that a high circulation was worth the price of moral compromise.

It is easy to argue that financial constraints and not moral scruples prevented the *Daily Herald*'s editorial team from producing a more commercially viable paper in the 1920s. With the exception of a brief period in 1923–1924, the paper lost money throughout the decade and required a continuous financial infusion from the trade unions and the party. At the 1922 TUC at Southport, the union members consented to triple their annual affiliation fee (from 1d. to 3d. per member), with the entire increase going to subsidize the *Herald*. In the following months, several of the larger unions committed to continuing the subsidy for a further five years, and the TUC sought to raise immediate funds for the paper by capitalizing these fees.[38] In addition, both the TUC General Council and the Labour Party executive made frequent grants and loans to the paper, with the cash-strapped party donating over £10,000 per year during the period of joint Labour Party–TUC ownership.[39] For the fiscal year 1922–1923 alone, the paper received £164,000 in subsidies.[40] Despite this substantial cash infusion, the paper's operating budget remained well below that of its rivals, and the *Herald*'s editors and directors frequently pleaded poverty in excuse for the paper's shortcomings.[41] While financial handicaps limited its ability to make needed improvements, those handicaps were compounded by the prejudices of the *Herald*'s trade union proprietors who refused, until 1928, to consider funding capitalization schemes through commercial banks or insurance companies, and who continued to rely on the dwindling reserves of the trade union, party, and cooperative movements to keep the paper solvent.[42] Further, it is highly doubtful that, even given a ready source of capital, the *Herald*'s editors and directors could have succeeded in producing a paper as palatable as its rivals without expanding its coverage to suit popular tastes.

In the 1890s, ILP leader Keir Hardie produced an amazing circular for his paper the *Labour Leader,* which bragged, "There is no other Paper like it. NO POLICE NEWS NO FOOTBALL NEWS NO CRICKET NEWS NO SOCIETY NEWS But it is full of news."[43] Twenty-five years later, the primacy that Labour pressmen had placed on moral uplift over commercial success was equally visible in the assessment which Philip Snowden offered for the chronically low circulations of Labour publications:

> A Labour Newspaper is at a disadvantage from the point of view of establishing a circulation by feeling under an obligation to maintain a higher moral standard than that observed by ordinary newspapers. The directors of a Labour newspaper regard it as inconsistent with their principles to give prominence to sensational news. . . . They have a gospel to preach. To them a newspaper is primarily a medium for propagating their ideas.[44]

While recognizing the deleterious effects of this attitude on press circulation, Snowden continued to feel that the Labour press could not and should not consider compromising its educative mission.

The content of the *Daily Herald*'s news columns reflected this near monomaniacal obsession with political education. Human interest stories were almost entirely absent. After the Labour movement assumed financial control for the paper in 1922, the board replaced George Lansbury as editor with Henry Hamilton Fyfe, a former journalist and editor for the Harmsworth press. But despite Fyfe's background in commercial journalism, the new editor did little to leaven the heavy dose of politics

Figure 5.1. Labour Leader circular, probably October 1891. (Courtesy of the Bodleian Library, Oxford)

and propaganda in the paper's columns. When confronted with the recommendations of the printers' union that the paper run more human interest stories, Fyfe cuttingly observed: "It is clear to me that the lament over the absence of 'human stories' simply means that we ought to have given the Russell divorce case as other papers gave it. I myself am persuaded that we gained far more than we lost over that."[45] Close supervision by the new union-dominated board of directors ensured that Fyfe did not continue with his predecessor's indulgence of left-wing and communist crusades, but it did not improve the pedantic tone of the paper.[46] As Huw Richards noted in his history of the *Herald*, "such phenomena as the four-column page two headline 'Sugar Subsidy Bill—3rd reading' . . . can have done little to encourage any wavering *Daily News* readers to switch allegiance."[47] Further, given that the stated policy of the postwar Labour Party was to represent the workers both "by hand and brain," the paper arguably devoted disproportionate space to industrial affairs, often at the expense of general interest news. Even Bevin, now vice-chairman of the *Herald* board, admitted in 1925 that "[w]henever a report is made of a conference or other industrial affair the D.H. always seems to want to import a scream into it and infer a crisis; it is everlastingly shouting 'fire' when there is not even smoke, with the result that people become indifferent to industrial reports and do not feel them reliable." As a result, "the paper is not an informative one. If one went away to a place where the D.H. was the only procurable paper, and returned after a period, one would be out-of-touch."[48]

Not only did the *Herald* fail to provide the same range of general interest news as its commercial competitors, it also failed to keep pace with other trends in popular journalism. Arthur Henderson "worried himself sick" over the *Herald*'s chronically low circulation in the 1920s, but he stopped short of advocating any concessions to the "New Journalism."[49] Like the *Herald*'s first editor, George Lansbury, he regretted the fact that the *Herald* felt compelled to run a racing tips column.[50] While Henderson and Lansbury "disliked horse-racing for religious reasons," many of their less religious colleagues similarly objected to the inclusion of a racing column on the grounds that such features were "trivial."[51]

Henderson's lack of interest in the commercial aspects of newspaper publication was similarly evident in his attitude toward the proposal for a *Daily Herald* insurance scheme. In a speech to the 1923 Labour Party conference in London, he supported the decision of the *Herald* board not to consider offering free insurance to subscribers, as many other daily and weekly papers were doing:

They felt—they might be too idealistic—but some of them felt that, at any rate, so far as the great Labour Movement was concerned, it was an exceedingly doubtful method of trying to get their rank and file to take the paper, which ought first of all—should he not say first and last—to be taken because it was the finest weapon that the workers could hope for in giving publicity to its own principles and ideals.[52]

Insurance schemes emerged as a tactic for securing loyal newspaper readership in the 1910s. Leading dailies began offering readers indemnities against death or injury in fires, train wrecks, and other spectacular accidents, and the papers' payouts for accidents became news items in themselves. The schemes were advertised in the pages of the press—both in a paper's own columns and in the advertising space of its rivals. A typical full-page promotion in the *Daily Mail* announced that readers could receive "£250 if killed while a pedestrian by any moving vehicle in the street, or while riding a bicycle, tricycle, or motorcycle for pleasure. Man and wife £500."[53] As a method for boosting sales, the schemes were remarkably successful. The *Daily News* doubled its circulation in the space of a year after introducing an insurance scheme in October 1921.[54] By 1925 such inducements had become so common that NEC member Herbert Morrison, who had worked on the circulation staff of the *Daily Citizen* ten years earlier, referred to them as "normal newspaper methods."[55] While its popularity boomed after the First World War, free insurance was already common enough by early 1916 to be served up for mockery in the pages of the satirical trench newspaper, the *Wipers Times*. The paper, produced by and for soldiers in the Ypres salient, offered a spoof insurance policy to its readers:

> OUR GREAT INSURANCE SCHEME
> INSURE AT ONCE BY PLACING AN ORDER
> FOR THIS PAPER WITH YOUR NEWSAGENT
> Why face the awful danger of submarine
> Without being insured. 10,000,000 (ten million), has been subscribed at the local bank to carry out the largest insurance Scheme instituted by any paper.
> In the event of death caused by a submarine, anywhere in the Wipers district, your next of kin will be entitled to 11s. 7d., if you had at the time of death, one of our coupons fully-signed, and bearing name of Newsagent.
> PLACE YOUR ORDER AT ONCE TO AVOID DISAPPOINTMENT!!![56]

Free insurance was arguably particularly attractive to a working-class audience that had been "taught thrift and the necessity for various forms of insurance . . . [by] Trade Unions, the Friendly Societies and the Co-op movement."[57] The *Daily Mail* and other major papers preyed upon such susceptibilities, employing paid canvassers to "make house-to-house visits, show the paper, and expatiate on the [financial] advantages of becoming a registered reader."[58] And national popular daily and evening papers were not the only ones to offer insurance schemes, though these were by far the most lucrative. In January 1927, the *Herald*'s circulation manager reported decreased sales in Lancashire as a result of a new insurance scheme in the *Manchester Daily Dispatch,* and the circulation of the "quality" daily the *Westminster Gazette* rose by a factor of ten between 1922 and 1927 "in spite of its unattractive character," largely as a result of the insurance scheme that accompanied its relaunch.[59] For a "majority of newspapers it [was] becoming more and more a question of buying circulation."[60]

The *Herald*'s annual directors' reports from the mid-twenties illustrate the perceived importance of insurance to the fate of the paper. Yet the majority of the TUC General Council, and of the rank-and-file, felt that the movement could not afford—either economically or morally—to support such a proposal. Hamilton Fyfe's attitude toward would-be readers put off by the *Herald*'s lack of an insurance scheme was typical: "It [the *Herald*] cannot offer you insurances against tumbling off the top of an omnibus or falling down in front of a motor lorry: if you feel inclined to do these things, you must take in some other paper."[61]

Even such seemingly innocuous commercial innovations as the publication of a picture page were initially resisted by the paper's backers, again for both moral and economic reasons. When the *Herald* finally introduced a picture page in February 1926, C. T. Cramp, on behalf of the board of directors, reported to the 1927 Labour Party conference that "a very large number of people were buying the *Daily Herald,* now that it contained pictures, who did not buy it before. It might be blameworthy that they should need to be attracted by pictures, but they had to take human nature into account."[62]

The paper did consent to run a special women's section, Home Rulings, of which Rebecca West was briefly editor. However, the page, unlike its commercial rivals, was much more concerned with housework than with conspicuous consumption, and occasionally sought to "distinguish itself from its competitors . . . by including socialist analysis of the housewife's position."[63] The page was little more than a perfunctory nod to the female readership, and it is hard to imagine an overworked mother, let alone a young modern girl, eagerly reaching across the breakfast table for the Home Rulings page. If a female reader were to look forward to this page, she could not even be assured of finding it, as the editors, spurred on by a board of directors which felt "the cost of producing the women's page [to be] high in proportion to the amount of space devoted exclusively to women's topics," often cut out the section when there was a high volume of trade union news.[64] Moreover, the *Herald*'s picture page was more likely to depict the plight of urban slum dwellers than minor aristocrats sporting the latest Parisian fashions. In fact, unlike the *Express,* which interspersed pictures of fashionable ladies' hats throughout its news pages, there was very little fashion—particularly young women's fashion—in the *Herald*.[65]

All in all, the movement-operated *Herald* never managed to replicate the popular package offered by its competitors, and its readership lagged accordingly. As Miners' Federation president Herbert Smith noted to the TUC in 1927, "The marvelous thing to me is that even coming into this Congress—and I want to tell you I am a close observer—I generally see about six *Daily Mails* to one *Daily Herald*."[66] The gap was even greater in terms of women readers, and the paper's failure to reach women was a particular handicap, given that these potential voters were less likely to be exposed to Labour views in the workplace or through their trade unions.

Unwilling to produce a commercially viable newspaper, the Labour leadership sought to boost sales of the *Herald* through a combination of hectoring, shame, and moral suasion. The *Herald* board constantly impressed party and trade union members with the "necessity of supporting a Labour daily newspaper" as "the larger its circulation grows, the greater becomes its power to stand up for the workers and the Trade Union Movement."[67] After the 1922 general election, Henderson sent a letter to secretaries of the divisional Labour parties and trades councils suggesting that they reiterate to their members that "subsidiz[ing] the parties which are doing their best to kill [the Labour movement], by taking in papers belonging to millionaires—papers which slander and abuse Labour daily—is a curiously muddle-headed way of undoing with one hand what they have done with the other."[68]

While such guilt-laden circulars were at best tedious, the constant abuse of non-*Herald* readers in the paper's "Henry Dubb" comic strip was downright insulting. The comic strip, in which a hapless worker is put upon by capitalists and Tories, was a British adaptation of a cartoon originally run in the American socialist press.[69] One typical cartoon has Dubb kissing a press lord's foot, with the title "Henry Dubb at his devotions" and the caption "The *Daily Herald* is the only daily paper owned by the workers themselves; yet the majority of workers do not read it." Another shows

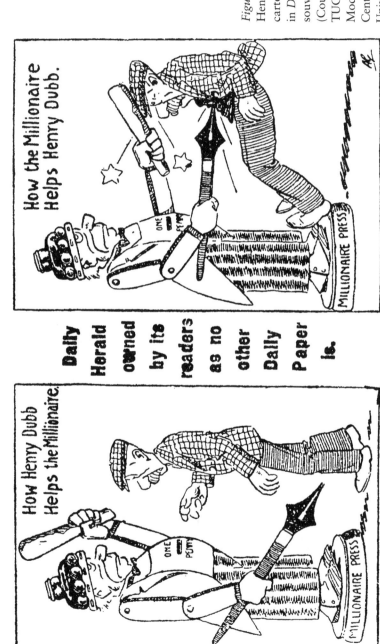

Figure 5.2. Henry Dubb cartoon, reprinted in *Daily Herald* souvenir book. (Courtesy of the TUC archive, Modern Records Centre, Warwick University)

two press lords, one the owner of the *Liberal Champion* and the other the owner of the *Tory Defender;* both papers carry headlines warning their readers of the "Menace of Labour." Between the two men, on the wall, is a framed picture of Dubb. The caption reads:

> Liberal Newspaper Owner: Henry Dubb is a good fellow. What shall we do for him, for all the pennies he has given us?
>
> Tory Newspaper Owner: Slander his Trade Union, defeat his Cooperative Society, smash his Labour Party.
>
> Both Newspaper Owners: Yes let's; he will still go on buying our papers instead of his own.[70]

Another equated a penny spent on the popular press with payment for a knock over the head. The cartoons were reminiscent of a priest preaching to the congregation about the evils of not attending mass, since the *Herald*'s audience was presumably not the Henry Dubbs of the world but its dutiful readers. Clifford Allen despised the cartoons, and advised his colleagues on the *Herald* board that "we should give up insulting the worker with 'Henry Dubb.' " R. B. Walker, secretary of the agricultural workers' union and a fellow board member, rationalized that the cartoon "doubtless appeals to some," though it was unclear to whom.[71]

Though the Labour movement turned away from mediated propaganda in the 1920s, the party still strove to "create a cross-class electoral appeal."[72] Much of the Labour literature from this period was targeted at nonmanual workers, including the following pamphlets: "The Financial Policy of the Liberal and Conservative Parties Is a MENACE to Labour Professional and Manual"; "Why Country Women Should Vote Labour"; "To the Women in the Home"; "A Call to Christians"; and "A Burden on the Rates"—the last of which was a direct appeal to the financial interests of the middle-class voter.[73] In the end, the party's failure to win over a broader section of the nonmanual workers in the decade after the war was not for lack of trying. However, the failure forced Labour to reconsider its publicity strategy and ultimately led it to accept the necessity of working through the mass media. By 1929, the Labour leadership had finally become convinced of the importance of support from the popular press to the party's political advancement, and that a successful left-wing journal would have to compete with the anti-socialist press on its own terms. "The heroic days of leftwing journalism were over. . . . [T]he only choice open to the movement was . . . to set up a popular paper of its own which met the other dailies on their own ground but kept open a channel for the Labour point of view."[74] It is illustrative of Labour's changed outlook that Ernest Bevin, who in 1919 denounced the commercial press as "the product of an evil system rotten at the base," solicited the sale of the *Herald* in 1929 to the commercial firm Odhams with the intention of re-launching the paper as a popular daily.[75]

The reversal took place gradually over the course of the 1920s. In many respects it reflected less an abandonment of earlier anxieties about the mass media and commercial culture than an acceptance that, in order to compete with the Liberals and Conservatives in the national arena, the party would have to embrace the new media of mass communication. While this change of policy was the result of a decade's worth of cumulative experiences and discouragements, the experience of the general strike in 1926 played a particularly important role in Labour's thinking about the mass media and public opinion. The strike was both the acme of the opponents of the mass media's influence and the turning point after which moral and political prejudices played a much smaller role in determining Labour's media policy.

CHAPTER SIX

Battling for Public Opinion

T HE TUC GENERAL COUNCIL'S DECISION to suppress and boycott the media during the 1926 general strike represented a triumph by those within the Labour movement who viewed the press (and to a lesser extent the BBC) as irretrievably biased against Labour, and who saw little hope or advantage to be gained from engaging with the commercial media. The decision to call out the printers with the first wave of strikers on 4 May 1926 and to refuse to cooperate with the BBC reflected the trade unionists' expectation that, absent the poisonous influence of the anti-Labour media, public opinion would automatically understand the workers' interests to be coincident with the national interest. However, the trade unionists' reasoning proved overly sanguine. For one thing, the printers' strike proved ineffective at stopping the presses, and pro-government journals and newssheets continued publication either overseas or using domestic scab (or "blackleg") labor. The TUC and Labour Party's boycott of the BBC similarly did not neutralize the role of the wireless in the conflict, and the BBC served as many people's primary source of information about the progress of the strike. For another, the Labour leadership's understanding of the formation and impact of public opinion proved excessively naïve. The leadership believed that the general strike was justified—that it was a legitimate response to the threat to the miners' wages and by extension to all laborers' wages—and refused to accept that the public could "come to any conclusion, but that the decision of the government . . . to break off negotiations was a crime against society."[1]

While the public may not have believed that the trade unionists were seeking to subvert the constitution, it did not necessarily follow that they would support the strike action as a legitimate response to the mine owners' proposals to further reduce miners' wages and extend working hours or to the government's unwillingness to enforce the Samuel Report's proposals for the reorganization of the industry.[2] The TUC's failure effectively to communicate their justification of the strike to the public made it easier for the government to take a hard line against the strikers, and helped to undermine any hopes for a more advantageous outcome to the dispute. This failure, in turn, proved to be a significant turning point in Labour's approach to the mass media in the interwar period. In the years that followed, the experience of the strike loomed large in Labour's rethinking of its publicity policy and ultimately helped spur the party and union leadership to adopt a more engaged approach to the mass media.

Since the 1889 dock strike, when Lord Rosebery responded to the perceived sympathy of the public for the dockers by unofficially mediating between the shipowners and the men, the influence of public opinion on the outcome of industrial action had grown appreciably.[3] Two decades later, Lloyd George similarly made himself a "popular hero" by intervening to resolve a dispute between railway owners and workers.[4] The trend toward government mediation of industrial conflicts (either official or unofficial) arguably increased the imperative to win over public opinion as government ministers had an electoral incentive to be seen to facilitate a "just" settlement between labor and industry.[5] The nationalization of the railways during the First World War put the government in a unique position of responsibility during the 1919 railway strike. Nonetheless, perceptions about public opinion remained critical to the government's attitude during the conflict. While actual public opinion about the railway strike remains difficult to gauge, the shift in press attitudes was indicative of a perceived shift in public opinion, and, as such, increased the pressure on the government to make peace with the railwaymen.

If public opinion was an important factor in the outcome of the 1919 conflict, its role in 1926 was arguably even greater, as both the trade unions and the government saw the general strike as a defining moment in the renegotiation of the balance of power among unions, industry, and the state. The idea of employing a general strike to paralyze society had originated with the anarcho-syndicalist movement in France in the late-nineteenth century, which expressly defined the general strike as a political weapon aimed at the suppression of the state.[6] The British government sought to depict the 1926 action in these terms, with Prime Minister

Stanley Baldwin defining the strike as a "despotic" abuse of power designed "to challenge the existing constitution of the country and to substitute the reign of force for that which now exists."[7] The leaders of the TUC General Council countered that the conflict was quantitatively but not qualitatively different from other sympathetic strike actions. The strikers were not out to "mak[e] war on the people" or to subvert the constitution, but merely to ensure that "the attempt of the mineowners to starve three million men, women and children into submission shall not succeed." In protecting the interests of the miners, the TUC saw itself as safeguarding the interest of all "workers of the country in the defence of the right to live by work."[8] To the General Council, the TUC was the defender of the national interest against the selfish sectional interests of the mine owners and their fellow capitalists.

In the opening days of the strike, it was by no means clear that the public would automatically reject the strikers' vision of the conflict. In Winston Churchill's estimation, by the fourth day of the strike, "large numbers of working people" still felt "quite detached from the conflict; and they are waiting, as if they were spectators at a football match, to see whether the Government or the Trade Union is the stronger."[9] Yet, as the strike wore on, the government increasingly secured the rhetorical high ground and succeeded in casting the strike as a "tragic" abuse of power by a section of the community at the expense of the broader nation.[10] While Baldwin, in his public pronouncements, sought to discourage "vindictiveness" and promised to work for a "square deal to secure justice between man and man," he nonetheless made clear his understanding of the strike as an attack on "the safety and security of the British constitution."[11] Baldwin's success in recasting the conflict in these terms was devastating to the trade unionists. As Philip Williamson has noted: "Once Baldwin translated the General Strike from an industrial dispute into a supposed threat to the 'basis of ordered government' and a 'challenge to Parliament and the road to anarchy and ruin,' the TUC leaders themselves grasped that defeat was inevitable."[12]

As with the 1919 railway strike, it remains difficult to assess public opinion about the conflict. Some scholars have emphasized the camaraderie and general lack of rancor between the public and the strikers.[13] But while volunteers' actions may have been driven less by "any strong political feeling" than by simple "Hurrah Patriotismus or fun," the willingness of thousands of citizens, particularly students and members of the middle classes, to volunteer as temporary dockworkers, bus drivers, and rail conductors suggests that the TUC failed to convince the public that the strike was an existential stand of organized labor against industrial greed and government lethargy.[14] In that the press can be assumed to reflect (albeit through a distorted prism) significant shifts in the public mind, there was little evidence that public opinion recoiled at the government's hard-line position. As the strike wore on, the press became, if less hysterical, no more sympathetic to the strikers' cause. When news of the TUC's capitulation to the government became known, the BBC reported that, in London, "the general public as a whole took no pains to conceal their satisfaction."[15] Yet, the public's hostility to the strike was not predetermined, and arguably was less indicative of the ingrained antipathy of the British public to the sectional interests of organized labor than of the failure of the TUC to present its position more successfully to the public.[16]

The TUC's publicity policy during the general strike reflected not only the hostility of many within the Labour leadership toward the commercial media but also their unwillingness to see the value of new techniques of political persuasion and their limited appreciation of the public's interests. The General Council's decision to call out the printers with the first wave of strikers to leave their posts on midnight, May 4, is telling. It did not naturally follow that, if a general strike were to take place, the printers should be in the first wave of strikers.[17] The strike, though "general," was not total, and the wave of strikers who left work on that first night were primarily those involved with the vital industries of transport and fuel. The printers could have been assigned to the second wave of industries (which were never ultimately called out), or an arrangement could have been instituted to ensure "unbiased" coverage of the dispute in the daily press. Several of the printing operatives, acting independently, had, in fact, attempted to institute such a policy on Monday, 3 May. While the members of the General Council and the government's negotiating committee were still attempting to find a way of avoiding the strike, the *Daily Mail* printers proactively refused to print the Tuesday morning edition of the paper unless the editors omitted the leading article titled "For King and Country," which argued that: "A general strike is not an industrial dispute. It is a revolutionary movement . . . which can only succeed by destroying the Government and subverting the rights and liberties of the people. This being the case, it cannot be tolerated by any civilized Government and it must be dealt with by every resource at the disposal of the community. . . . We call upon all law-abiding men and women to hold themselves at the service of King and country."[18] Their efforts backfired. The government, which had arguably given up hope of finding a solution to the impasse, seized upon the action by the *Daily Mail* printers as a pretext for calling off negotiations, announcing, in a clever public relations coup, that talks could no longer be continued as the printers' act was a "gross interference with the freedom of the Press, [which] . . . involves a challenge to the constitutional rights and freedom of the nation."[19]

The government's representation of the printers' action as an attempt to subvert the freedom of the press revealed the risk to the trade unions of attempting to censor press content. Nonetheless, in the days leading up to the strike, local printers' chapels had successfully instituted an unofficial censorship regime. The *Sunday Express* printers forced the amendment of what they perceived to be biased reporting on the strike negotiations; the *Evening News* staff managed to stop the paper from quoting the *Daily Mail* editorial in its Monday-evening edition, and the printing of the *Evening Standard* and the *Star* were both brought to a halt on Monday afternoon as a result of conflicts between the editorial staff and the printers over the depiction of recruiting scenes in Whitehall.[20] Such action was not atypical among the printers' unions. Sixty years later, when Rupert Murdoch moved his printing facilities to Wapping and sacked all of the Fleet Street printing staff, sympathetic colleagues at rival papers exercised an unofficial censorship over press content related to the dispute.[21]

The TUC General Council could have attempted to institute a policy of limited control over content, wherein papers would be allowed to maintain production if they included trade union as well as government perspectives on the strike. Such an approach was in fact advocated by Lloyd George. Responding to a speech by Arthur Henderson in the House of Commons on the second day of the strike, the former prime minister claimed:

> I should have thought honestly from the point of view of the Labour party, it was to the advantage of everybody that you should have a Press, and I have no doubt at all if conditions were imposed on the press that there should be columns representing the Labour point of view . . . because it is fair in a great conflict like this that the Press should represent the position fairly, in news, showing the contentions on both sides. . . . I think it was a mistake to suppress the papers.[22]

Henderson might fairly have responded that Lloyd George's position was inconsistent at best, given his attitude toward the media during the 1919 railway strike. Yet the former prime minister's statement was indicative of the position that the *Daily Chronicle,* whose editorial policy his family controlled, might have taken toward the strikers but for the printers' strike. Other sympathetic editors and publishers similarly condemned the trade unionists' decision to shut down the press. Upon hearing that the movement intended to call out the printers, The *Manchester*

Guardian editor C. P. Scott cabled to MacDonald to warn him against such a policy, arguing that the "saner part of the press" might do much to "brin[g] pressure to bear on the Government . . . in the interests . . . of the Unions and the nation."[23] On the fourth day of the strike, the progressive journal the *New Statesman,* which successfully printed a strike edition, ran a leading article claiming that the decision to call out the printers was "short-sighted" and cost the strikers potentially valuable publicity.[24]

Thus, it was not only in hindsight that members of the Labour movement were given cause to question the decision to call out the printers. However, the impetus behind the callout was not merely to silence the anti-Labour voices in the daily press but also to punish the popular press and their anti-Labour readership. Seeking to justify the General Council's decision in the months after the strike, the TUC's research officer, Walter Milne-Bailey, wrote: "The main arguments in favour of the complete stoppage of the Press are that the anti-labour parties are deprived of their biggest medium of publicity and therefore of propaganda, and that the psychological effect on the 'bourgeois' classes is more immediate and more striking than that of almost any other stoppage."[25] The decision marked the culmination of years of hostility toward the "capitalist" press, which had given Labour tepid support when it suited their interests, and "attempt[ed] to set groups of Trade Unionists against each other, by running campaigns in favour of some Trade Union demands and denouncing others."[26] It further underscored the depth of union antagonism toward the "bourgeois" classes, who took their news from capitalist papers and supported the capitalists against the workers in industrial disputes.

The TUC and Labour Party's boycott of the BBC during the strike similarly reflected a long frustration with the broadcaster's treatment of industrial and political news. The TUC publicity committee had staked out its position in regard to the BBC three days before the strike began. At their first meeting, the committee drafted a message to be sent to all trade union secretaries instructing them to inform their unions that "[i]n view of the fact that the government is understood to have commandeered the British Broadcasting Company, . . . the General Council warns the Trade Union and Labour movement to take no notice of any statement that may be broadcasted by wireless."[27] Their decision can be faulted on several grounds, the most obvious being that it was based on false intelligence: the government had not actually commandeered the BBC, nor did it at any point during the conflict, despite pressure from Churchill to do so.[28] Left to their own devices on the question of broadcast policy, the

TUC publicity committee reached the conclusion that broadcasting was not likely to play a central role in the conflict, and that "it was easy to exaggerate the effects of propaganda by wireless."[29]

The committee maintained their suspicions of the BBC even after they learned that it had not in fact been commandeered. When suggestions were put forth that the TUC lift its boycott, they held fast, declaring: "If the BBC were once given authority to speak in the name of the TUC it would be very difficult to control statements the BBC might make later as purporting to issue from the General Council: the Publicity committee would have no guarantee that at a possibly critical stage of the stoppage statements might be made by wireless in the Council's name to sabotage the stoppage at the instigation of the government."[30] This declaration echoed the concerns expressed by Charles Trevelyan, Labour representative on the Sykes committee on the future of broadcasting, three years earlier.

The fear that the BBC, controlled by private commercial interests and indebted to the government of the day for its right to broadcast, could not be trusted to behave objectively presented a legitimate concern. Nonetheless, it did not necessarily mean that the best way to counter this concern was to boycott the airwaves. Trevelyan himself thought otherwise, as did his colleague William Graham, who was then serving on the second committee on the future of broadcasting. Several of the two men's colleagues within the General Council and the Labour Party also shared or came to share their view, but their attempts to influence the TUC's broadcast policy proved ineffectual.

The General Council's initial attitude toward the press and the BBC reflected the extent of the anger, resentment, and suspicion within the movement toward these organs of the mass media which for years had failed to give the workers a fair hearing. In this light, the General Council's decisions are understandable, if arguably ill-advised. However, the General Council's complete failure to consider constructive policies for getting its message across to the public during the strike suggests an inability to appreciate the role of the media in public opinion formation, and the importance of public opinion to the strikers' cause. Depriving the enemy of their weapons to use against you should logically be accompanied by hitting them hard with your own weapons, and the TUC strike committee was slow to recognize the importance even of putting out its own daily news bulletin.

The seeming obliviousness of key members of the General Council to the role of publicity in shaping the outcome of the conflict alarmed many members of the movement. On the early afternoon of 4 May, a deputation from the National Union of Railwaymen and the London Trades Council impressed upon the TUC publicity committee the urgent need for a strike bulletin, as did a subsequent deputation of representatives of the various printing and paper workers' unions. The next day, the Paddington central strike committee wrote to "urge upon [the General] Council the extreme need of some sort of publication of news for those on strike."[31] By the time that this letter reached Transport House, the decision to publish a strike bulletin had already been taken. However, it is not clear that the committee would have gone ahead with the publication of the *British Worker* had it not been for the government's decision to publish the rival *British Gazette*.[32]

Whereas the trade unions were slow to recognize the importance of publicity and public opinion to the course of the conflict, the government paid close attention to the press and broadcasting before and during the stoppage. At a 27 April meeting of the government's supply and transport committee—the emergency committee that had been appointed to draft contingency plans in preparation for a general strike—the deputy chief civil commissioner, J. C. C. Davidson, was put in charge of publicity preparations, and appointed a small staff based at the admiralty. The decision to publish the *British Gazette* was taken even before the cessation of negotiations, and the machinery for the publication of the government's strike bulletin was firmly in place before the first workers left their posts.[33] In addition to publishing the *Gazette,* in at least one instance the government sought to influence press coverage in the independently operated press through informal contact with the paper's editor.[34]

In contrast, the trade unionists did not print a union newssheet until the second day of the strike. The editor of the *Daily Herald,* Hamilton Fyfe, had long been convinced of the need for a trade union paper in the event of a strike and had pressed for such arrangements to be made earlier.[35] He had even gone so far as to ask his staff to remain at the office on the first night of the strike, "expecting that the General Council might require at very short notice the production of a strike bulletin."[36] Nonetheless, the decision to produce the *British Worker* from the *Daily Herald* facilities was not taken until late Tuesday evening, after a deputation from Fyfe, the *Herald*'s general manager Robert Williams, and the night editor William Mellor met with the full General Council and firmly impressed upon them the need for such a publication.

The meeting underscored the haplessness of the General Council's publicity and communications subcommittee. Publicity and communications were put under the charge of two minor members of the General Council, E. L. Poulton, the secretary of the National Union of Boot and Shoe Operatives, and J. W. Bowen of the Post Office Workers' Union. Poulton could claim some knowledge of the press as a member of the board of directors of the short-lived *Daily Citizen,* but neither proved to possess a particularly sophisticated understanding of the media, and their selection to head the committee is further evidence of the low priority placed on publicity by the General Council. It is clear from this committee's minutes that their decision to publish the *British Worker* was almost entirely reactive. As the committee secretary recorded, "in view of the public receiving information through a bulletin to be issued by the government, *it had been forced upon the General Council to consider the possibility of issuing a bulletin daily."* Having accepted the need to "consider the possibility" of producing such a publication, the committee remained so unattuned to the propaganda importance of a widely-circulated paper giving the trade union version of events that they contemplated hand-stenciling a strike bulletin so as not to raise issues about using trade union labor to produce the paper.[37]

This failure to appreciate the link between effectively distributed publicity and public opinion was equally apparent on the political side of the movement. MacDonald's first official statement to the press was not issued until the third day of the strike, after the general manager of the London Press Service sent the following message to the opposition leader:

> You no doubt know that the views of Mr. Baldwin, Mr. Winston Churchill, and Sir Austen Chamberlain on the Strike are being distributed throughout the Continent and in America. I think it most imperative that counterviews should be distributed . . . I would strongly advise immediate action, and on the chance that you recognize the importance of my proposals I am instructing the bearer of this letter to await a reply.[38]

The failure of the Labour leadership, industrial and political, to make appropriate publicity preparations meant that the first edition of the *British Worker* did not roll off the presses until Wednesday evening, 5 May. In the meantime, the *British Gazette* had appeared on Wednesday morning. This first issue of the *Gazette* was not without its problems. The four-page broadsheet only contained two pages of printed text, with its middle two pages blank, and not all 232,000 copies made it out of the warehouse.[39] However, it enjoyed the advantage of being one of the few London newspapers circulating that morning, and one of only three printed national dailies, the other two being a thirteen-by-eight inch miniature version of the *Times* and the *Continental Daily Mail,* flown in from Paris. The *Daily Mirror* produced a mimeographed bulletin, and provincial papers such as the *Yorkshire Post* and a special *Manchester Guardian Bulletin* floated through the city, as did several homemade strike bulletins. Nonetheless, news remained scarce.

As a result, those who managed to get their hands on a newspaper or strike bulletin during the day on Tuesday were presented with a nearly uniform denunciation of the strike. The *British Gazette* put the case most stridently with their headline: "HOLD-UP OF THE NATION: Government and the Challenge: No Flinching: The Constitution or a Soviet." An editorial written by Winston Churchill, who acted as the unofficial editor of the *British Gazette,* outlined the paper's mission as a "Reply to Strike Makers' Plan to Paralyse Public Opinion." Churchill lamented that, as a consequence of the "violent concerted action" of the trade unionists, "nearly all the newspapers have been silenced . . . and this great nation, on the whole the strongest community which civilization can show, is for the moment reduced in this respect to the level of African natives dependent only on the rumours which are carried from place to place." The *Gazette*'s mission was to bring civilization back to the benighted masses.[40]

Both contemporaries and subsequent historians have commented on Churchill's unsuitableness as editor of the *Gazette.* Lloyd George accused the paper of being "first-class indiscretion," but "third-rate journalism." TUC general secretary Walter Citrine complained to his diary that Churchill's singularly biased reports of the negotiations leading up to the strike were "a poisonous attempt to bias the public mind." In his history of the strike, Julian Symons described the chancellor as "by temperament peculiarly unsuited" to run the *Gazette.*[41] All of this is true if one believes that the purpose of the *Gazette* should have been to help maintain order, and to further a peaceable end to the strike. However, by calling out the printers, the trade unions created the opening for a publication that refused to remain "impartial as between the fire brigade and the fire."[42]

In contrast to the shrill and militant tone of the *Gazette,* the *British Worker* strove above all else to be a voice of moderation. Its three principal goals were to reiterate the industrial, as opposed to constitutional, nature of the strike; to encourage orderly conduct and dispel rumors of rowdyism; and to hearten the strikers through articles emphasizing the uniform success of the call out and the solidarity of the men. The first issue exemplified this threefold agenda. Its lead article was headlined "WONDERFUL RESPONSE TO THE CALL: General Council's Message: Stand Firm and Keep Order." At the bottom of the page, a bold-typed "Message to All Workers" read:

> The General Council of the Trades Union Congress wishes to emphasize the fact that this is an industrial dispute. It expects every member taking part to be exemplary in his conduct and not to give any opportunity for police interference. The outbreak of any disturbances would be very damaging to the prospects of a successful termination of the dispute.
>
> The Council asks pickets especially to avoid obstruction and to confine themselves strictly to their legitimate duties.

Articles in the inside pages emphasized the success of the call out in regions across Britain, and several articles underscored international support for the strikers, including "India Wishes Success"; "Japan Says 'Fight On!' "; "French Unions to Act: Railmen, Dockers, Seamen and Miners Declare Solidarity"; and "Canada's Full Support: Financial Assistance If It Is Needed."[43]

The paper's moderate tone probably served to its advantage, in that it appeared a more credible publication than its government competitor. As the journalist Kingsley Martin wrote of the *British Gazette* and the *Daily Mail:* "It seems probable that Mr. Churchill grew daily less popular during the strike and Lord Rothermere less influential" as "even the suburban housewife (probably the lowest type of intelligence in England) has spoken to a busman or Underground conductor and will feel doubtful of his murderous intentions." It simply was not a plausible project to "persuade Englishmen that their compatriots had similar habits [to the rapacious Huns]."[44] The Cabinet at least, if not Churchill himself, absorbed this lesson as the strike wore on, and the later issues of the *Gazette* were remarkably less hysterical in tone than their predecessors.[45] By the sixth day of the strike, headlines such as "NEGOTIATIONS UNDER MENANCE" had been replaced by the more upbeat "VITAL SERVICES BETTER EACH DAY" and "MR. BALDWIN AND THE NATION: A CONFIDENT APPEAL."

While the reaction of the *British Gazette* in toning down its rhetoric is perhaps one sign of the *Worker*'s success, the impact of the TUC publication remains hard to gauge. Because of limitations on printing capacity, the paper's circulation never reached beyond around 700,000, with the majority of its copies printed in London;[46] with the abridged versions of the *Manchester Guardian* and *Manchester Evening News*, whose circulations ranged in the tens of thousands, this represented nearly the totality of the pro-Labour press.[47] The Conservative papers, in contrast, were more successful in bringing out strike editions than their Liberal and Labour rivals. The *Daily Mail*, the *Daily Mirror*, the *Daily Express*, the

Evening Standard, the *Yorkshire Post,* and countless other regional Tory papers managed to produce at least abridged versions.[48] The *Times,* though assiduously fair in its reporting, supported Baldwin in its editorials.[49] And the General Council faced press competition from the left as well as the right. The Communist *Workers' Daily* was quickly suppressed by the government, but supporters of the Minority Movement around the country were active in the production of strike sheets whose militant message was perhaps more frightening to the General Council than the rhetoric of the *British Gazette.*[50]

All these papers competed directly with the *British Worker* for circulation, and many made more of an effort than the *Worker* to appear attractive to their readers. The *British Worker* was less a newspaper than a propaganda sheet, a reality underscored by the fact that every issue of the paper reprinted the "Message to All Workers" on its front page. While it contained uplifting stories of international support, as well as amusing anecdotes from C. L. Everard in his trademark "Gadfly" column and several lighthearted poems by "Tomfool" (Eleanor Farjeon), it contained very little hard news. Even the "confused and frightened" members of the General Council came to "rel[y] more on the very heavily slanted reports in the *British Gazette,* with which the hurriedly improvised TUC paper, the *British Worker,* never caught up."[51]

The paper obviously had solid reasons for not publicizing information such as which train services the government had managed to get back up and running; yet, it was just such news that was of most interest to the majority of readers. The paper's attractiveness was further undermined by its publishers' refusal to allow the inclusion of any non-strike related news in its pages. On the third day of the strike, Fyfe requested permission from the publicity committee to include more general interest items in the *Worker*'s pages, in particular cricket scores. The committee responded by stating that "all information of a general character must be secondary and should only be admitted if there is no further information relative to the industrial situation available."[52] Its refusal to countenance the publication of cricket scores reflected the long-held aversion of many within the movement to the supposed frivolities of popular journalism. The TUC's unwillingness to pander to popular interest in subjects non-industrial distinguished the *Worker* from the *Gazette,* which prominently ran sports coverage, and from such publications as the emergency strike edition of the *Manchester Evening News,* which, despite being produced by mimeograph, included "a full service of cricket scores," or the miniature strike edition of the *Times,* which devoted a full column to cricket, lawn tennis, golf, and other athletics.[53]

Fyfe noted in his dairy that "[t]he demand for the *British Worker* is insatiable. We could sell to purchasers at the doors three times as many as we print, and we are printing half a million."[54] But sales of the *Worker* were more a reflection of the public's hunger for news than their hunger for Labour views. Even with most papers producing blackleg strike editions, newspapers remained so scarce that "late on Tuesday afternoon copies of newspapers which had appeared that morning were selling briskly at 2d. each [twice their face value]."[55] A better, but unfortunately unavailable, figure would be the resale value of the *Worker* versus the *Gazette* or the *Continental Daily Mail*. Nonetheless, given the chaos wreaked on the rest of the printing industry by the strike, the General Council would have been in an exceptional position had they arranged for the *Daily Herald*'s printers to remain at their posts at 12:01 AM on May 4. That they did not even consider such a course of action reflects the extent of their failure to appreciate the value of press publicity.

The TUC's approach to press publicity was mirrored in its attitude toward the BBC. In its defense, it is seriously doubtful that the BBC's bias in favor of the government and "the constitution" could have been changed by any action on the part of the General Council. For one thing, the BBC was constrained in its attitude by the constant threat that Broadcasting House would be commandeered if the company deviated too far from government prerogatives. But government pressure notwithstanding, the politics of the BBC mediated against overly sympathetic treatment of the strikers. The broadcaster's loyalties were succinctly summed up by its director-general: "Assuming the BBC is for the people, and that the Government is for the people, it follows that the BBC must be for the Government in this crisis."[56] As Reith wrote in a postmortem on the company's strike coverage, "There could be no question about our supporting the government generally, particularly since the General Strike had been declared illegal. We could not therefore permit anything which was contrary to the spirit of that judgment, which might have prolonged or sought to justify the strike." He went on to claim that, despite these constraints, the BBC gave "authentic impartial news of the situation throughout"—a contention with which many did not agree.[57]

The government was quick to appreciate the potential role that broadcasting could play during the strike. On 1 May, Davidson met Reith (who was, conveniently, his next door neighbor) for lunch to discuss the position of the BBC in the event of a strike. The deputy chief civil commissioner told Reith that he hoped to keep the BBC in private hands.[58] This was what Reith wanted, as he felt that the integrity of the BBC would suffer irreparable damage if it were to be commandeered by the government. However, in the ensuing days, Reith's desire to maintain the BBC's autonomy in name led him to accept an increasing number of "hints" and "suggestions" from the government that so compromised the company's impartiality that it may perhaps have been better for the BBC to have unambiguously surrendered control of the airwaves to the government.

Beginning on 4 May, the BBC stepped up its news bulletins from twice to five times a day. At Davidson's suggestion, an office was set up to allow continuous BBC representation at Davidson's temporary headquarters in Admiralty House, and secure phone lines were installed connecting it to the BBC headquarters at Savoy Hill. In this office, the BBC representatives worked with a member of Davidson's staff to compile the news bulletins from a combination of Reuters and the civil commissioner's reports. The final drafts were then submitted to Davidson for approval.[59] The process of comprising these reports ensured that—unlike the articles in the *Daily Mail* or the *British Gazette*—they did not contain many intentional inaccuracies. The bulletins even included occasional TUC news, as the General Council's press briefings were covered in the Reuters wire reports. The general tone of the bulletins was pacific and optimistic. However, they also contained a large number of government announcements, such as the daily repetition of the civil commissioner's assurance that

> [w]hen the present strike is ended His Majesty's government will take effectual measures to prevent the victimization by Trades Unions of any man who remains at work or who may return to work, and no settlement will be agreed to by His Majesty's government which does not provide for this for a lasting period and for its enforcement, if necessary, by penalties. No one who does his duty in the present crisis will be left unprotected by the State from consequent reprisals.[60]

In addition to these and similar messages that clearly delineated the duty of all citizens during the strike, the BBC gave open access to government speakers and pro-government Liberals including Baldwin, the Home Secretary Joynson-Hicks, and former Foreign Minister Lord Grey.

The government exerted its prerogative not only in demanding access to the airwaves for pro-government speakers but also in keeping "antigovernment" speakers off the airwaves. The most infamous occasion of this was the BBC's refusal on 7 May to allow the archbishop of Canterbury to broadcast a joint proposal from the nation's church leaders encouraging an immediate resumption of negotiations between the two

parties on the lines of the Samuel Report. The government objected to
the bishop's pronouncement on the grounds that it did not stipulate that
the strike be called off before negotiations were resumed. As the first lord
of admiralty commented, "I wish our Church could be a little more clear
in discerning fundamental right from fundamental wrong—& not always
trying to condone the unchristian behaviour of the mob, because they are
poor."[61] After ascertaining the prime minister's position, and that Baldwin did not want the political baggage of personally crossing swords with
the Church of England, Reith took it upon himself to cancel the archbishop's broadcast on his own initiative—"to cover the PM."[62]

Reith was put in a similar position on 10 May when Ramsay Mac-
Donald submitted a script to the director-general and requested permission to broadcast that evening. The tenor of MacDonald's draft broadcast echoed the columns of the *British Worker*. He proposed to "give the
public a most categoric assurance that it never entered into the mind
of the Trades Union Council to challenge the Government or the constitution. It is not a political strike nor has it in any sense a revolutionary
significance. It can and will be terminated the instant the Trade Unions
have some certainty that . . . protection will be afforded against a further
lowering of the standards of the lives of the miner, his wife, and his children."[63] Reith himself found the script innocuous and felt that the opposition leader should be allowed to speak. But the government was "quite
against MacDonald broadcasting" and again made Reith "take the onus
of turning people down."[64] In a conciliatory letter, the BBC director-general
sought to make the opposition leader "appreciate the somewhat deli-
cate position in which the BBC has naturally been placed" by the strike.
Needless to say, MacDonald was not overly sympathetic to Reith's plight.[65]
The incident drove Reith to vent his spleen against the government in
his diary: "I do not think they treat me altogether fairly. They will not
say that we are to a considerable extent controlled. . . . They want to
be able to say that they did not commandeer us, but they know they can
trust us not to be really impartial and they will put all the responsibility
on me."[66]

Given the constraints placed on Reith by the government, it is unclear
that any action the General Council could have taken would have secured
the strikers better representation on the BBC. Nonetheless, the General
Council's failure to initiate any engagement with the BBC indicates a lack
of appreciation of the importance of the medium. On the first day of the
strike, the *Daily Herald* editorial board recommended that the General
Council at least try to give the BBC a message for broadcast, similar to

the messages being broadcast by members of the government. Several members of the General Council supported their suggestion, and they actually decided to send such a "trial" message to the BBC. However, the TUC publicity committee vetoed the scheme on the grounds that the issuance of official trade union news via the airwaves would confuse the strikers, who had already been told not to trust the BBC.[67] On 5 May, Charles Trevelyan came to inform the committee that he intended to see Reith and discuss the broadcaster's pro-government bias. The next day, he and his colleague William Graham met with Reith, who attempted to pacify them by explaining that the BBC was acting as impartially as possible in a situation where it was threatened with government seizure. Despite Reith's cautious tone, Graham was clearly heartened enough by this conversation to write to Reith on 7 May and ask him if the Labour Party could make arrangements for one of its members to broadcast.[68] In the following days the scandal over the suppression of the archbishop's broadcast eclipsed other concerns, although MacDonald did follow up Graham's letter with his request for access to the microphone, though, as we have seen, the government intervened, and MacDonald was kept off the air. Given this interdiction, it is perhaps irrelevant that the TUC publicity committee refused the suggestion of Bevin and party leaders R. B. Walker and Arthur Greenwood that the General Council attempt to secure airtime for one of its members to present the strikers' position. If a speech by MacDonald was considered too risky to be allowed on the air, there was no way that Bevin or Arthur Pugh would ever have secured access to the microphone. Nonetheless, the General Council's passivity unquestionably made the government and Reith's job easier.

There has been significant debate over the position of the BBC, and particularly its director-general, during the crisis. Reith's apologists have stressed the fact that the BBC was operating under a real threat of being commandeered by the government, and that within that constraint the company attempted to be as impartial as possible.[69] Others have pointed to the essential conservatism of the Reithian BBC, and have suggested that even in the absence of external constraints the company would not have acted impartially between the two sides in the dispute.[70] A further debate exists about just how impartial the BBC managed to be, and it is this debate that ultimately had the greater impact on the history of political broadcasting. The Labour Party and the trade unions viewed the BBC's coverage as profoundly biased. In the decades that followed the strike, they lobbied fiercely to create an institutional framework within the BBC that would eliminate the possibility of a repetition of 1926. For both the government and Labour, the general strike provided a brilliant illustration of the advantage that a pliant broadcasting monopoly under the suzerainty of the government could be to those in power.

It is hard to argue that the attitude of the TUC General Council toward publicity and propaganda during the strike did not have a detrimental impact on public understanding of and sympathy for the strikers' cause. Despite the pronouncements of pro-government spokesmen that the public was obviously on the side of the government and would not "patiently suffer any self-constituted authority, however well organized, to supercede Parliament and to over-ride the will of the people," it is not clear that public opinion was automatically against the strikers.[71] And, as we saw in the case of the 1919 railway strike, it is conceivable that the General Council, through a well organized publicity campaign, could have made substantial inroads into public opinion and brought pressure to bear on the government. In 1919, as in 1926, the government had begun the battle with the strikers by proclaiming the unconstitutionality of the strike, the impossibility of negotiation, and the severity of the strike's implications for the future of British politics. However, the ninth day of the 1919 strike saw the government capitulate in the face of significant media and public sympathy for the strikers' cause. In contrast, the ninth day of the 1926 conflict saw the General Council's surrender and, ultimately, the proposal and passage of harsh anti-union legislation. The general strike was not only a disastrous failure from the point of view of industrial organization, it was also a disastrous failure from the point of view of publicity and public relations.[72]

The general strike has been characterized as having forced a "sharp and fundamental" break in Labour's attitude toward industrial action by "reveal[ing] the bankruptcy of a purely industrial strategy . . . , and in doing so caus[ing] a constriction in the minds of the workers of the 'limits of the possible.' "[73] The strike had a similarly profound impact on Labour's thinking about political communication. In the decade and a half after what seemed a stunning setback for traditional industrial action, Labour came to learn that it must succeed not as a working-class vanguard, but as the representative of the progressive forces of the British nation, to whom and with whom it must learn to communicate successfully.

CHAPTER SEVEN

Rapprochement with the Media

WHEREAS THE TRADE UNION LEADERSHIP had largely ignored advice from advocates of a more aggressive media strategy during the nine days of the strike, the months immediately following saw a good deal of introspection over the conduct of the stoppage, including the media boycott. The TUC research department compiled a massive memo entitled, "Chief Criticisms of the General Strike," which was composed of excerpts from the major daily and weekly journals.[1] Several entries addressed the General Council's media strategy. The right wing of the press establishment was, of course, of the view that the printers' strike was a reprehensible move. However, the left-wing press was almost equally united in its censure. Kingsley Martin expounded his opinions about the decision to call out the printers' union in a book-length study, *The British Public and the General Strike,* published several months after the conflict:

> When we consider this story it becomes, I think, clear that the TUC made a tactical error in calling out the printers. . . . [T]hey needed as much middle-class support as they could get. But it was impossible to build up a favourable public opinion upon a single Labour paper. It is probable that they would have gained a fair measure of publicity in all the Liberal papers if these had appeared. Moreover, even the most hostile papers might have felt it good business to give the strikers' case prominence.[2]

In an article published on the last day of the strike, the ILP publication the *New Leader* similarly denounced the decision as a tactical error, claiming: "It is certain that, had the Press been free, the Archbishop's effort for peace would have found in some newspapers effective support. The shutting down of the Press gave some small excuse for the Government's charge that the strike was, in fact, political."[3] In a signed editorial, the paper's editor, H. N. Brailsford, further criticized the General Council for what he saw as its paranoid attitude toward the press. The Labour movement, he argued, "gravely underestimate, now and always, the extent to which, by alert and confident publicity, we could win a hearing in the rest of the Press. . . . With all our faith in democracy, we take singularly little trouble to perfect our technique of persuasion. The Labour Government ignored the Press: most of the Unions do the same."[4]

The publicity and communications committee of the General Council took the criticisms of Martin, Brailsford, and others to heart. In its internal review of its performance during the strike, the committee confessed that the press shutdown had been in retrospect unwise: "It is unquestionable that, as a measure of policy, the closing down of the press intensified feeling against the General Council." In the future, if confronted with the prospect of another general stoppage, the General Council should demand that the newspaper proprietors agree to give "full publicity . . . to the Trade Union case whilst the dispute lasts, that the case as presented should be published by the newspapers, and that subject to strict observance of this condition there should be no interference with freedom of the press." Such a policy would better secure that "the Trade Union case . . . be properly stated in the newspapers."[5] The publicity committee's conclusions reflect the TUC's perennial preoccupation with directly controlling media discussion of industrial news; but, within these constraints, they indicate a much more conciliatory approach toward the "capitalist" press.

The committee did not come to the same conclusion in assessing its decision to boycott the BBC. In its postmortem memorandum, it argued that "it is easy to exaggerate the effects of propaganda by wireless; and that the harm done by wireless propaganda from the Government side was largely minimized by the official warning issued by the General Council [not to trust the BBC]." However, the statement reads as special pleading, as the committee clearly anticipated criticism for its attitude toward the BBC, and expressed a defensive "wis[h] . . . to place on record its opinion that having warned the movement against Government propaganda by wireless and having stated that the BBC would not be used for broadcasting statements from the Trade Union side, it would have been a cause of confusion, and perhaps worse mischief, to change this policy in the midst of the stoppage."[6]

Certain observers concurred with the publicity committee's assessment—Kingsley Martin dismissed the propaganda value of the

BBC as "doubtful" and its utility as a means to reassure the middle classes as limited. Others disagreed. Beatrice Webb described her experience of the strike as "centr[ing] around the head phones of the wireless set." She later asserted that broadcasting had made a profound impact on the outcome of the strike, seeing the medium as a "new instrument of power" that the state could deploy against the trade unions. After the nationalization of the BBC, she advised the TUC general secretary, Walter Citrine, that "Broadcasting is a public service now, and you should insist upon your right to put the trade union point of view. What you get are employers' views, thinly disguised; the trade unions should have the right to put their point of view as well." Ramsay MacDonald believed the BBC to have acted as "an agent in misleading the public." In a letter to BBC director-general John Reith, he compared the role of the BBC during the strike with the roll of the commercial press in distorting and undermining Labour's cause: "We have been so accustomed to unfair play in publicity that we are beginning to take it as an ordinary experience, but I regret that this new form of publicity seems to have already yielded to tendentious propaganda." Ernest Bevin freely admitted that it was a "mistake" to call out the printers "since the absence of newspapers hit the trade unions more than the government which was able to rely on the BBC." Several Conservatives recorded their views that the BBC had played a pivotal role in the strike's outcome. And Reith believed that the BBC broadcasts had been critical to the early termination of the strike.[7]

Whether or not the broadcasts actually influenced a significant portion of the population, the attitude of the BBC during the strike rankled the Labour Party. MacDonald felt that the BBC had been "biased and an agent in misleading the public." Labour MP Ellen Wilkinson wrote to Reith that she "fel[t] like asking the Postmaster General for my license fee back as I can hear enough fairy tales in the House of Commons without paying ten shillings a year to hear more." Hers and other correspondence led the director-general to complain in his diary, "We are properly in bad with the Labour Party." The anger persisted. Six years after the strike, a delegation to the BBC from the National Joint Council of the Labour Party and Trade Union Congress (NJC) asserted, "They were not people who felt resentment very long, but on this [the issue of the BBC's strike coverage] they felt it very deeply, very seriously." Their subsequent relationship with the broadcaster had not erased the memory of the "unfair advantage taken of a position held to make an attack upon people who were at least entitled to fair play."[8]

But while many within the Labour movement continued to harbor a deep resentment toward the BBC, the party and TUC leadership came to appreciate the importance of broadcasting to Labour's political and industrial future fortunes. As Conservative Party chairman J. C. C. Davidson noted to Prime Minister Stanley Baldwin in 1928, "The Labour Party has a powerful organization in this country, but no Press. . . . The Conservative Party, on the other hand, has the best and strongest organization of the three parties, and is supported by a very large section of the Press. In such circumstances it is clear that it is to the advantage of [Labour] to have a system of political broadcasting, as it provides them with better opportunities of propaganda than they enjoy at present."[9] In the late 1920s, Labour sought to increase its "opportunities of propaganda" through the expansion of political broadcasting. The media and Labour scholars Jean Seaton and Ben Pimlott have noted that the strike "marked a turning point in Labour thinking about broadcasting," after which they could no longer "shru[g] off the BBC's partiality as an irrelevance."[10] At the same time, Labour attempted to redress the political imbalance within the popular press through a policy of renewed cooperation with the Conservative and Liberal papers, and ultimately through the commercialization of the *Daily Herald*. The party had long realized that, in order to win a parliamentary majority, they would need to "appea[l] to each section of the electorate in the language which that section understands; emphasizing just the points in which that section is interested; subordinating the question that each section finds dull or unpleasant; addressing to each section the literature most appropriate to it."[11] By the end of the decade, Labour had come to appreciate the importance not only of a national political appeal, but of the effective propagation of that appeal through the national media.

The internal review conducted by the TUC after the strike was the first step toward the realization that the movement could never hope to obviate the "advantage the other side possesses in its wealth and its ownership of . . . a score of important newspapers having an aggregate circulation of many millions" through such negative methods as a printers' strike.[12] Martin's observation on the inadequacy of both the *Daily Herald* and the *British Worker* to affect public opinion resonated uncomfortably with the Labour leadership. It underscored the fact that, while the paper's mere existence might ensure that the capitalist press did not "go the length they otherwise would," without a larger circulation the paper would never make a significant impact on public opinion.[13]

Prior to the strike, not everyone had agreed with the leadership's policy of seeking to ignore, or at least to circumvent, the commercial press. MPs J. R. Clynes and Ellen Wilkinson, in particular, frequently contributed articles to the anti-Labour press throughout the interwar period. Even opponents of such practices acknowledged that "if their leaders did not take advantage of the opportunity, the Movement would lose a good deal of publicity."[14] The year after the strike, the railway leader C. T. Cramp, a sometime *Herald* board member and longtime critic of the capitalist press, conceded that "[e]veryone knew that to preach to the unconverted was the best propaganda work. The articles which appeared [in the capitalist press] were rather elementary so far as their own people were concerned. . . . But to the man who merely got, say, his Sunday newspaper, they were valuable information and performed a valuable service to the interests of Labour."[15]

This recognition that pro-Labour articles printed in capitalist papers could perform a valuable service for the party reflected the growing acceptance within the Labour leadership of the need to make use of the mass media in order to broaden the party's support outside its industrialized male base. Labour leaders recognized that "the political problem of the middle classes [was] of real importance, demanding careful attention," and that a successful Labour policy could not be limited to the employment of continental socialist rhetoric or the language of class solidarity which "may be unintelligible or repugnant to [a nonworking-class audience]."[16] A successful Labour appeal would have to address the disparate sectors of the electorate not with socialist "jargon," but using "the English that people outside the movement understand."[17] And it would have to take advantage of the media through which people outside the movement took their news and formed their views.

The process by which the majority of the Labour leadership came to accept the necessity for such engagement was, however, gradual. Longheld antagonisms were hard to abandon, and Labour publicists remained wary of cooperating with the commercial press or the BBC. While the TUC was willing to spend thousands of pounds on its "Mines for the Nation" publicity campaign in 1920–1921, the press and publicity committee chose not to advertise its cause in 1926, even as mine owners relied heavily on press advertising to persuade the public of their arguments against reform.[18]

In 1927, the TUC and the Labour and Cooperative parties led an extraordinary campaign against the trade disputes and trade unions bill. Yet, although the campaign committee prepared a series of newspaper advertisements and special articles explaining the evils of the "Anti-Trade Union Bill," these were run primarily in union and local party publications, and to a lesser extent in provincial papers.[19] The movement did not take out advertisements in the national press, and, with a sole exception, the opinion pages of the major dailies did not carry any Labour response to conservative characterizations of the bill as designed to "protect honest trade unionists from communists and extremists."[20] The limits of the "Trade Union Defense Campaign" illustrate the difficulties of reversing the movement's long-held prejudice against the mass media.

Nonetheless, as daily press readership and radio listening continued to increase while attendance at public meetings and speeches declined, party leaders began to fear that they were "delud[ing] [them]selves that press influence was played out—that people read the newspapers but did not follow them politically."[21] Whereas, in 1928, Herbert Drinkwater, the editor of the *Labour Organiser,* had dismissed the importance of cultivating the press, claiming that "personally, I think a quarter of an hour of my time in one day for this purpose is rather a trifle too much," by 1935 the *Labour Organiser* was advocating that election agents "set aside a definite hour each day for press communications," and that they take steps not to antagonize national press correspondents. A guide to the *Conduct of Parliamentary Elections,* produced in 1945, advised Labour Party agents to "[w]elcome all the Pressmen . . . and give them proper attention. Don't blame the reporter for the bias of his paper, and don't be too sensitive about alleged 'distorted' reports. Remember that what appears unfair to Labour people may not be at all unfair as tested by the canons of even a generous opponent. In any case, even opposition advertises Labour."[22]

The TUC and the Labour Party press offices both increased their efforts to improve Labour and industrial coverage in the popular press in the late 1920s. The TUC press department updated and expanded its daily précis of "Industrial News: For the Use of the Press," which included a list of trade union and party activities and a general Labour gloss on the events of the day. By 1934, they were able to report that "[c]ontact with newspapers, especially the Industrial Correspondents and specialized writers on Trade Union and Labour politics, is now a matter of routine . . . , and those relations have continued during the year with a mutual appreciation of their usefulness."[23] The TUC's press officer, Herbert Tracey, who was referred to by the members of the Industrial Correspondent's Group as "The Voice of the TUC," developed close relationships with this group of young men, which included Ian Mackay at the *News Chronicle,* Trevor Evans at the *Express,* and Hugh Chevins at the *Daily Telegraph.* The correspondents "did the rounds in pursuit of news . . . at countless conferences . . . from Brighton to Blackpool, from Copenhagen to Rome . . . [and] lobbied Transport House and trade union headquarters all over the country."[24] Some of these reporters, like Mackay, were

Labour sympathizers. But even those who did not share their convictions came to respect the union leadership, and could be relied upon to produce straightforward and objective accounts of union activities.

A similar rapprochement was visible within the political side of the movement. Whereas, in the 1920s, the party had limited itself to providing weekly notes to "Labour and Trade Union papers and to Labour correspondents to provincial papers," during the 1929 general election Labour's press department prepared pre-written articles for the "important provincial papers"—a policy that had long been followed by their Conservative opponents.[25] By the 1930s, the department, like its TUC counterpart, was in regular communication with the principal national dailies. Individual Labour leaders also increased their contributions to the capitalist press. MP Philip Snowden occasionally wrote for the *Express* while in office, while Ellen Wilkinson continued her earlier relationship with the Beaverbrook papers, writing a series of profiles of prominent politicians for the *Evening Standard* during the second Labour government.[26] She also wrote the novel *Clash,* her literary début, and followed it with *The Division Bell Mystery,* a fictionalized tale of murder in the House of Commons featuring a young female Labour MP much like Wilkinson, which was serialized in the *Express* from August through October 1931. As with *Clash,* the novel was serialized during a general election, giving publicity to the author and her party. Beaverbrook's willingness to serialize the novel during the campaign perhaps reflected a desire to appear evenhanded and not to alienate Labour readers. On the other hand, it may merely have reflected his eccentric personality which often led him to privilege friendship over politics, as in his postwar funding of his ex-employee Michael Foot's journal *Tribune.*

While Labour leaders wrote for both Tory and Liberal publications, the rapprochement was most visible between Labourites and the Liberal press. In this Herbert Morrison was particularly notable. A fellow Labour MP described Morrison as "one of the first Labour politicians deliberately to court the press."[27] A former *News Chronicle* journalist recalled that Morrison "took trouble to cultivate" the lobby men. Morrison particularly courted the *News Chronicle,* the Liberal journal formed from the merger of the *Daily News* and the *Daily Chronicle* in June 1930. Whereas, in the 1920s, Labour had lambasted the false sympathies of these papers, Morrison exploited their willingness to give a "great deal of space to Labour." He would often give them advance notice of questions he planned to ask in the House. And the journalists, while they "never felt they were being used, . . . realized that they were advancing a cause."[28] Morrison held joint meetings with the editors of the *Daily Herald* and the *News Chronicle* to devise press policy before the 1935 election, and after the *Daily Mirror* abandoned its previous conservative stance in favor a broad populist and anti-appeasement critique of the government, he became a columnist for that paper.[29] He also courted the local London press and had a close relationship with Sir Walter Layton, chairman of both the *Chronicle* and the London *Star*.[30] Morrison was one of the most vocal supporters of the need for Labour to make a broad appeal to the electorate in the interwar period.[31] Both in his personal activities and in his capacity as a member of the NEC's publicity committee in the 1930s, he demonstrated a commitment to using the mass media to further this end.[32] While both were exceptionally prolific, Wilkinson and Morrison are merely the most high profile examples of a broader shift in Labour's approach toward the mass media in the late 1920s.

Figure 7.1. Sidney Strube cartoon depicting Morrison as the Duke of Wellington, triumphantly breaking ground on the Waterloo Bridge. The cameramen set up behind him are a reference to his love for media attention. (© *Daily Express*, 22 June 1934)

The 1929 General Election

The party's determination to make a broad appeal to the electorate through the mass media was visible during the 1929 general election campaign when the party successfully presented an "image which convinced many more people that it could be 'their' party . . . a practical party, capable of providing security and opportunity."[33] In terms of seats contested and won, 1929 was Labour's most successful election in the interwar period. The party contested 570 seats, more than at any other interwar election, and saw 287 MPs elected. Of course, Labour's exceptional showing was not solely attributable to the popularity of its policy proposals or the success of its campaign, for 1929 was the last interwar election in which the Liberal Party participated on a truly national scale. The party ran 511 candidates, all in contested seats; 444 of those constituencies saw three-cornered contests. Whereas, in earlier elections, three-cornered contests had been seen to benefit the Conservatives by splitting the left-wing vote, in 1929, Liberal intervention played to Labour's favor for, despite the pronounced progressivism of the 1929 Liberal campaign, the result of the three-way contests tended to be a splitting of the anti-socialist vote.[34]

Labour also benefited from a general frustration and exhaustion with the Conservatives, who, by May 1929, had been in power for five and a half of the previous six and a half years. This weariness was evident in the frayed relationship between the conservative press and the party going into the election. While the *Daily Express* and the *Daily Mail* may have endorsed the Conservatives in both 1924 and 1929, the papers' frequent hostility toward the government in the intervening years made their support ring somewhat hollow. Even before the launch of their "Empire Crusade" on 8 July 1929, the press barons had sought to undermine the authority of Baldwin's government to speak for conservatism. During the campaign itself, they presented the election as an opportunity for Baldwin and his cronies to reform their incompetent ways, and their support of the prime minister was so conditional that Lloyd George quoted appreciatively from a *Daily Express* editorial in his election broadcast.[35] Lords Rothermere and Beaverbrook, and particularly the latter, had little love for the Conservative leader, and the animosity was mutual—Baldwin privately referred to the two men as "lunatics" and expressed the view that "to call them swine . . . was to libel a very decent, clean animal."[36]

Many voters doubtless developed their own suspicions of the adequacy of Baldwin's leadership without the help of the press barons. Though overall unemployment figures declined slightly during the last years of the 1924–1929 government, unemployment in certain key sectors remained near or above 20 percent at the end of that term, and it did not take a convinced socialist to share Snowden's conclusion that the Conservatives had had their chance and failed.[37] Although structural factors and weariness with the present government may have helped, "Labour's victory cannot simply be explained as a consolidation of support combined with a measure of good fortune. It was less dependent on its 'core' supporters than ever before. Something had expanded the party's appeal."[38] While much work remains to be done on what exactly the "something" driving this surge in Labour support was, the following section argues for the importance of party publicity and propaganda to the expansion of Labour turnout in 1929.

Labour's 1929 election campaign focused on the party's national appeal, and in particular its appeal to the middle classes and the new women voters. The party's election manifesto, based on the tellingly named 1928 party platform *Labour and the Nation,* clearly shows the scale of the party's ambitions. *Labour and the Nation* begins by stating that "the long-awaited opportunity has now come for the Nation to give its verdict on the present Government."[39] The Labour Party gave the document prominence in its speeches and print propaganda throughout the campaign. One party poster showed an earnest MacDonald standing in front of John Bull being interviewed for the job of prime minister. John Bull has in hand MacDonald's resumé—a copy of *Labour and the Nation.* The caption reads: "John Bull—Credentials excellent! Just the man I want."[40] While the *Daily Mail* attempted to downplay the manifesto's appeal, characterizing it as "The Socialist Programme: Bigger Doles, Relations with Moscow," the fact that the NEC managed to sell nearly nine million copies to constituency organizations suggests a considerable interest in the publication at the local level.[41]

The *Daily Express* special correspondent, H. V. Morton, who followed MacDonald's motorcade tour during the election, wrote an article on the "Changing Face of Labour":

> [T]he Labour movement, like all communities destined to achieve respectability, is developing a middle class. . . . A big mass meeting in a great city is the time to sum up a Labour crowd. Take Birmingham and Bristol. Here were thousands of ordinary middle-class men, women, and girls. There were, I would say, more clerks, typists, shop assistants, and school teachers at these meetings than artisans and manual workers. The neck-cloth has almost disappeared from Labour meetings except at wayside gatherings which naturally attract all the local unemployed and every lounger in the district. . . . I must perhaps be forgiven for the impression that it will soon be unfashionable to be Conservative or Liberal.[42]

This emphasis on reaching out to a broad audience was not merely evident in the party's print propaganda and speeches, but was also reflected in its media campaign. While Labour's full-on embrace of the mass media would have to await the 1930s, the party's 1929 election campaign highlights the role that the popular press and the BBC had come to play in Labour politics.

Labour's determination to use the *Daily Herald* as a platform to appeal to readers and would-be supporters outside of the party's traditional base was in strong evidence in 1929. During the election campaign, the *Herald* showed the same attention to audience differentiation and subconscious appeal that the Tory press had previously deployed so successfully. Whereas, in 1924, the *Herald* had directed its campaign coverage almost exclusively at manual laborers, in 1929 the paper's election coverage was appreciably more diverse. Just as the Labour publicity department in 1919 had prepared a series of columns for the *Daily Mail* that dealt with the reasons why different sectors of the population should vote Labour, the *Herald* in 1929 ran a series of "Little Letters" on its front page, addressed to, among others, a shopkeeper, a doctor, a young mother, and "Miss 1929," or the newly enfranchised "flapper voter."[43] These appeals to traditionally conservative demographic groups emphasized the ill-effects of Conservative policy on consumer demand and public health, and sought to counter negative stereotypes about trade unionism. They also underscored the lackluster performance of the Tories in office, and the bankruptcy of "Safety First" as an argument against political change.

The paper's news and editorial columns similarly evinced a desire to appeal outside of Labour's traditional strongholds. While the emphasis of the election coverage was on the government's record on unemployment, the paper also dealt prominently with farmers' wages and with the exclusion of shopkeepers from the Tories' derating bill. The competence and success of Labour in government was hammered home in a series of photos of municipal pools and dentistries in Labour-controlled boroughs, and houses built "to let—not 'for sale' at high prices" under the Wheatley Housing Act. Conservative manipulation of the specter of "the tragedy of 1926" was confronted head on in a series of articles on "How the Tories Caused the General Strike." And the paper pulled no punches in attempting to depict Baldwin not as an avuncular and conciliatory head of state but as a man whose "brazen ignorance" had led to "five years of footling and fumbling."[44]

Further, the *Herald* made significant play of the news of Conservative campaign improprieties, such as the use of the civil service to produce rebuttals to Liberal and Labour propaganda and the anonymous distribution of anti-Labour leaflets to Catholics which allegedly misrepresented statements made by Cardinal Bourne. These disclosures were accompanied by large sensationalist headlines denouncing "SECRET TORY PLOTS" and "TRICKS" with the intent of prejudicing the casual viewer against "these bad sportsmen."[45] The rhetoric of trickery and untrustworthiness was also deployed against Lloyd George, and considerable mileage was made of the former prime minister's unfulfilled promises after 1918, and of the mutual antipathy and distrust of the Liberal leadership. In addition, the usual assaults against the viability of the Liberal Party were trotted out against Lloyd George and his band of "clever lads."[46] However, the comparatively slight attention paid to the Liberal program suggested a confidence that voters recognized that "the Labour Party offers the only serious alternative to the existing Conservative Government."[47]

Labour's press campaign was not limited to the *Daily Herald*, but was part of a broader Labour attempt to capitalize on the weaknesses of the Conservatives' political record and electoral strategy. The contradictory nature of Conservative strategy in the 1920s, in which the party sought simultaneously to legitimize the parliamentary Labour Party as a respectable party of government and the natural successor to a played-out Liberalism and to demonize Labour as an alien movement led by irresponsible and incompetent would-be revolutionaries, has been detailed elsewhere.[48] During the 1929 election, Labour sought to play up its own legitimacy as "a practical, responsible and effective party of reform," and to expose Tory accusations to the contrary as hypocritical scaremongering.[49] They also made considerable mileage out of the government's failure to solve the nation's problems during its previous terms in office, as well as its failure in the realm of foreign affairs.

This last theme formed the focus of Ramsay MacDonald's pre-election article in the *Daily Mail*, in which he articulated the party's support for the Kellogg-Briand Pact, and its commitment to international disarmament. The article was part of an eleven-part series that ran in the *Mail* in the weeks before the election and included contributions from Churchill, Lloyd George, Joynson-Hicks, Snowden, Samuel, Thomas, Simon, Chamberlain, Worthington-Evans, and the editor of the *National Review*, L. J. Maxse. The other two Labour articles, by Snowden and Thomas, dealt respectively with taxation and unemployment. Snowden's article made no mention of the politically unpopular capital levy proposals that had been a staple of Labour's platform in earlier elections and instead focused on the use of the surtax and death taxes to effect a "readjust[ment of] taxation according to means" so that "the middle and working classes [no longer] contribute more than their share." Thomas's article on unemployment

Figure 7.2. Front page cartoon by "Pip" (Philip Youngman Carter), *Daily Herald*, 21 May 1929, attacking Lloyd George for his history of "selling the public a pup," or cheating them through unfilled pledges and false promises. (© Mirrorpix)

stressed the need to raise the school leaving age and to lower the retirement age, as it was indisputably smarter to "supplement the pension to enable the aged to retire from industry than to pay money to unemployed young men," a conviction which he claimed accorded with the views of the sensible tax-paying public. The tone and tenor of these articles reflected the party's determination to, in the words of the *Mail*, "mollif[y] moderate opinion by [its] dignified and restrained attitude on important and difficult questions."[50] The fact that the articles were published in the *Mail* reflects the newfound willingness of the Labour leadership to make use of the very medium that it had long excoriated as "the principal manufactory of that unscientific bias called 'Public Opinion' which is the despair of progressive minds" in order to popularize its policies and turn public opinion to its favor.[51]

The party also sought to make use of the wireless to broadcast its message to the widest possible audience. The 1929 party election broadcasts proved to be a particularly successful aspect of the party's election campaign. In 1924, the Labour postmaster general had unilaterally authorized a single election broadcast for each of the three party leaders; in 1929, the distribution of airtime in the month before the election was a matter of considerable debate, and one to which the Labour Party devoted energy and attention. Despite the government's reluctance to open up the airwaves to its opponents, Labour succeeded in arguing that, in addition to the proposed pre-dissolution rota of four government broadcasts to two each for the Labour and Liberal parties plus one broadcast from each party in the week before the election, "in view of the importance of the woman voter, a series of three addresses be given to women voters strictly on women's questions, by women representatives of the three parties."[52] Conservative reservations notwithstanding, this proposal was accepted by Reith, changing the broadcast ratio to a more advantageous 6:4:4.

Labour's broadcasters—Henderson, Snowden, Margaret Bondfield, and MacDonald—did not repeat MacDonald's mistake of 1924 of broadcasting from a public platform; each recorded his or her speech from the studio. And while Henderson was not a particularly inspired broadcaster, according to one listener, "Labour did right in selecting Mr. Snowden to address us via the microphone. A masterly speech, likely to gain the approval of the most exacting accountant." The *Daily Express* described Snowden as being "magnificently intimate with the needs of his audience," and Reith felt him to be Labour's strongest broadcaster.[53] His broadcast opened by noting that Churchill's speech three nights prior had contained almost no mention of the budget or of Conservative taxation policy and commenting that "in this matter, Mr. Churchill evidently thought that silence was the best policy." He then went on to outline the details of Labour's fiscal and monetary proposals, successfully showcasing his skill at combining a clear exposition of facts and figures with a dry and cutting wit.

Conservative critics of the 1928 franchise reform argued that newly enfranchised "flappers"—single women allegedly more intent on fashion and socializing than responsible citizenship—would vote Labour out of a sense of perversity and contrarianism.[54] Given this focus on the perils to Conservatism of unmarried women voters, it is noteworthy that Bondfield's election broadcast was directed primarily not at single women, but at young mothers. Bondfield sought to depict the Labour Party as a defender of the family. She directly attacked the Conservative

Figure 7.3. Labour Party election poster, 1929. (© Labour Party. Courtesy of the Cambridge University Library)

propaganda of the 1920s which elided Labour policy with the atheism and alleged anti-family ethos of the Russian Bolsheviks, and denounced such tactics as a "scandalous violation of decent electioneering." Instead, she argued, Labour was an advocate for mothers and families. In a campaign pledge that prefigured the New Labour slogans eighty years later, she promised that, if elected, "Labour will build a broad highway for all children from the nursery school to the University."[55] This emphasis on the Labour Party as the party of the children was evident in several of the party's posters as well, including "Women Vote Labour for the Children's Sake." While the direct effect of the Labour's media campaign on public opinion about the three political parties is difficult to gauge, the party's determined exploitation of the mass media in 1929 is an important indicator of its shifting attitude toward political communication in that period. The full impact of this shift is exemplified most visibly in Labour's changing attitude toward the *Daily Herald* in the late 1920s.

The Transformation of the *Daily Herald*

Nearly a year after the formation of the second Labour government, the Trades Union Congress officially relaunched the *Daily Herald* as a pro-Labour rival to the Tory and Liberal popular press. Agitation to reform the *Herald* along popular lines had begun even before the general strike underscored the need for a more successful paper. By 1924, Hamilton Fyfe had become despondent over the paper's ability to win readers through exhortation, concluding that if the movement continued to tell people that "it was their duty to take the paper . . . they would regard it as a medicine."[56] The *Herald*'s directors increasingly shared their editor's discouragement, and in 1925 they convened a subcommittee to look into editorial policy. The committee was composed of board chairman Ben Turner, vice chairman Ernest Bevin, and board members Clifford Allen and Dr. Ethel Bentham. As discussed in Chapter 5, Allen believed that the "paper [was] in its nature wrong," and that instead of being a Labour daily, it should strive to be "an attractive general newspaper."[57] Allen's views were (at least in 1925) outside the mainstream of the movement; the other board members did, however, agree that efforts should be made to make the paper more commercially competitive.

The committee passed on its suggestions for revamping the paper to Fyfe, who exposed the limits of his commitment to reform by responding that "it is quite impossible that a paper which exists in order that the Labour point of view may be represented in the Press should serve up its news and comments exactly as the *Daily News* and the *Daily Mail* do. If it did, what need would there be to keep it going?"[58] Despite Fyfe's hostility, the committee persuaded the General Council to earmark funds to expand the paper from eight pages to ten, including one page of pictures. The *Herald* advertised these new improvements on its front page, instructing existing readers to "Tell Your Friends Please that tomorrow's issue of the *Daily Herald* will be improved, enlarged, illustrated. Our paper will be of better quality, we shall always be ten pages, and one page will be devoted to pictures of the world's happenings."[59] The first *Daily Herald* picture page ran photos of the previous day's record-breaking floods, the new baby fox at the London zoo, a play at the Wyndham, the Oxford crew team, and a stylish new Parisian hat.[60] The *Herald*'s chairman, the trade unionist and sometimes newspaper editor, Ben Turner, found the necessity of bribing readers with pictures "lamentable," but the new page helped to boost the paper's circulation back above 300,000.[61]

Over the next few years, the board introduced several other editorial changes. Fyfe resigned shortly after the general strike and was replaced by William Mellor, who had served as deputy editor of the paper since its takeover by the movement. Mellor's appointment was strongly supported by Allen, who saw in him a kindred spirit.[62] While himself a leftist who would go on to join the Socialist League, Mellor did not share the same hostility toward popular journalism as many of his fellow left-wing intellectuals. His willingness to combine educationalist journalism with commercial appeal would later be evident in his editorship of *Tribune* in the 1930s. At the *Herald,* the new editor allowed several concessions toward popular taste that had been resisted by his predecessor. The picture page upped its complement of pretty ladies, and the news content of the paper was diversified to include more human interest articles. On 3 January 1929, for instance, the stories on the front page included, in addition to political news: "Workhouse 'Mint' Discovered in Boiler House: False Florins: Inmate Accused of Possessing Them" and "Attack on Shop: London Man Struck on Head." Inside the paper, a story on Germany's financial recovery was juxtaposed with "Indian Archers Repel Monkeys: Wood-Tipped Arrows for Sacred Beasts," and an article on the threatened censorship of Labour organizations in Mexico ran alongside news of a kissing ban in Vienna. These human interest stories were intended not only to amuse Labour loyalists, but also to draw in apolitical readers who might then be persuaded by the paper's political coverage.

Unfortunately, editorial changes were not enough to boost the *Herald*'s flagging circulation. The continued decline in sales was partly attributable to the inadequacy of the paper in providing up-to-the-minute news, particularly in the north. Unlike its larger rivals, the *Herald* published only three editions, all produced in London—an early "Northern" edition, a second edition, and a late London edition, with the result that, as one Bolton resident stated to the 1926 party conference, "anything which happened anywhere in Britain late in the evening was not to be found in the *Daily Herald* of the following morning."[63] Furthermore, the increased spending by the *Herald*'s commercial rivals on exclusive photographs and special features was believed to have enticed readers away from the *Herald*.[64]

But while news and features played a role, the *Herald*'s lagging circulation was largely attributable to the increasingly elaborate bribes that the paper's rivals offered to subscribers. Then as now, large newspapers' profitability depended more on advertising than on sales revenue, and advertising revenue in turn was directly linked to circulation. In 1914, newspaper baron Lord Northcliffe began issuing net sales certificates for his papers, certified by chartered accountants.[65] The sales certificates were intended to illustrate the value of the *Mail* and the *Evening News,* at that point the largest daily and evening paper respectively, as advertising media. While the practice of issuing sales certificates was initiated by the press, by the mid-1920s it was "big commercial advertisers who force[d] [papers] to issue these net sales certificates so that they may judge of the paper's value as an advertising medium."[66] As a result, rival dailies were willing to go to great lengths to increase their circulation, primarily by offering fabulous insurance schemes and other free giveaways to subscribers (discussed more fully in Chapter 5). The *Herald*'s directors initially resisted proposals for a *Daily Herald* insurance scheme, both on the grounds that bribing readers with such "baits" as free insurance was unworthy of a movement-owned paper and, more pragmatically, on the grounds of cost.[67] Financial constraints were similarly used to rationalize the paper's lack of a Manchester edition and its inability to provide "the most up-to-date news from every corner of the world."[68] But whereas the paper's directors had previously been more concerned with economy than adequacy, in the second half of the decade several members of the *Herald* board began to argue the need for large-scale investment in the paper in order to attract a mass circulation on par with its commercial rivals.

The Labour movement had long recognized the link between circulation and agenda-setting power. A 1922 party publication argued that the lack of a widely circulated Labour corrective in the daily press allowed the "capitalist" papers to distort news of the movement: "Headlines are used to suggest untruths, vital facts are omitted, weaker aspects of the workers' case are unduly emphasized, and in some cases resort is made to downright lying." The *Daily Herald* exercised a "valuable and increasingly corrective influence," but only a very large circulation would be sufficient to "act as a bulwark against capitalist misrepresentation."[69] In the battle for public opinion, the movement needed a paper that could "fire for every shell the other side fired into them, two shells back again." Only if the paper's circulation were made "pre-eminent" could "its influence be most effectively used on occasions when issues of policy involving the Labour movement are at stake."[70]

With this end in mind, the *Herald* board appointed a subcommittee to consider all possible methods of increasing "the circulation and influence" of the paper. The subcommittee included both Bevin and Morrison, who had joined the *Herald* board in 1926. More than any other of the directors, these two men were convinced of the importance of publicity to the future of the movement. And while both had begun their journalistic careers imbued with the educationalist ethos of Edwardian Labour journalism, by 1927 they had reached the conclusion that only commercial methods could achieve the results that the movement required. Given their convictions, it was not surprising that they recommended that the *Herald* should bow to competitive pressure and launch "an insurance scheme which, while not as pretentious as the schemes of our competitors, would offer genuine benefits to readers."[71] This recommendation did not please everyone. When confronted with the subcommittee report, Turner expressed his view that an insurance scheme was not "a proper and honest thing." To Turner, the paper's problems lay with its readers, or more accurately with those who refused to read it. His pronouncement that "until we are ourselves satisfactory we shall not have a satisfactory newspaper" reflected the outlook of the early 1920s wherein the failure to "take the Labour daily first" was seen to illustrate a lamentable lack of class consciousness.[72]

Yet the forces of change were against Turner and his sympathizers. No additional money was voted to fund reforms of the *Herald* that year, in large part because many of the unions were strapped for cash in the wake of the general strike. Bevin, however, did not let the matter drop. By the next year's congress, he had managed to line up several key members of the General Council in support of outside investment for the *Herald*. The Transport leader came to the TUC hell-bent on securing a large sum of money—at least £1 million—to revamp the

Herald and fund an insurance scheme in order to boost it into the league of the *Daily Express,* the *Daily Chronicle,* and the *Daily Mail.* In a private session on the future of the paper, Bevin made a tour-de-force speech in which he impressed upon the unions the need to get their hands on the necessary funds at any cost, even through the open market: "[T]here is need for capital. . . . It may mean going to the market for money; it may mean using affiliation fees in the future to guarantee the interest on that money, but we must get sufficient at least to launch out on a wide footing."[73]

In support of this view, which would have seemed treasonous only a few years earlier, stood many of the most influential members of the movement. MP Fred Roberts, of the typographical association, who had served as the Labour Party representative to the *Herald*'s board of directors and was a longtime chairman of the NEC's press and publicity subcommittee, seconded Bevin's views. He argued that the trade union representatives present at Congress had a responsibility to "ge[t] our people to understand that if the directors deem it fitting to raise the money essential for our purposes in the open market, we will not criticize them but hold them up and give them all the assistance in our power." Walter Citrine rose to explain the practicalities of obtaining a commercial loan assured by the TUC affiliation fees. Finally, Jimmy Thomas spoke on behalf of the General Council. The time had come for change: "There will be a scheme brought to you, a big scheme, a scheme that you have never before considered, a scheme that I repeat is going to be a capitalist scheme, because you cannot run the *Herald* on sentiment." The message was clear: moral scruples would no longer prevent the commercialization of the paper. Congress gave its support to the board's proposals.[74]

The following year a joint subcommittee of the *Herald* board of directors and the General Council's finance committee, including Bevin, Citrine, Thomas, and Allen, set about seeking financial backers for the *Herald.* After exploring several options for a loan, the committee, through Bevin, arranged for the sale of 51 percent of the paper's shares to Odhams Press, the publishers of the Sunday *People,* with the understanding that editorial control of the paper would remain with the TUC. Odhams provided the funds to relaunch the paper on 17 March 1930, complete with a large-scale insurance scheme and a Manchester plant for the printing of a northern edition.[75] The new publishers triumphantly advertised the paper's relaunch in the columns of its rival dailies. Giant display ads appeared in the *Mail, Express, Chronicle,* and *News* announcing the arrival of "LABOUR'S GREAT

NATIONAL NEWSPAPER . . . THE NEW DAILY HERALD . . . £10,000 FREE FAM-
ILY INSURANCE."

Whereas in earlier years the *Herald* directors had exhorted the paper's readers to "persuade your friends and fellow workers to do the same," the new proprietors resorted to the more surefire method of paying readers to enroll their friends as *Herald* subscribers.[76] These *Daily Herald* "helpers" were paid one shilling for every new reader they registered. The paper even produced a special journal, *The Helper,* which included such canvassing tips as "Hunt in Pairs—You will find it a very good plan to work with a pal. This gives added confidence and is far more pleasant than playing a lone hand."[77] The new *Herald* proved a commercial success—the paper was the first to pass the two million mark in the press circulation wars of the 1930s—but it did so by exploiting the very commercial methods that Labour had long condemned.[78]

Many Labourites in fact continued to condemn the crass commercialism of the new paper. Shortly before the paper achieved its two million circulation mark, the Tottenham plumbers union wrote to their local trades council asking them to "submit a resolution to the General Council urging them to sell their interest in the present *Daily Herald,* and to start a new paper on the basis of the old *Daily Herald.*"[79] One Labour activist bemoaned that "the prestige of the *Daily Herald* has dwindled amongst the party membership chiefly because it has ceased to be a political organ and become a popular newspaper."[80] Another argued that, while he was "aware that for business reasons it is not at present desirable to emphasize the Trade Union and Labour connection of the paper[,] . . . I think there is room for much more discussion of economic and industrial matter"; this despite the fact that the *Herald* continued to carry, on average, more than 300 percent as many column inches of industrial and Labour news as the *News Chronicle* and 900 percent as much as the *Express.*[81] The *Daily Express* gleefully exploited the discomfiture of its rival, publishing a leading article in 1932 that admonished workers "not [to] allow yourselves in any circumstances to be placed under the guidance of capitalist newspapers which call themselves Socialist journals. . . . *The entire daily Press of this country is under capitalist direction. There is no exception to this.*"[82]

In an attempt to combat rank and file discontent, the paper's directors produced a leaflet for distribution to trade union secretaries, outlining "How the *Daily Herald* Helps Labour." The circular emphasized that the directors were "anxious that our people should realize the full value of the *Daily Herald* to the Movement generally. The conversion of its circulation from 250,000 to 1,000,000 was a great and unrivalled achievement . . . we shall [now] have a first-class newspaper going into more than a million homes to counter the attacks and misrepresentations of our opponents and to tell the truth about Labour policy."[83] Yet they were unable to stanch the flow of complaints. Three years later, in response to yet another complaint from a Labour reader, fellow *Daily Herald* board member Arthur Pugh expressed his frustration to Citrine: "If every objector and crank had their way, the *Herald* would soon be published as a blank sheet. I personally strongly object to the *Herald* being used as a medium for gambling and betting tips, but I know that it is common to the daily press of the country and that it has been demonstrated that you cannot maintain a circulation without it."[84]

While the continued complaints of objectors and cranks discomfited Pugh, the majority supported the board of directors' decision. Even the *Labour Organiser,* long a staunch critic of commercial journalism, grudgingly reconciled itself to the necessity of tolerating the populist pandering of the new *Daily Herald*. In the April 1932 issue of its advice column for local organizers, the paper admonished readers who "don't like the *Daily Herald*" and find in it "too much Davidson [the former director of the Conservative Party organization]":

> O fie! Don't you realize you cannot have all the paper for Socialism? The new readers are not all Socialists, are they? And we suppose the *Daily Herald* knows what pleases the people. So don't complain. . . . Let us understand clearly that a newspaper is a newspaper and a propaganda sheet is a propaganda sheet. The one sells and the other doesn't. . . . Take our tip. Don't cry for the moon. Don't pine because the *Daily Herald* isn't the holy bible of Socialism.[85]

Despite continued reservations about the methods of commercial journalism, by 1930 the Labour leadership had given up "crying for the moon." Labour's leaders, if not all of the rank and file, had come to see the benefits of modern methods of mass communication. The Labour Party of the 1930s was determined that, if they could not change the system, they would at least be as successful at it as their rivals—they would "pla[y] Beaverbrook at his own game," and play to win.[86]

The party also made significant strides with broadcasting, and with incorporating new marketing and publishing techniques in the production of party propaganda in an attempt to bring its message to the broadest possible audience. The Labour leadership remained wedded to an inclusive national policy throughout the interwar period, and the lessons learned by MacDonald's Labour Party were not unlearned by the leaders of the National Council of Labour in the 1930s. The post-MacDonald Labour Party was, in many respects, more attuned to the potentialities of mediated communication than their National Government rivals.[87]

CHAPTER EIGHT

Experimenting in the 1930s

THE LABOUR PARTY'S APPROACH to political communication in the 1930s reflected its sophisticated awareness of the importance of the mass media to the party's political fortunes and its willingness both to embrace existing opportunities and experiment with new avenues of national political outreach. While the 1931 crisis dealt a serious blow to Labour both in parliament and in the country, the decision by the Liberal Party (with the exception of the small clique of Lloyd George supporters) to join the National Government effectively sounded the death knell of Liberalism as a national political force. The Labour Party, albeit reduced to a rump contingent of fifty-two MPs, retained its *de jure* status as the official opposition and solidified its position as the second party of the state.[1] In the decade that followed, the party sought to rebuild a broad national constituency around a democratic socialist program of government planning, progressive municipal governance, and international anti-fascism, and the mass media played an increasingly central role in its strategy for communicating this agenda to the British nation.

Anxieties about the corrupting influence of commercial culture and intense suspicions of the capitalist-controlled media continued to plague Labour leaders, but by the 1930s these anxieties had been overwhelmed by practical considerations of the value of mediated communication.[2] Whereas tirades against the popular press had once been a standard element of Labour stump speeches, such criticisms were now more likely to be heard in Cambridge quads than in local Labour halls.[3] The post-MacDonald Labour movement fully accepted that "[p]arty propaganda services have to be kept efficient and up-to-date, and the party must be ready to adopt modern instruments and to make use of new methods," and the years before the Second World War saw an expansion of Labour's efforts at mediated political outreach.[4]

While the interwar popular press had an extremely heterogeneous readership, the Labour leadership recognized that it was insufficient to base its media strategy solely on the promotion of the *Daily Herald,* or on Labour contributions to rival papers. The NEC and the TUC General Ccouncil actively sought to exploit broadcasting, a medium that the party perceived to be particularly useful in communicating its message to middle-class voters, who were more likely to own a radio and to listen to political broadcasts, and to women, whose domestic commitments often prevented them from participating in public politics. Many of the new middle-class leaders of the party, particularly Clement Attlee, Stafford Cripps, and Hugh Dalton, recognized the central role of the radio in middle-class family life. The party's emphasis on issues affecting middle-class voters in its 1935 election broadcasts is indicative of their conscious attempt to communicate with this constituency via the airwaves. Additionally, the party made innovative use of print propaganda in the 1930s to bring its message to a wider audience.

The post-MacDonald Labour Party made use of the press, broadcasting, and print propaganda to appeal to the nation on a broad productivist platform of full employment and social welfare. Although the impact of Labour's media strategy on public opinion in the 1930s is not easily measured, it is clear that the party was remarkably successful at making its ideas heard by a wide audience. Even if Labour's media campaign did not succeed in convincing the majority of the electorate to vote Labour by 1939, it arguably made many rethink previous conventional wisdoms about the anti-social nature of the so-called socialist party, and to consider the party's policies on their merits.

In August 1931, the newly formed National Government was quick to present the Labour Party as "ha[ving] changed into something much more dangerous than it had shown itself to be in the 1920s. It had become an overtly class party, sectional, irresponsible, confiscatory, 'revolutionary.'"[5] The resignation of the Labour ministers at the height of the August crisis, the confusion of the Labour movement in the months after the formation of the National Government, the expulsion of MacDonald and his supporters from the party (they re-formed as the National Labour Party), and the rushed nature of the general election meant that the Labour Party was largely unsuccessful in countering "the government's claim to embody 'national unity' . . . [and] 'patriotism.'"[6] In Arthur Henderson's words, 1931 "was a 'khaki' election on the slogan of 'Stand by the Nation' and the issue was presented as the Nation versus party."[7]

Despite Labour's efforts, almost every organ of the media was united against the party in 1931. The entirety of the national press, with the exception of the *Herald,* the Cooperative-owned Sunday paper *Reynolds News,* and the *Manchester Guardian,* supported the government. The *News Chronicle,* which had shown sympathy for the challenges facing the Labour government the previous spring, declared Labour's program to be "a menace."[8] Even the support of the *Herald* was initially in question, as members of the editorial staff evinced sympathy for MacDonald, and the advertising department feared that support for Labour would cause the paper to lose advertisements. It was largely due to Ernest Bevin and the other trade union members of the board of directors that the paper remained loyal to the party.[9]

The National Government's post office savings bank "canard"—the government put it out that Labour, if elected, would confiscate pensioners' savings—was picked up and run by all the national dailies.[10] The BBC's allocation of election broadcasts was "little short of disgraceful. . . . [and] indefensible in any argument about balance." The BBC granted two election broadcasts apiece to the National Labour and Conservative parties, as well as one broadcast to the Simonites and one to the Samuelite Liberals, while only allowing three to Labour, despite the party's outraged protests that, as the official opposition, they had a constitutional right to equal access to the microphone with their government opponents. In the period between the formation of the National Government and its dissolution, the prime minister, Sir Arthur Steel-Maitland, and Professor Henry Clay of the Bank of England, each broadcast once, and the chancellor of the exchequer twice, while "not one single opportunity was afforded to the Opposition to indicate its attitude or present its case to the public." Additionally, at the end of the evening news bulletin on the eve of the election, the newsreader declared to listeners, "On your action, or your failure to act, may depend your own and your children's future and the security and prosperity of your country," a statement which the party took as a thinly veiled inducement to vote National. Labour supporters' assertions in the wake of the election that the BBC was "virtually a Tory platform" were difficult to dismiss.[11] Finally, the newsreels, while not overtly political, were pro-National in tone. Pathé, in particular, showed a strong anti-Labour bias, as did Movietone, perhaps a reflection of the attitude of one of its principal financial backers, Lord Rothermere.[12] October 1931, more than any previous point in Labour's history, seemed to prove the contention that the commercial media was controlled by and "for the advantage of very rich men, who have been made rich by the present social and economic system, and who are determined to use every means in their power to prevent that system from being in any important direction changed."[13]

Although the Labour Party failed in 1931 to convince electors that its interests were coincident with the national interest, it did not abandon its policy of seeking to influence political discussion within the commercial media. Nor did the party abandon its broader strategy of national outreach and revert to a dependence on its unionized industrial base.[14] The distinction between pre-1931 and post-1931 Labour policy was less in its professed aims than in its commitment to devising "a constructive policy [to implement socialist reform] complete in every detail and ready for use."[15] Despite many Labour supporters' hysterical rhetoric about the crisis of capitalism in the immediate wake of the 1931 crisis, the failure of the capitalist system to implode and the need to win over moderate voters soon led the party to focus both its rhetoric and its policy not on the endemic contradictions of the capitalist system, but on the need to implement concrete socialist reforms.[16]

Ben Pimlott begins his study, *Labour and the Left in the 1930s*, by stating that "[s]ome left-wing ideas appear in retrospect blinkered or utopian; others were far-sighted and highly practical. We are concerned, however, not with judging policies, but with political action; with attempts to put favoured policies into practice."[17] But while, as Pimlott rightly points out, the Labour Left was handicapped by its willingness to defy party loyalty and publicly flaunt its disagreements with the leadership, it also suffered from the perception within the party and trade unions that its policies were unlikely to win public approval. TUC secretary general Walter Citrine, for example, dismissed the proposals of the Socialist League for the introduction of emergency powers by a future socialist government on the grounds that the adoption of such proposals would scare the electorate "out of their wits," and that the mere talk of such ideas was "damaging to Labour's prospects of electoral victory." Threats of unconstitutional action, he admonished, were "[not] the way in which the middle class would be converted."[18]

The Society for Socialist Inquiry and Propaganda's first report, *A Labour Programme of Action*, was rejected by the NEC as being "over-ambitious, impractical, and *likely to frighten the electorate*."[19] The party was so alarmed by Labour MP Sir Stafford Cripps's statement in November 1934 that he "regarded a financial crisis as inevitable" if Labour were to come to power, and its implication that such a crisis would be a necessary step on the road to socialism, that they took the extraordinary step of issuing a press release that directly repudiated responsibility for Cripps's remark:

> The NEC takes the view that in the event of a victory at the polls, a Labour Government is entitled to rely and can count upon the loyal support of the people. It does not regard a crisis as 'inevitable.' The National Executive expresses the belief that the minority would bow to the will of the majority, but it wishes to make it clear that a Labour Government would take prompt and effective measures to deal with any crisis by financial or other private interests.[20]

Hugh Dalton had already lambasted Cripps for similar statements, arguing that the socialist barrister was "damaging the party electorally" and "stabb[ing our candidates] in the back and push[ing them] on to the defensive." Dalton's diary records his fury at the adverse effect of Cripps's statement on Labour's electoral prospects, and he doubtless fumed when the *Daily Express* observed that "Cripps, promising Crisis and Crash" had contributed significantly to Labour's poor showing in 1935. Two years later, Richard Crossman criticized the left-wing of the party for "neglect[ing] the simple fact that it is not they but the Tory voters who must be converted." Crossman recognized that "[i]t was time to develop from a sectional movement into a national one. The appeal to the manual worker was not enough—We must approach the blackcoated workers." The young backbencher was not the only member of the party to voice such views. Herbert Morrison had long held that Labour propaganda should seek to reach beyond the party's traditional industrial base to the clerical workers and the professional classes. He was exceptionally optimistic about the party's prospects for success, arguing as far back as 1923 that "there is no insurmountable difficulty which prevents us in due course securing a considerable number of supporters from among the middle classes and those who are workers on their own account." Even members of the political left, such as Margaret Cole, recognized the imperative to "win the middle class on the slogan of 'England for All.' "[21]

As in the 1920s, the post-1931 Labour Party's program for winning over middle-class Britons focused on the embrace of a politics of production which pitted "all who work, whether by hand or brain," against "the small minority (less than 10 percent of the population) who own the great part of the land, the plant and the equipment without access to which their fellow-countrymen can neither work nor live." During the 1929 election campaign, the party had positioned itself as the representative of "all who bring their contribution of useful service to the common stock."[22] As discussed in Chapter 7, Labour propaganda in 1929 repudiated the Conservative Party's assertion of its right to represent "the public" or "the nation" against the sectional interests of organized labor, and emphasized the coincidence of interest between many of the manual and professional classes. During the 1931 crisis, "[t]he point is not just that each party, institution, group or individual had their own view of the national interest, but that each presumed an identity between their own higher interests and those of the nation."[23] The same point holds true throughout the interwar period. While the party briefly fled to the left in the aftermath of the 1931 crisis, the leadership quickly resumed their centrist commitment to promoting policies that would appeal not only to union workers, but to a broad coalition of voters. Although Labour's support throughout the period remained largely working class, and strongly regionally based, its political appeals were consistently national and consistently voiced through the national media.[24]

The Press

Despite its interest in other media, the conquest of the popular press remained the primary focus of Labour's media strategy throughout the 1930s. To a certain degree this reflected the arguably atavistic preoccupations of many members of the movement who remained convinced of the direct link between newspaper coverage and electoral support presupposed by Victorian politicians.[25] However, it is also true that the popular press remained the most important medium of political communication throughout this period. Although the number of radio listeners increased exponentially between the two world wars, the amount of political coverage on the airwaves remained limited. With the exception of two fifteen-minute evening news broadcasts and the Week in Westminster, there was no regular political programming on the BBC. Broadcasting on political and controversial industrial issues was limited to occasional talk series such as the Time to Spare series on unemployment or the series on the India Round Table discussions, both of which aired in 1934; the special series of political broadcasts arranged between the BBC and the parties in the 1930s; and the party election broadcasts.[26] In contrast, the popular press brought the world of Westminster into the homes of the vast majority of the British public on a daily basis.

The party recognized this and sought to maximize its exposure both through the promotion of the *Daily Herald* and through the dissemination of Labour views in the Liberal and Conservative press. After the relaunch of the *Herald* in March 1930, Bevin, as the paper's vice chairman, made use of the organizational apparatus of the party and trade unions to reinforce the efforts of the *Herald*'s circulation department in its fierce battle with the four rival broadsheets—the *Daily Chronicle,* the *Daily Express,* the *Daily Mail,* and the *Daily News.* In addition to the grand insurance scheme which accompanied the relaunch, the *Herald* offered a bevy of other bribes to potential readers, including, most famously, a cut-rate collection of the works of Charles Dickens. The paper's rivals responded in kind. The *Herald*'s aggressive circulation push had an immediate and fatal impact on the two main Liberal dailies, which were forced by economic necessity to merge, reconstituting themselves as the *News Chronicle* on 2 June 1931.[27] The paper's impact on the right-wing press was also keenly felt, though largely among the lower socioeconomic end of those papers' readerships.[28]

Lord Beaverbrook, who had a controlling interest in the *Daily Express,* was so concerned about the decline in working-class readership of the *Express* that he resorted to the expedient of publishing direct appeals "To Working Men and Women of Britain," "To Trade Unionists," and "To Co-operators" in an attempt to convince them that the *Express* understood working-class interests, and asked "for sufficient support, strength and sustenance from the working classes" to enable the paper to continue to champion their cause.[29] For several weeks in the autumn of 1932, the *Express*'s front page was adorned with "news" stories on the free giveaways and competitions that the paper was offering as its latest salvo in the "newspaper competition war." Beaverbrook and Beverley Baxter, the paper's editor, were acutely concerned about the impact of the *Herald*'s circulation push on the *Express.* One of the many front-page stories explained: "A great newspaper competition war is waging. It is being fought with energy, resolution and astonishing ingenuity. . . . No matter in what direction this phase of newspaper activity is developed the *Daily Express* is determined to remain the unchallenged leader so long as newspaper competitions are continued."[30]

The circulation wars became so fierce that the interwar social chroniclers Robert Graves and Alan Hodge have suggested that, at their height, "[a] great many families . . . subscrib[ed] to two or three papers—for the bribes, not for reading."[31] So intent were the managers of the new *Daily Herald* at beating the anti-Labour press at their own game that Beaverbrook ultimately attempted (unsuccessfully) to convince the head of Odhams Press, J. S. Elias, to end this "unnecessary expenditure in newspaper competition."[32] But Elias and Bevin were not about to quit while they were ahead; the *Herald* passed the one million mark in circulation within two weeks of the relaunch. While one million readers would have seemed incredible to Bevin only months before, the transport leader immediately began organizing a campaign to reach the unprecedented readership of two million.[33] In 1933, the paper became the first to attain this holy grail of press circulation, making it the largest circulating paper not only in Britain but in the world.

Even if many subscribers were taking the paper for the bribes, not for reading, the fact that the *Herald* now went "into hundreds of thousands of non-Socialist homes" inevitably increased the likelihood of the unconverted coming into contact with pro-Labour arguments and opinions.[34] The historian Martin Pugh has suggested that the interwar readership of the *Herald* was largely limited to that part of the "working-class community associated with the institutions of the Labour movement" and entrenched in the "serious-minded political culture of working-class radicalism and socialism." He argued that the party had to await the leftward shift of the *Daily Mirror* in the late-1930s to secure itself sympathetic coverage from a newspaper read by that portion of the working classes who were not already Labour voters.[35] Interwar readership data, however, does not bear out this assertion, but instead indicates that the *Daily Herald* of the 1930s was read by a broad national audience, which was not limited to members of the unionized working class.

The *Herald*'s former editor Francis Williams has done significant damage to the paper's historical reputation with the publication of his oft-quoted autobiography in which he denounced Elias for his supposed lack of interest in the news value of the publication and his repeated cuts in the editorial budget in the 1930s. But Williams's statements should be taken with a grain of salt. The editor blamed Elias for his dismissal in January 1940 and clearly had an axe to grind with the man who he admitted to "hat[ing] more than any man I have ever known."[36] In fact, the paper continued to run a greater proportion of industrial news than any of its rival dailies.[37] As one reader noted in a backhanded compliment to his morning paper, "I read the *Daily Herald* because it gives full account of the news. [Although] it is rather inclined to be 'party' and sometimes rather dull."[38]

The paper also actively sought to cater to a wider audience by including more sport and features columns, and by upping the paper's society coverage—which Bevin had previously denounced as the "caprices of princes and lubricities of courts."[39] The content of the *Herald*'s women's page changed markedly after the relaunch, as advice for housewives and mothers was increasingly displaced by articles on women's fashion, which appealed to a younger female audience as well as to the imaginations of housewives who, while they may have been stuck at home clad in aprons and overalls, still liked to imagine themselves in the latest evening fashions.[40]

The *Herald*'s discussion of political and industrial issues further shows an attempt both to present the party as responsible and to appeal to a broad-based electorate. The paper's coverage of the 1935 municipal election campaign addressed themes such as "Value for Money," claiming that "[t]hose who predicted that the advent of Labour meant soaring rates have been falsified by facts. In many towns which have been under Labour government for several years the rates are now actually lower than when they were governed by Tories."[41] The *Herald* ran extensive and supportive coverage of the League of Nations Union (LNU) peace ballot initiative between its launch in November 1934 and the publication of its results in June 1935. While the paper's high-profile support for the peace ballot reflects the sincere support of its then editor Francis Williams, its coverage of the LNU initiative arguably helped to attract a broader pro-peace, but not necessarily pro-Labour, readership to the paper.[42]

The *Herald*'s 1935 general election coverage did not replicate the 1929 feature of open letters to constituent groups. It did, however, make explicit reference to the benefit of Labour's proposals to groups other than the working classes and the unemployed in articles such as "Shopkeepers Rally to Labour's Policy: Higher Wages Mean More for Food," which noted, "There are more shopkeeper members of the Labour party today than ever before in the Movement's history."[43] Herbert Morrison wrote an opinion piece for the paper titled, "Security for all who work: Why the 'middle-classes' should vote Labour."[44] The principal themes emphasized in the *Herald*'s election coverage were collective security and disarmament in foreign policy, abolition of the means test as a method of administering unemployment benefits, nationalization of major industries, and development schemes to alleviate unemployment in the domestic arena. Yet the paper did devote considerable attention to economic issues affecting the middle classes, such as the record of rate abatement in Labour-controlled councils, the security of financial assets under Labour rule, and Labour's promotion of home ownership.[45] The content of these articles makes it clear that their intended audience was not just the party faithful but also the unconverted middle-class electorate. As the *Herald* journalist, Hannen Swaffer, wrote after the election:

> Labour's vote was increased by nearly 2,000,000. . . . It is surely unnecessary to stress the point that this splendid recovery . . . was due in good measure to

the *Daily Herald*'s steady and continuous advocacy and explanation of Labour's practical plans of Socialist reconstruction and policy for international co-operation; its day to day treatment of the work of Parliament; its regular supply of information regarding the political and industrial activities of the Labour Movement; and its special accounts of Labour's efforts in municipal life.[46]

Labour's use of the *Daily Herald* as a platform to appeal to voters outside of its core constituency indicates its awareness of the need to reach out to the wider electorate through the mass media. The leadership further recognized that if it were to maximize its reach, it could not rely on the *Herald* alone. Among lower-middle-class and middle-class readers, the four most popular newspapers were, in order of their percentage of the market in 1939, the *Daily Express,* the *Daily Mail,* the *News Chronicle,* and the *Daily Mirror*.[47] The most conservative of these papers was the *Mail,* which continued to rail against the Soviet Union even as its largely middle-class readership became more interested in consumption than in the threat of communism. However, the *Mail*'s increasingly niche market of "middle-aged and elderly middle-class women living in the provinces" arguably limited the impact of its anti-Labour reporting on general public opinion, and was largely offset by the increased exposure that the TUC and the Labour Party managed to secure in the other organs of the national press.[48]

In 1937, the party's publicity department reported that "[a] considerable volume of work that falls under the head of 'Press Publicity' has been done by the Department. It has prepared and issued official communiqués for the National Executive Committee and dealt with the press in relation to all party declarations, statements of Policy, [etc]. It has also dealt with a wide range of press enquiries, conducted personal interviews with many Foreign and British newspaper correspondents; and issued special articles and news items."[49] Although Bevin showed a proprietorial anger when the TUC's press department arranged for TUC president Andrew Conley to write an exclusive retrospective on the Tolpuddle martyrs for the *News Chronicle* instead of for the *Herald,* the article and others like it played an important role in educating non-trade unionists about the trade union movement. More generally, Labour benefited from an increasingly close relationship with the *News Chronicle* in the 1930s. Hugh Dalton's diary contains a typically cryptic and scheming reference to meetings between himself and Morrison and editors from the *News Chronicle* to discuss anti-Conservative strategy during the run-up to the 1935 general election.[50] The *News Chronicle* came out in strong support of the LLP during borough and county council elections in the 1930s as well. On the eve of the 1937 London County Council (LCC) election, the paper ran an "Open Letter to Londoners" by Morrison on its opinion page, complete with a large smiling photo of the Labour leader.[51] The willingness of members of the *News Chronicle* staff to coordinate with Labour was driven by the near visceral hatred for the National Government that pervaded the *News Chronicle*'s offices in the 1930s. The National Government was only ever referred to in the *News Chronicle*'s columns in inverted commas, and the Conservatives were invariably referred to disrespectfully as the "Tories," even in news columns. A typical headline, which appeared on 12 November 1935 over an article on proposed tariffs for foreign poultry, read "'Tories' Tax Poor Man's Christmas Dinner." In the face of persistent Liberal decline, the paper's editor, Aylmer Vallance, turned to Labour as the best hope to oust the so-called National Government from office.

In the conservative press, the ever prolific Ellen Wilkinson substantiated the *Express*'s claims that while "Socialism is attacked with great violence [in the newspaper's columns,] the Socialists will not be denied a chance to reply," by writing articles such as "Well, Lord Beaverbrook, What Now?" on the fate of the Labour Party after the 1931 election.[52] Morrison did not become a regular weekly columnist for the *Daily Mirror* until October 1939; however, the London Labour leader wrote occasionally for the paper beforehand, in addition to his frequent contributions to the *News Chronicle* and the *Star*.[53] The increase in sympathetic Labour coverage in the *Mirror* in the late 1930s arguably played a role in changing *Mirror* readers' opinions about the party even before the paper adopted a more consistently progressive stance during the Second World War.[54] Even the *Daily Mail* was not immune. On the eve of the 1935 election, the paper ran an opinion piece by Morrison outlining the "Case for Labour," albeit alongside an op-ed piece that declared that "our reckless Socialists" were "out to confiscate the property of the public" through a program of "robbery" and, to boot, were also seeking to "kill forever" the spirit of British patriotism by selling out the nation's foreign policy to the League of Nations.[55]

Radio and Film

Labour publicists and publicity-savvy politicians successfully engineered several high-profile media events throughout the 1930s. In 1922, the American commentator Walter Lippmann had condemned the activities of professional publicists, saying that, in the modern era, "the verdict [in political or industrial conflicts] is made to depend on who has the loudest or the most entrancing voice, the most skilful or the most brazen public-ity men, the best access or the most space in the newspapers."[56] For Lippmann, and for many others on the political left in the 1920s, this constituted a breakdown of the democratic process. Less than a decade later, the Labour movement itself was committed to obtaining not only "the most space in the newspapers" but the most airtime and access to the newsreels in order to secure itself a favorable verdict. While Labour leaders had not given up the belief that the ultimate aim of publicity was the political education of the masses, they had come to accept the reality that education could not occur without exposure, and that exposure in-creasingly meant not only space in the newspapers, but publicity on the airwaves and in the cinema.

Perhaps the most famous interwar publicity stunt was the Jarrow Hun-ger March, wherein two hundred men, led by a group of local politicians including Ellen Wilkinson, then MP for Jarrow, marched the three hundred miles to Westminster in October 1936 to present their "right to work" petition to parliament. The marchers sought government intervention to alleviate unemployment in the city which, despite the broader economic recovery, remained above two-thirds. Wilkinson was a canny publicist, and her self-professed intent in orchestrating the march was to stop "the National Government [from] getting away with its talk of national pros-perity."[57] The emphasis by the crusade's leaders on its allegedly apolitical character and the pointed exclusion of known communist agitators from its organization meant that it was not subjected to the same government censorship as the frequent demonstrations of the National Unemployed Workers' Movement, and footage of the workers in dignified procession was featured in all the major newsreels.[58] The march was organized by local leaders of all political parties, and remained ostensibly not party-political. Wilkinson, however, proved remarkably successful in identify-ing the march both with her own personality and with her party's cam-paign for relief of the distressed areas. The four foot eleven inch redhead was the only politician to appear in the *Pathé Gazette* newsreel of the march, and the *Daily Express* of 29 October featured a photo of Wilkin-son, cigarette in mouth, being taught to play the drums by a group of her fellow crusaders. Despite, or perhaps because of, being the only woman to participate in the march, Wilkinson became the media face of the Jar-row Crusade.[59]

The party and trade union leadership's determination to make use of the mass media to reach those members of the voting public who might otherwise come into little contact with Labour views was equally visible in its relationship with the BBC. In key respects, Labour's attitude toward the BBC mirrored its approach to the "capitalist" press in this period. As with the press, the party and trade union leadership remained suspicious of and hostile toward the BBC, which they viewed as being run by a board of governors who, while claiming to act in the national interest, were in reality often Tory satraps who possessed few qualifications beyond having "filled some important office in the Primrose League."[60] Despite this, the majority gradually came to accept that the propaganda value of the wireless outweighed its desire to snub an institution which it perceived to be inveterately biased against the interests of Labour.

Hints of the change in Labour's attitude were evident shortly after the general strike. As early as November 1926, Labour's spokesmen in a House of Commons debate on the future of the company advocated the expansion of controversial and political broadcasting once the BBC was reconstituted as a public corporation on the grounds that the new entity would have a "duty to the public" to put forward both sides of arguments over important social and political questions, in order that, through debate, "the truth may emerge." Despite anxieties concerning partisanship in access to the airwaves, Labour denounced the government's decision to "maintain the existing restriction upon the broadcast . . . of matter on topics of political, religious or industrial controversy."[61] Once the government ban on controversy was lifted in March 1928, the party pushed hard to increase the number and scope of political reports and debates, and to secure equitable access for Labour.[62]

Although certain Labour leaders, most notably George Lansbury, continued to believe that the best way to deal with the BBC was to pretend that it did not exist, the official attitude was that such a policy was more likely to hurt Labour's cause than to help it.[63] And while Lansbury's personal convictions may have been hostile toward the BBC, as party leader from 1932 to 1935, the old radical accepted the views of his deputy leader and his colleagues on the NEC and pursued a policy of cooperation with and conciliation of the organization.[64] The Labour leadership recognized that their ability to influence the BBC's political coverage was limited since the allocation of political broadcasts was largely left to the discretion of the corporation, with the government exerting an important indirect influence by merit of its right of veto.[65] What is most notable about the Labour leadership's approach to broadcasting in the 1930s is their willingness to accept what they perceived to be iniquitous compromises rather than risk losing access to the airwaves. Not even their indignation over the BBC's conduct during the 1931 election campaign could derail the party leaders' determination to cooperate with the corporation. Two years later, when the three parties met with the BBC to discuss the proposed distribution of political broadcasts to be aired that autumn, Labour accepted the rota 5:3:1 (Government: Labour: National Liberals), albeit only after protesting:

> We are strongly of the opinion that the Official Opposition are entitled to an equal number of dates with the Government. It should be 5 and 5 or 4 and 4. Whilst the position of [the National Liberal leader] Sir Herbert Samuel may complicate matters from the point of your Corporation, it offers no complication to the Labour Party. If Sir Herbert Samuel is to broadcast and he cannot have one of the Government dates, he should have a date separate and distinct from either the Government or the Opposition.[66]

By 1935, when hearings were held to discuss the renewal of the BBC's charter, Labour's conviction had hardened: "The official opposition should be treated in this connection [i.e., in determining access to the airwaves] as it is in the House of Commons, with rights and privileges not accorded to other groups in the House. Other minorities should be accorded opportunities in relation to their respective strength in Parliament."[67] In addition to an equal distribution of airtime for government and opposition in political broadcast series, Labour also pushed for an opposition right of reply to any broadcasts made by the government, especially the chancellor's "explanatory" budget broadcast.[68] The party lodged a vehement protest against the BBC's decision to allow Herbert Samuel and Philip Snowden, who resigned from their respective positions as home secretary and lord privy seal in the National Government in response to the Ottawa Agreement on imperial preference in August 1932, to broadcast their views on the agreement, followed by a government reply. In their protest, the party "claim[ed] their right as the official opposition to broadcast in reply to whatever statements were put forward on behalf of the Government."[69] As Lansbury emphasized to the party conference that year, "whatever our numbers in the House of Commons, we are His Majesty's Opposition, and as such we claim that our voice in this business should be heard."[70]

While the BBC refused to recognize this official right of reply,[71] they did seek out consultation with Labour on issues concerning political broadcasting, and in 1937 they put substantial pressure on Harold Webbe, the leader of the London Municipal Reform Party, to accept a schedule of LCC election broadcasts that privileged Labour as the governing party.[72] Thus, though Labour's ambitions for equality of access were never fully met, as Lansbury told the party conference in 1933, "We are doing a little better with the BBC. . . . We have made some advances, and, having made some advances, we think the next step will be easier."[73]

Labour similarly worked hard to improve its radio coverage in other areas. Both the party and the TUC proved willing to cooperate with the BBC by participating on various advisory councils and committees in the 1930s. The National Council of Labour (NCL), the coordinating body of Labour Party and trade union leaders, had initially taken the position that Labour representatives should not sit on these panels, as for them to do so would indicate acquiescence in what it perceived to be the biased and anti-Labour attitude of the BBC in political and industrial broadcasting.[74] However, once it became clear that obstruction would not result in the discontinuance of such consultative committees, but would only mean that Labour's voice was excluded from any discussions over broadcasting, they changed their position. In 1936, the party agreed to send representatives to a BBC conference on broadcasting and women's issues.[75] The TUC had already appointed Alec Firth, Citrine's acting under secretary, to serve on the central council for broadcast adult education, and trades council representatives were represented on the various local adult education advisory councils.[76] Both Citrine himself and Labour colleague Margaret Bondfield served as members of the BBC's general advisory council (GAC) in the 1930s. The former was a particularly active member of the GAC, and on his recommendation George Isaacs, the general secretary of the printers' union , was appointed to the new talks advisory committee in 1937, a position that he used to advocate the inclusion of trade union voices in talks series on a wide variety of domestic and international issues.[77]

Even before the ban on controversial broadcasting was lifted, the TUC had come to appreciate the importance of full and favorable coverage of trade union activities in BBC news bulletins, and adopted a policy of liaison with the BBC news desk. As a result of their efforts, the TUC press and publicity department was able to report to the 1928 Congress that "[m]ention may be made of the increased interest in Trade Union affairs which the British Broadcasting Corporation has permitted to the compilers of its wireless bulletin, who now broadcast very fair and full statements of news and official statements issued on behalf of the General Council."[78] In encouraging cooperation between the unions and the BBC, Citrine's professed goal was to ensure that the General Council "be consulted about matters where the presentation of Trade Union opinion or views is involved."[79] As the NCL argued in a 1933 memorandum to the

BBC: "Just as the official opposition should be given a right of reply to all government broadcasts, where broadcast speeches are made by politicians, economists and employers on any topic affecting Trade Unionism, ... [t]he equality of opportunity should be extended also to the Trade Union Movement in order that it may present its views on questions of economic, industrial or social interest dealt with in broadcast speeches."[80] Although this right was not conceded, the BBC did consult with the General Council in many important areas, including the BBC's ten-part series in commemoration of the Tolpuddle martyrs in the spring of 1934, "From Tolpuddle to TUC: 100 Years of Trade Union History," and its series of talks by unemployed persons in their "Time to Spare" series that summer.[81]

The Labour leadership had come to recognize that "the British Broadcasting Corporation is one of the greatest mediums of propaganda in this country," and one which they could not afford to ignore: "Wireless [had become] one of the most decisive factors for the working class and the development of the Labour Movement. After the press, it is the most important way of reaching the great mass of people. Just as the existence of the Labour Movement is today unthinkable without its press, so the Movement of the future will have to make use of the wireless."[82] This conviction sustained their determination to cooperate with the BBC, despite ongoing disputes.[83]

It is notable in this respect that the leadership never seriously entertained suggestions that the party take "direct action" against anti-Labour broadcasters by attempting to oscillate the BBC's signal. At the 1933 party conference, George Lansbury summarily dismissed a delegate's proposal that the NEC circumvent the BBC's broadcast monopoly and hire airtime from one of the commercially operated continental stations, such as Radio Luxembourg, which could be heard in the British Isles. Three years later, a suggestion by a member of the Amalgamated Engineering Union that the trade unions "buy time from a continental station in order to popularize the workers' demands for shorter hours and larger wages" was similarly dismissed.[84] While the idea of sidestepping the BBC's monopoly and broadcasting to Britain from the Continent was in fact pursued by Oswald Mosley and the British Union of Fascists, as well as by the British Communist Party, it is a testament to the Labour leadership's view of both the BBC and itself as integral members of the British constitutional structure that the party never explored such possibilities.[85]

Labour not only abandoned its previous obstructionist attitude toward the BBC in the 1930s, but it also showed a strong interest in maximizing the political impact of its broadcast opportunities. Much has been written of the Conservative Party's political perspicuity in exploiting the microphone in this period, but the Labour Party, though lacking in personalities with Stanley Baldwin's ability to appeal to the "honest, homely, hearth-and-home English emotions" of the electorate, showed a near equal concern with the medium.[86] The party devoted considerable attention to the texts of political broadcasts, which were consciously directed to a broad democratic audience. Although 1929 was the only year in which special party election broadcasts were set aside to address women voters, in succeeding years, Labour broadcasters continued to engage specifically with the female electorate.

Such appeals were particularly crucial during the 1930s, as the party's post-1931 policies in many respects privileged the interests of the male-breadwinner over the interests of wives and, particularly, single women. Labour's failure to support abortion law reform and its hostility toward proposed family allowances schemes, which the party feared would cut salaries of single working men on the pretext of funding social programs for children, have been singled out by historians as particularly women-hostile policies.[87] Such policies may help explain the documented gap between male and female support for Labour in the 1945 general election (the first election for which such data is available). In 1945, 54 percent of men voted for the Labour Party, compared with only 45 percent of women.[88] This gap widened at successive postwar elections, a phenomenon that historian Ina Zweiniger-Bargielowska has attributed to the Conservatives' exploitation of a highly feminized "politics of consumption" in the postwar period.[89]

The clash between productivist and consumerist visions of politics likely affected gendered patterns of party support in the interwar period as well. Given the lack either of poll books, which Victorian scholars used to reconstruct patterns of party support, or modern methods of opinion polling, it is dangerous to make inferences about interwar voting patterns. It is noteworthy that, while in 1929 many in the Conservative Party, including Baldwin, believed that they had been adversely affected by female enfranchisement, in the 1930s women voters were seen as an asset to the party.[90] Yet, as recent research has emphasized, millions of women also supported the Labour Party in the 1930s.[91] One explanation for this is that working-class women put class before gender and voted for the party of workers against the party of capital. Class politics did undoubtedly play a role. But the post-1931 Labour Party also sought to appeal across class lines to female voters as women and mothers and to target their perceived greater sympathy for social welfare.[92]

Labour's pictorial propaganda directed at women was essentially emotive, designed less to provoke a reasoned response than a visceral reaction. In 1935, the party produced a highly controversial poster of a baby wearing a gas mask that was intended to suggest that National Government policies would lead to war, as well as a more upbeat poster in which a young mother holds her baby aloft alongside a caption exhorting viewers: "For Your Children's Sake, Vote Labour." Such propaganda was largely devoid of intellectual content, but Labour did also seek to engage women in a serious discussion about the role of government. Scholars have noted the Conservative Party's attempts to use the analogy of the "domestic chancellor of the exchequer" to sell female voters on the necessity for economic retrenchment in the interwar period.[93] However, the Conservatives did not hold the monopoly on such discourse. In his 1935 party election broadcast (PEB), Clement Attlee denounced the National Government's policy of cutting wages and restricting production in an attempt to raise prices by declaring: "It sounds quite mad, doesn't it? If you had too much food in the house, you would not put the children on half rations and destroy the food." He ended his broadcast by asking that the voters "apply to the affairs of State the same commonsense and ethics that you apply in your family life."[94] Here was the same language of the domestic chancellor turned on its head, and used against its inventors.[95]

Labour's broadcasts provided a forum for the party to challenge other aspects of the Conservative assault on the "perils of socialism," and to present their own inclusive vision of the Labour nation to an audience that might be unreachable by traditional methods of party propaganda. Labour broadcasters in 1935 specifically rebutted National Government insinuations that a Labour government would lead to financial collapse and Soviet-style immiseration. Where Conservative leaders sought to equate Labour with Bolshevism, they drew parallels with the Socialist government in Sweden.[96] Where Conservative leaders depicted Labour as hysterical pacifists, they emphasized the coincidence of their position with that called for in the peace ballot.[97] And, in what was a prominent party strategy from 1934 onward, the Labour speakers sought to underscore the party's responsibility and credentials by drawing attention to the success of the London Labour Party (LLP) in government. This strategy was expounded most clearly by Morrison, who wound up Labour's series of PEBs in 1935. The London leader began his broadcast by stating: "The choice you have to make is quite clear. Just as last year London had to choose between a Conservative County Council which could not make up its mind about anything, and a Labour Council that knew what to do and how to do it, so the nation must now decide between Tory negation and the positive and constructive policy of the modern Labour party." Morrison's broadcast also explicitly embraced one of the other themes of 1930s Labour publicity: the coincidence of interest between the working and middle classes as against the privileged few. "What," he asked his listeners, "of the insecurity of middle-class people, as well as working-class? Where is the Government's positive, constructive policy?" He ended his broadcast by asserting, "The working and middle classes love their country with love that is real and enduring. Their patriotism is the patriotism of service and not that of possession. . . . That is the patriotism of the Labour party."[98]

Morrison was exceptional in his consistent attention to middle-class electors, both in his broadcasts and in his speeches and writings. Nonetheless, an attention to middle-class listeners is evident in the subjective emphasis of all four of the party's PEBs in 1935, as well as in Labour's other broadcasts during this period. The party was keen to maximize the propaganda impact of its broadcasts, and the more successful were often reprinted as party pamphlets, such as Ernest Bevin's contribution to the BBC's 1934 "Whither Britain" series.[99]

In addition to content, individual broadcasters also devoted attention to the art of radio broadcasting. Clement Attlee asked Reith if he could come by the studio and rehearse before appearing on Week in Westminster in 1931, and throughout his career remained solicitous of advice given by BBC producers regarding his scripts and style of presentation. Hugh Dalton was similarly "very keen" on rehearsing his broadcasts, though his openness to direction was occasionally limited when "vanity step[ped] in the way." Morrison, who appreciated the value of well produced publicity, would, according to one BBC producer, go to "any amount of trouble" to get his broadcasts just right.[100]

Stafford Cripps, though occasionally a political liability, was an invaluable asset at the microphone. Cripps recognized that radio could "make a politician overnight by giving him an audience of 5,000,000 or 6,000,000," and worked hard to translate his skills at the bar into success before the microphone. He proved to be both an "excellent" and "brilliant" broadcaster whose radio popularity helped catapult him to number two in a series of wartime polls on who respondents would most want to replace Winston Churchill as prime minister. Between November 1941 and April 1942, Cripps shot from 1 percent to 34 percent in the Gallup survey of whom voters would most prefer as prime minister if anything were to happen to Churchill, making him a close second to Sir Anthony Eden, who scored 37 percent. The spike in his popularity coincided with his series of "Postscript" broadcasts on the BBC Home Service.[101]

In contrast, Walter Citrine's first contribution to the trade union centenary broadcast series was considered by the head of the talks department to be "extremely pompous," "unhappy," "long and tedious." Although the BBC producers' criticisms greatly wounded his pride, Citrine agreed to collaborate more closely with the talks department before his second broadcast in the series, and the resultant cooperative effort yielded a more "informal, personal style of ... talk" that was deemed to be much more effective.[102] The willingness of most Labour leaders to take direction from BBC producers on matters of style suggests the extent of their determination to make the most of their opportunities before the microphone.

Posters and Propaganda

While the party made significant strides in its exploitation of broadcasting in the 1930s, the area in which Labour most vividly outstripped their Conservative opponents was print publicity and advertising. At first glance, their continued emphasis on leaflet and pamphlet production suggests that Labour remained "wedded to traditional concepts of publicity."[103] However, a closer consideration of party propaganda in this period reveals a willingness to experiment with and invest in new methods of presentation and packaging, and to learn from the lessons of commercial advertisers and marketing agencies. Labour's print propaganda was more strikingly modern in its presentation than that of its competitors, and it is not coincidental that many of those involved with its production ended up as government propagandists during the Second World War.[104]

The media historian Dominic Wring has emphasized the limits of Labour's efforts to produce "persuasionalist" party literature in the 1930s, citing the comments of the *Daily Herald*'s Labour Party liaison, Maurice Webb, at a 1937 conference on "Selling Socialism" as evidence of the party's failures. Webb attacked Labour's propaganda literature as being "too diffuse and lacking in simple central ideas; tend[ing] to be gloomy and out of touch with human interests, [and] too obviously propaganda and often directed to the politically interested section of the population only."[105] However, the very fact that Labour had organized such a conference, at which leading members of the publicity industry such as George Wansborough of the London Press Exchange brainstormed ideas on new methods of publicity and propaganda with future party leaders such as Hugh Gaitskell, Richard Crossman, and Michael Stewart, indicates the extent of the party's commitment to the commercial aspect of political electioneering in the 1930s.[106]

The NEC's interest in new methods of "selling socialism" was evident later that year when it appointed a technical expert from the publishing industry to consult on the production of *Your Britain,* a sixteen-page "pictorial presentation of *Labour's Immediate Programme* in colour and photogravure" to be distributed to a mass audience. *Your Britain* truly was an "entirely new kind of political document."[107] The publication resembled an issue of the *Picture Post,* the photo-filled weekly which became the second most popular periodical in Britain within a year of its launch in October 1938, particularly among younger and more affluent audiences.[108] The party evidently hoped that *Your Britain* would appeal to a similarly broad demographic. As Herbert Morrison bragged, "It is more than politics—it is human. Its beautifully printed pictures, its spirit of hope and good cheer will make *Your Britain* a best seller of wide popular interest."[109] And indeed it was. The NEC successfully sold over six hundred thousand copies of the publication to local party organizations—well above the sale of any previous party publication during a non-election year—and its success inspired the party to produce several successive editions.

Though the magazine was conceived as part of the party's "Socialist Crusade Week," and not as election propaganda, observers within and outside of the party believed that *Your Britain* had aided Labour in the 1937 municipal elections. A *Times* editorial instructed the paper's conservative readership to "stud[y] the tactics and methods of the opposing party." The Labour Party, the paper reported,

> [p]repared attractive and persuasive publications which sold by the hundred thousand [which] . . . had direct reference to the politics of the locality and the home. . . . Nor should it pass unnoticed that the title of this publication, outlining the Labour programme, was "Your Britain"—that is to say the Britain to be won by votes.
> Without regard, for the moment, to the merits of the Labour programme itself, here was a meritorious way of presenting it.[110]

Five years later, the slogan "Your Britain" would be used again by the army bureau of current affairs (ABCA), this time to signify not the Britain to be won by votes, but the Britain to be won by bullets. In 1942–1943, the ABCA commissioned a series of posters with the slogan "Your Britain . . . Fight for it Now" for display in army barracks and canteens. The posters were produced by two noted commercial artists, Frank Newbould and Abram Games. While Newbould's posters displayed bucolic scenes of Sussex downs and village fairs, those produced by Games depicted the new urban Britain that would emerge after the war, with accompanying captions extolling the virtues of state welfare. One poster

A Labour Council has built this pleasant estate of happy homes for the people. (Vivex Natural Colour Photograph)

Figures 8.1 and 8.2. Front and back covers of *Your Britain*, no. 1. The caption on the lower right corner of the front cover reads, "A Labour Council has built this pleasant estate of happy homes for the people." (© Labour Party. Courtesy of the People's History Museum, Manchester)

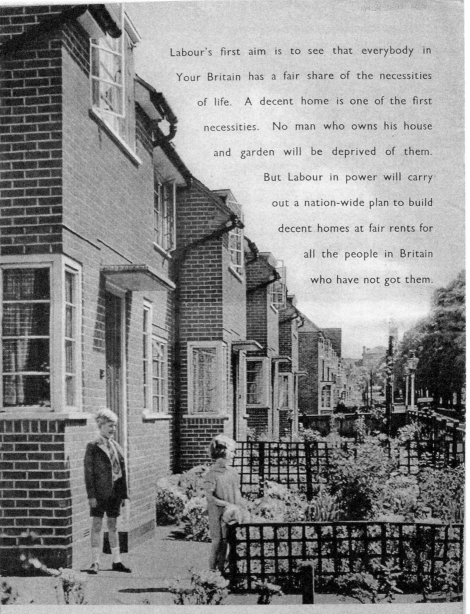

Labour's first aim is to see that everybody in Your Britain has a fair share of the necessities of life. A decent home is one of the first necessities. No man who owns his house and garden will be deprived of them. But Labour in power will carry out a nation-wide plan to build decent homes at fair rents for all the people in Britain who have not got them.

Help Labour to Build YOUR BRITAIN

showed a new block of council flats, with the caption: "Clean, airy and well planned dwellings make a great contribution to the Rehousing movement. This is a fine example of a block of workers' flats built in London in 1936." Another, showing the Finsbury health center built in 1938, read: "Modern medicine means the maintenance of good health and the prevention and early detection of disease. This is achieved by periodic medical examinations at Centres such as the new Finsbury Health Centre, where modern methods are used."

It is unclear whether the ABCA's use of the phrase "Your Britain" was a conscious attempt to play on the popularity of Labour's 1937–1938 campaign, though the resonance of the phrase is noteworthy. Games' intentions are less easy to discount. The illustrator was a Labour supporter, and was almost certainly aware of the *Your Britain* journals.[111] And the language of the captions on his posters strongly mirrors that of the captions in the Labour publications. Further, the images used are of municipal

Figure 8.3. Artwork by Abram Games depicting the Finsbury Health Centre, from poster produced for the Army Bureau of Current Affairs, 1942.
(© Estate of Abram Games. Courtesy of Naomi Games)

buildings built by the Labour-controlled LCC. It is hard to view Games's posters as anything other than a conscious attempt to build on the success of the earlier Labour Party propaganda campaign. Churchill, in fact, regarded them as such, and banned the display of the Finsbury health center poster.[112] The links between wartime propaganda and the 1945 election victory are discussed more thoroughly in Chapter 9. However, given the emphasis that scholars such as Paul Addison have placed on the centrality of the war experience in transforming public perceptions of social welfare, it is worth emphasizing the continuity between pre-war Labour propaganda and the propaganda produced during the war.

Your Britain was only the beginning of the party's foray into photojournalism-style propaganda. Within a year, the NEC produced three further editions of the journal, focusing on specific aspects of domestic and foreign policy, all of which sold hundreds of thousands of copies. In addition to *Your Britain,* the party also produced other photo-based propaganda, such as the pictorial-letterpress magazine titled *We Saw in Spain* detailing Attlee's visit to Republican Spain in December 1937, which sold out quickly through two large editions.[113]

The use of pictorial propaganda was not Labour's only overture to the world of political advertising in this period. In 1937, Herbert Morrison employed a group of outside consultants from the London Press Exchange (LPE) to advise on campaign strategy during the LCC elections, with impressive effect. The party's publicity budget for the election was nearly ten times that spent in previous years. The LPE team crafted a campaign based around the personality of the party leader, including an advertisement which ran in the Conservative press headlined, "Why Morrison gets our vote today, by 'two fair-minded Conservatives.'" The text of the advertisement relates a conversation in which a normally Conservative voter explains to his friend why he has decided to give Morrison his vote this time around. It ends with the undecided man pronouncing "True enough. They're doing a good job. I'm fair-minded. I'll give them a chance to finish it." The Conservative politician Cuthbert Headlam noted the impact of the Labour campaign on the LCC election outcome: "Herbert Morrison has got away with it: not entirely surprising . . . his propaganda was excellent—that of the Municipal Reformers futile."[114]

Taking a cue from London, in December 1937 the NEC put together "an advisory panel of publicity experts and journalists . . . to assist in press and publicity work."[115] The following spring, the NEC press committee secured the hefty sum of £250 pounds for the production of "first class" party posters, and looked into having the posters designed by a commercial agency.[116] These posters joined the stable of those that the party had commissioned before the 1935 election, including the famously disturbing poster of the gas mask-clad baby with the caption "Stop War," and the skull and crossbones emblazoned "War Sower and Reaper," designed by the railway poster artist R. G. Praill.

The party continued its emphasis on "stratified electioneering," or the policy of differentiating appeals to different target audiences. In 1937, the NEC publicity committee published two leaflets produced by the Fabian Society to appeal to civil servants and municipal officers, and commissioned the production of its own series of "middle-class leaflets" directed at teachers, business executives, and civil and municipal servants. These leaflets, which made "a direct appeal to the black-coated workers," were subsidized by the NEC to ensure a national distribution.[117] Furthermore, the movement had begun publishing a special monthly magazine for women, the *Labour Woman,* in 1911; from 1934, this journal became the first party publication consistently to turn a profit.[118] It is easy to quote individual party critics who assert that "Labour as a whole has a very poor appreciation of the values of publicity or publicity experts," and chide the party to "brighten up its propaganda and publicity ideas to reach a [new younger] population."[119] However, similar quotations can be found in Conservative Party publications from the same period,[120] and an examination of the production and reception of Labour propaganda in the mid-1930s illustrates that the party was not as behind the times as its critics contend. In fact, during the Second World War, the party built upon and perfected the publicity techniques pioneered in the 1930s to put its message across to the electorate much more successfully than its partners in the coalition government.

CHAPTER NINE

Election Victory

LABOUR'S PUBLICITY CAMPAIGN in the 1930s played an important role in re-legitimizing the party in the eyes of the public and helping Labour to broaden its base of support. Yet, although Labour's electoral progress in the 1930s has arguably been underestimated, the party would not have won the landslide victory it did in July 1945 had it not been for the social and political realignments that occurred during the Second World War.[1] Even those scholars who have questioned the extent of the "swing to the left" or the impact of the "spirit of Dunkirk" acknowledge that the experience of the war created an enthusiasm for state planning and support for a state-guaranteed social minimum, or at least for a greater degree of "social justice" than had existed beforehand.[2] In historian Kenneth O. Morgan's assessment, Labour won the 1945 election because "the perceived beneficial thrust of wartime planning and controls was largely identified in the popular mind with the Labour ministers."[3]

Yet, it is still worth asking *why* the achievements of the cross-party coalition government were identified with the Labour ministers. In the late 1960s and 1970s, a body of scholarship emerged that emphasized the degree of consensus between Labour and Conservative ministers over the direction of social change during and after the war.[4] Through a detailed analysis of Labour Party policy, scholars such as Stephen Brooke, Martin Francis, and Richard Toye have shown how this literature overstated the cross-party consensus and argued that the development of the postwar welfare state was much more contingent on Labour's victory than had previously been appreciated.[5] But while these scholars have illuminated the ideological differences between Labour and Conservative cabinet ministers, there has been little attempt to understand how such differences were communicated to the public and how the Labour Party managed to win public opinion to its side. Given that opinion polls showed a continued preference for Conservative government as late as May 1943, this is a significant question. We cannot simply assume an inevitable progression from the public furor over the publication of the Beveridge report in December 1942 to the election of the first majority Labour government two and a half years later.[6] The Labour Party needed actively to persuade the public of its qualifications to build the "New Jerusalem" after the war.

To a certain extent, this process of public conversion was done on Labour's behalf by organizations like the Left Book Club, publications such as the *Daily Mirror,* and the by-election campaigns of Common Wealth and "Independent Labour" candidates such Fred Wise at King's Lynn and Charlie White in West Derbyshire, whose unendorsed candidacies nonetheless generated significant publicity for the party.[7] The belief that Labour benefited from the "fifth column" work of organizations such as the Left Book Club, Penguin Books, the *Daily Mirror,* the army bureau of current affairs (ABCA), and the BBC (in particular J. B. Priestley) was strongly held within the Conservative Party both during and after the war. In August 1943, the party researcher-turned-Conservative MP, Henry Brooke, reminded the BBC's director of talks of the "immense and lasting harm which the BBC did to its reputation in Conservative circles by inviting Priestley to do six postscripts [short broadcasts after the evening news] running away back in 1941."[8] According to the Conservative MP, party organizer, and later cabinet minister R. A. Butler's memoirs: "The forces vote, in particular, had been virtually won over by the left-wing influence of the Army Bureau of Current Affairs."[9] In June 1947, the Conservative Party held what it termed a "Trust the People" exhibition at the Dorland hall in Regent's Street. The exhibition, opened by party chairman Lord Woolton, was an unsubtle piece of propaganda that recast the history of modern Britain in a Tory-tinted light, claiming that, to quote the *Times* reviewer, "all the successful housing measures have been passed by Conservative governments; that the Conservatives were the godfathers of British trade unionism, and that the party was the prime mover in abolishing child labour in factories, and that it succeeded in doing so in the face of opposition by left-wing economists."[10] Given the extent of Conservative achievements, the 1945 defeat could only be explained in terms of left-wing chicanery. In a section of the exhibit entitled "How the People Are Told a Story," the party claimed that "Socialist propaganda was 'put across' in spite of the party truce" by left-wing individuals, organizations, and journals allegedly independent of the Labour Party.[11]

It would be difficult to argue that these progressive publications and organizations did not benefit the Labour Party, though scholars have expressed skepticism as to their impact on both public support for Labour and public opinion more generally.[12] Similarly, it would be absurd to claim that no one voted Labour in 1945 to punish the "guilty men" of Munich, or simply from a desire for change.[13] Yet, historians' focus on the propaganda work of such nonparty organizations and individuals has obscured the degree to which the Labour Party itself actively worked to convert public opinion to its cause during the Second World War. In part, this is the by-product of earlier studies that have discredited Conservative accusations about Labour's superior organization at the constituency level. Historians from Paul Addison to Andrew Thorpe have emphasized the continued organizational advantage of the Conservatives over Labour. According to Thorpe, while the greater atrophy of Conservative organization may have resulted in a comparative improvement by Labour, the "Conservatives tended, *post hoc,* to overstate the extent of their wartime organizational collapse, in part because it allowed them to avoid damaging recriminations about the real reasons for their defeat."[14] The resulting picture has been of the two political parties entering the general election on relatively even footing.

Although the Conservative Party retained an organizational advantage—if a narrowing one—at the constituency level, Labour's national propaganda organization remained much more active than that of its rivals. While the Conservative Party largely allowed its publicity apparatus to go into abeyance during the war, politicians and publicists at Transport House devoted substantial attention and money to wartime publicity. Labour's wartime campaign showed the extent to which the party's approach to publicity and public relations had evolved over the previous two decades. While it would be an overstatement to attribute the swing to Labour in 1945 solely to such activities, an exploration of Labour's wartime publicity offers new insight into the process of political realignment during the Second World War.

Like subsequent historians, the Labour leadership was not unaware of the growing radical feeling in the country in the early years of the war. However, unlike retrospective scholars, they did not take for granted that this left-wing sentiment would redound to the benefit of the party come election time. In October 1942, the *New Statesman* opined that the party was leaving "this growing movement of political awakening without any encouragement or direction." The journal expressed a frustration that was to remain prominent within Labour circles throughout the war. The following March, MP George Ridley, chairman of the Workers' Film Association, the film distribution company jointly owned by the TUC and the party, and a member of the NEC's publicity and organization committees, wrote to the party's national agent expressing his fears that "although there is undoubtedly a body of leftish opinion thinking largely in our terms, it is not at the same time thinking about *us*."[15] The following week he drafted a memorandum in which he expounded his views on the action the NEC needed to take to "link to the party in an organisational and electoral sense that large body of opinion which I am convinced is thinking unconsciously in our direction."[16] A report by the Parliamentary Labour Party from June 1943 emphasized that "if the Labour Party desires to secure government with power in the future, a large part of this awakening public opinion must be enlisted to its side." The following February, the Clapham Labour Party wrote to the NEC expressing their "fears that the enthusiasm, which is ours by right is being bypassed by people who are using our phrases, and our ideas."[17]

Yet, although party supporters in parliament, the constituencies, and the press continued to think that Transport House should be doing more to grasp the reins of popular radicalism, the party leadership was working as actively as it felt that it could, within the constraints of the electoral truce that the three parties entered into on 8 September 1939. Despite its agreement not to contest by-elections during the war, the party continued the campaign of public meetings in the constituencies begun in preparation for an expected general election in 1939. While Conservative operatives expressed skepticism as to the impact of these meetings, they feared that Labour's propaganda activity "create[d] an unfortunate impression in the mind of the man in the street who is only allowed to hear one side." One Conservative area agent "remark[ed] that if we are not allowed to state our case we shall lose the support of all but confirmed Tories."[18]

In April 1940, the party published a statement of its postwar policy, titled simply "Labour's Home Policy." In February, the *Daily Herald* had run a series of articles cast as a public forum on the drafting of a "New Declaration of the Rights of Man." The forum's chairman, H. G. Wells, posited that man's "fundamental rights" included the "Right to a common inheritance." Wells asserted that "every man in this world is joint heir to all the resources, powers, inventions and possibilities accumulated by our forerunners, and is entitled without distinction of race, colour or professed belief or opinions to the nourishment . . . [and] medical care and attention needed to realize his full possibilities of physical and mental development and to keep him in a state of health from his birth to death."[19] Over the next several weeks, the *Herald* used discussion of the "New Declaration of Rights" to forward the Labour Party's agenda on the importance of social welfare in a new postwar society.

After Labour's entry into the coalition government on 10 May 1940, the party, like their Conservative and Liberal allies, initially put party politics on hold. Expenditure on party literature fell from nearly £11,000 in 1939 to under £5,000 in 1940, and to under £4,000 in 1941.[20] But, by the end of 1941, the leadership was beginning to rethink its attitude toward party politics. In December, the NEC's organization subcommittee considered the state of party propaganda since the outbreak of the war. The memorandum on the subject posed the rhetorical question: "What would be said by the Labour Party if the Conservative Party were to set about a widespread campaign demanding the maintenance of Capitalism?" It concluded by recommending, not that party propaganda cease, but "that speeches and platforms devoted to an exposition of our proposals . . . be so conditioned that the proposals are accepted as a contribution to a discussion and not as the spearhead of an attack on one political or economic institution by another."[21] The die was cast. The Conservatives might justifiably complain that Labour was not "adher[ing] loyally to the spirit as well as the letter of the Truce."[22] Nonetheless, from late 1941 onward Labour determined to resume party political activity on a level nearly indistinguishable from the pre-war period.

The party's first priority was to draft a general statement of Labour's proposed policies for postwar change which could serve both as "a rhetorical framework on which to hang more specific policy" and as a statement to the British people of the party's intentions.[23] In January 1942, the party approved Harold Laski's draft of the "interim report on reconstruction," *The Old World and the New Society*. The interim report was as much for public as for party consumption, and the NEC garnered extensive publicity for the document. An abbreviated version, intended for "cheaper and wider circulation," was published as a pamphlet under the title "Labour Looks Ahead!" The press and publicity committee courted publicity for the document through press conferences, advertising in Labour and trade union journals, and the preparation of several pre-written articles by Labour heavyweights for distribution to the local and specialized journals.

In addition to press coverage, Labour also pushed for coverage of and publicity for the report on the BBC. While the daily press, whose circulation surged during the war, was a valuable forum for propaganda, the previous decade had taught the party the unparalleled utility of the BBC as a vehicle for reaching the broadest possible cross-section of society.[24] As such, Laski contacted the BBC about the possibility of a talk or talks series being given on the report, potentially with "a representative of the Conservative or Liberal parties expressing their views on the document."[25] His professed willingness to allow for a commentary by Labour's political opponents suggested a recognition that, in an environment where popular opinion was demonstrably to the left, any critical comment by their opponents was likely to redound to Labour's credit. And, as the party agent Harold Croft would write in 1945, "[i]n any case, even opposition advertises Labour."[26]

Laski's suggestion did not meet with an enthusiastic audience at the BBC. The BBC talks director felt that any such program would be "quite out of the question" as: "Since the outbreak of war we have, in the interests of national unity, ceased to broadcast talks and discussions which would emphasize divergence of opinion along party lines; and it seems to us that either a talk or a discussion on the subject of the Labour Party's report on Reconstruction would, however carefully prepared, tend to contravene this principle."[27] That said, the BBC did agree to provide full coverage in their news briefings of the debates on the report at the party conference that June.[28]

Labour's wartime party conferences provided a valuable publicity opportunity for the party, and one that was not shared by their Conservative rivals, who did not hold a party conference from 1938 to 1942. While conference was often a fractious event, and while the wartime conferences routinely served to show up the rank-and-file's frustration with Labour's presumably supine role within the coalition, they were also a forum for presenting Labour's distinctive position on postwar Britain. In a sense, even the public wrangling over Labour's role in the coalition benefited the party as it allowed Labour "to behave like a party of government and a movement of opposition at one in the same time."[29] Both the daily press and the BBC provided consistently good coverage of these conferences—much to the frustration of the Conservatives. When the BBC governor and Conservative Party member Sir Ian Fraser met with the 1922 Committee (the caucus of Conservative backbenchers) in June 1942, several MPs complained of the publicity that the BBC gave to Labour's conferences. Fraser replied with some exasperation: "The Conservative party had not had a conference, and do not make so many speeches in the House. Consequently they do not provide the matter out of which broadcasts are made. [It's] not for me to say that it would be wise for them to have a Conference, but in the absence of the basic matter there can be no broadcasts."[30] The absence of the basic matter did not prevent the party from taking the issue up with the BBC, with the result that the broadcaster "guaranteed similar opportunities by the BBC for broadcasts of reports of the proceedings at future Party meetings, whether these take the form of an actual Party Conference or not."[31] The Conservatives felt similar frustration at the publicity given to the annual Trades Union Congress. In October 1941, the TUC was held simultaneously with a meeting of the National Council of Conservative Associations, with the result that coverage of the former more or less swamped reporting on the latter event. Sir Robert Topping, the director-general of the Conservative Party organization, complained: "I suppose we must admit that in present circumstances there was more general interest taken in the TUC Congress than in our Party gathering. [But,] there is strong feeling in our ranks about the attitude of the BBC at the present time and it is a matter which is exercising our minds here and must continue to receive attention."[32]

The Conservatives' frustration with the BBC was partly sour grapes—the party resumed holding annual conferences in 1943 in part because they too wanted the publicity that a conference brings.[33] It was also partly a legitimate reaction to the fact that the BBC frequently gave the Labour Party and the TUC what was arguably preferential treatment during the war. This preferential treatment was less the result of left-wing sympathy within the BBC (though this was doubtless a contributing factor) than of the TUC and Labour publicity departments'—as well as several members of the Labour and trade union leadership's—practice of lobbying the BBC and pushing the broadcaster for every concession they could get.[34]

This aggressive behavior was arguably a form of revenge, as the Labour leadership, and particularly Walter Citrine, remained resentful of the BBC for its behavior during the general strike of 1926.[35] Many at the BBC believed this to be the case. When the National Council of Labour sent a deputation including Hugh Dalton and Citrine to protest over the BBC's decision not to air a Labour address to the German people in August 1939, "Sir Richard [Maconachie, the Home Controller] told [his colleague Andrew Stewart] that it was a display of power politics. They made it clear to us, as they did to the Cabinet, that without their support the war would stop, and although the composition of the Churchill Government is much more to their taste than the Chamberlain Government, that interview and its results are worth bearing in mind."[36] Although the trade unionists' often abrasive and contemptuous attitude toward the BBC chafed with the program producers and staff—Citrine at one point denounced the

BBC staff to their faces as "a collection of anarchists who didn't understand the team spirit"—the TUC did successfully ensure that workers' views and voices were adequately represented on the airwaves during the war.[37]

But the BBC's concessions to Labour were not all extracted via bullying. In mid-1942, Laski, Will Henderson, and the chairman of the NEC's publicity committee, Barbara Ayerton Gould, met with the directors-general and chairman of the BBC to press upon them the wisdom of running more programs on postwar reconstruction. The Labour delegation, while emphasizing that they were concerned with the national interest, and "not concerned with Labour propaganda at all," impressed upon the BBC their belief that the corporation should make more effort to hold a "national debate on national problems . . . considering the main problems with which the world would be faced after the war and how these could be settled in a truly democratic way."[38] The Labour leadership got its wish four months later when the BBC ran a series of features on the contents and consequences of the Beveridge report, which attracted an exceptionally high audience interest.[39]

Nearly all analyses of Labour's election victory note that the public associated the party with Beveridge, despite Beveridge's standing as a Liberal candidate. This was not coincidence. From its conception, the party actively sought to associate itself in the public mind with the Beveridge committee and its conclusions. When the committee on reconstruction was first established in May 1941, the minister of health Arthur Greenwood immediately set out to give it the widest possible publicity. Greenwood had long served as the secretary of the Labour Party's research department, and, as such, worked in close cooperation with Will Henderson, whom he invited to serve as his parliamentary private secretary when he became minister of health. It is not unlikely that Henderson provided the inspiration for Greenwood's efforts, which included feeding Fleet Street the line that the committee was a "harbinger of social security for all," and giving a broadcast on the BBC's North American service to the same effect.[40]

On the day that the report was published, nearly a year-and-a-half later, the Labour-controlled *Daily Herald* devoted almost the entirety of its four pages to a nine-point summary of the contents of the report, under headings such as "For Children" and "Housewives' Charter: Husband and Wife as Sharing Team." The accompanying editorial stressed that "Trade Unionism and the Labour Party feel a special satisfaction at its appearance. For it was the insistent pressure of the Trades Union Congress upon the Government Departments that made plain the need for such an investigation as Sir William has conducted."[41] The following day, the *Herald* advertised its exclusive sale of a three-penny pamphlet summarizing the contents of the report. Stephen Brooke has suggested that the editors of the *Daily Herald* showed an increasing "restless[ness]" with the leadership's support for the coalition and party truce, and that the paper "was ceaseless in its criticism of Tory politicians and groups and continued to remark that it was 'spoiling' for a fight."[42] The *Herald* did occasionally act as a thorn in the side of a party leadership eager to secure rank-and-file support for the continuation of the coalition. In December 1942, however, it served as a tool of the party leadership, allowing Labour to show its difference from the Conservatives without openly breaking the terms of the party truce.

Herbert Morrison used the report's publication as a pretext to make a series of dramatic speeches on Labour's vision for postwar Britain, speeches which the Conservative press viewed as thinly veiled party propaganda. The day after Morrison's speech on "the control of industry after the war," the *Daily Sketch* ran an editorial that asserted that "it is 'grossly and culpably irregular' for a Socialist minister to talk socialism 'in these days of political truce.'" The *Daily Herald* responded the next day with an editorial maintaining that, although there was an electoral truce in place, the so-called political truce was "a pure fiction—a hypocritical distortion of the purposes of the electoral truce. The 'political' truce has been concocted by Diehard Tories for use as a Muzzling Order against Socialist speakers."[43] This sentiment should be interpreted as representing the view of the NEC. The paper remained in close contact with the party executive throughout the war and from November 1942 onward, the *Herald*'s editor Hugh Cudlipp even sat in on the meetings of the NEC's publicity committee. The following January, the NEC made manifest its conviction that Morrison's speeches were within the acceptable boundaries of patriotic party politics by publishing them a pamphlet entitled "Spearhead of Humanity."[44] The backbench rebellion over the vote on Beveridge may or may not have been a political "accident,"[45] but the party's efforts to steal the thunder of the coalition over the report were certainly intentional. The Workers' Film Association even distributed a promotional package of films "on aspects of Social Security" for rent to local Labour parties, trade councils, and co-operative societies in connection with the report's publication.[46]

The party's publicity campaign in December 1942 is notable for its emphasis on the practical benefits of social welfare and state direction of the economy not only to the working classes, but to the nation as a whole. In his classic study *The Middle-Class Vote*, John Bonham noted that the

Labour Party vote rose among each of his five London regions (Westendia, Suburbia, Blackcoatia, Artisania, and Eastendia) in the general elections of 1923, 1924, 1929, 1935, and 1945, and fell in all five regions in 1931. This coincidence led him to conclude the bankruptcy of class politics for a national party—"if you make yourself unpopular with one class, you cannot expect the other class to swing in your favour."[47] Labour's determined appeal to a broad cross-class and cross-gender constituency throughout the interwar period has been emphasized in the previous chapters; this national appeal was similarly evident in the party's wartime propaganda. The *Herald*'s emphasis on the benefits of the Beveridge plan to the housewives of Britain is an example of this policy. So too is Morrison's treatment of the subject of industrial control, which argued for nationalization in terms of industrial efficiency, and pointedly not in terms of the ideological imperative for the socialization of the means of production. Further, the party's election manifesto was "skilfully . . . designed to draw in the uncommitted voter: each proposed measure of nationalization was justified in terms of practical arguments for efficiency."[48] As Morrison argued in 1945: "Labour has a programme which can and must appeal to workers by brain as well as by hand. Our appeal is to the community as a whole, including the great numbers of progressive-minded professional people, for there is no cleavage of interest between hand workers and brain workers, factory workers or office workers."[49]

This national appeal was made explicit in the publicity campaign launched by the party in the autumn of 1943. At their 20 July 1943 meeting, the NEC's publicity subcommittee agreed on a two-stage plan of literature production: the first stage, to run from September to December 1943, would focus on Labour's policies for health and housing; the second phase, to run from January to May 1944, would focus on the less immediately tangible questions of the national minimum, workers' control, and the "new world order." The following week, the NEC's organization committee proposed a plan for the "intensive development of Party activity commencing in the autumn, consisting of policy conferences, public meetings and the promotion of study and discussion groups."[50] The organization committee was headed by Morrison, who would go on to chair the campaign committee appointed after the 1944 party conference. In his memoirs, Butler wrote of Morrison's party political activity during the war: "[He] had taken advantage of his position on the Home Front to roll out pamphlets and speeches which gave a very firm impression of leading to the left. He recorded in his biography that [when I became director of the Conservative research department,] I carefully examined what he had done for the Labour Party prior to and during the

1945 election and told my staff that I wanted to do the same for the Conservative Party. This information was correct."[51]

Butler's comments illustrate the lengths by which Labour outstripped their Conservative rivals in terms of publicity and propaganda during the war. However, his suggestion that Labour's superior publicity apparatus was attributable to Morrison's position as home secretary and minister of home security is disingenuous. Butler himself served as president of the board of education for the majority of the war, and he used his "position on the Home Front" to spearhead several Conservative committees on postwar social policy and party propaganda. He served as chairman of the postwar problems committee, was a member of the Tory reform committee, and coordinated the informal committee for future policy in 1940. The remit of the postwar problems committee, which was established in the summer of 1941, included "watch[ing] with the utmost care both the Press and the BBC with a view to seeing what is being said by those holding different political opinions . . . and to consider methods of immediate steps being taken to counter in the most effective and prompt way these activities."[52] Left propaganda was meant to be countered by Conservative propaganda articulating the party's own vision for postwar Britain. But while Butler and others were full of ideas for postwar Conservative policy, such ideas came up against hostility from certain corners of the party. Butler's efforts in 1940 to set up a brainstorming group including representatives from the press, nonpartisan think tanks, and even National Labour to help the party "adjust its outlook and policies to meet the social changes of the moment" were dismissed by the party vice chairman, Lady Hester Bourne, as "a movement which is certainly not Conservative, but rather pseudo-intellectual and educational and certainly non-party."[53] As a result, Conservative candidates in by-elections were "handicapped . . . by the lack of a positive policy on home affairs. The Independent or Common Wealth candidates present programmes of 'a new and better world' but the Conservative has little more to offer in comparison than vague promises." They were faced with "the growing apprehension of an electorate which, seeing the end of the war in sight, is beginning to wonder what lies beyond."[54] Despite Butler's best efforts, his party could not even agree on a postwar policy, let alone a strategy for publicizing that policy.

Labour, in contrast, was exceptionally united during the Second World War. While party activists (and some party leaders) disapproved of Labour's presence in the coalition and the ministers' failure to push for more radical social reform during the war, nearly all Labour supporters were united around a postwar program of planning and social welfare.[55]

This consensus would begin to unravel before the end of Clement Attlee's first administration, but in 1943 it meant that the Labour leadership could be assured that nationally produced publicity would be well received in the constituencies, and complement the efforts of local activists.[56] Buoyed by this assurance, the publicity department set upon the first stage of their 1943–1944 campaign with gusto, quickly preparing two pamphlets "in the popular style" on health and housing. Notably, they decided to call the housing pamphlet *Your Home*—an allusion to the enormously successful *Your Britain* series published in 1937–1938. By the end of October, the committee had a draft version of the publication in hand. Notably, though, they decided to consult with outside publicity experts before committing to publication.[57]

The party's emphasis on housing is significant, as the Gallup poll identified housing as the most important election issue in 1945. One historian has suggested that the voters trusted Labour to deliver on homes for heroes because of memories of the Wheatley Housing Act of 1924, but this is doubtful.[58] For one thing, more homes had been built under Neville Chamberlain's tenure as minister of health than by the first Labour government; and, for another, the majority of younger electors who voted for the first time in 1945 would not have remembered the Wheatley Act—a significant point, as Labour was seen to benefit disproportionately from the youth vote.[59] It is more plausible to argue that the public believed that Labour was more committed to home building because it spent more time shouting about its commitment to building homes.[60] *Your Home* was followed up a few months later by a summary of Labour's reconstruction policies entitled *Your Future*—the party was clearly determined to ride the popularity of the *Your Britain* series for all it was worth.

The publicity committee also undertook to produce a series of "discussion pamphlets" on reconstruction, and arranged with the managing director of Odhams Press (publishers of the *Herald*) to secure their subsidized production.[61] In the political environment of wartime Britain, in which 635,000 copies of the Beveridge report were sold to individual citizens, and the government was compelled to produce a condensed version of the white paper—the "Beveridge Report in Brief"—to meet public interest in the report, the party had reason to hope that these discussion pamphlets would not only be read, but actually stimulate real discussion among potential voters.[62] The publicity department further assisted in producing literature and "talking points" for Labour speakers at the conferences and public meetings arranged by their colleagues on the NEC's organization subcommittee.[63] While the body of "Labour in the War

Government: A Record of Things Done" was written by Evan Durbin, Will Henderson also contributed to ensure that the document packed the intended political punch.[64] The final draft began with an introductory note which prodded speakers to "direct attention to positive social, industrial, economic and other achievements for which Labour's representatives in the Government are rightly entitled to a large measure of credit." The pamphlet emphasized: "Whilst it would be unfair to deny to Conservative and Liberal Ministers their full share of credit for good work done. . . . These achievements can justly be presented as examples of the value and influence both of Labour's direct participation in the Churchill Government and of the Labour Movement's powerful contribution to the national war effort."[65] The NEC's publicity committee even mooted the idea of producing an illustrated chronicle of the party's contributions to the coalition.[66]

In early 1944, Labour moved its publicity operations onto a general election footing. A membership campaign was put into effect with the result that, between 1944 and 1945, party membership rose by 366,000.[67] The party's national agent, George Shepherd, contacted the chief agents of the Conservative and Liberal parties in February to discern their views on the use of state-owned loudspeakers and vans by the parties during the election, as well as the "question of the equitable use of Aeroplanes for transport purposes." Later, Shepherd approached his counterparts about arranging for the filming of cinema messages by the three party leaders, as had been done in 1935. The party also decided in February to put together an "informal consultative group of experts" to advise them on political broadcasting.[68]

By May, the publicity department had compiled a detailed estimate of the measures it would need to undertake, and the money it would need to spend, in order to run a successful election campaign. The estimate ran to £150,000; in contrast, the party spent £13,641.9.8 during the 1935 campaign.[69] Even taking into account wartime inflation, this still represented a more than sevenfold increase.[70] When one looks at the details of the publicity department's proposals, the reasons for this surge become clear. They included proposals for the "preparation of a special documentary film on the lines of *Your Britain*," and the hire of 60 mobile film units to display this documentary in marginal constituencies; six mobile vans; a national bill-posting scheme including eight-, sixteen-, thirty-two-, and forty-eight-sheet posters (these last measuring in at over six meters by three meters); twenty million election leaflets; the inevitable sixteen-page illustrated publication "along the lines of *Your Britain*"; miscellaneous leaflets and pamphlets, "party political advertising in national and provincial newspapers"; and the possible employment of additional staff to consult on the party leaders' election broadcasts.[71]

In both scale and scope, the publicity committee's proposals—which were signed off on by the full-NEC—represented a huge leap over the party's election activity in 1935. They also represented an enormous imaginative and organizational edge over the Conservatives. This reflected, in no small part, the improvement in the party's financial position during the war. As a consequence of both curbed expenditure and fundraising, the party's balance sheet went from a debt of £6,045 in 1939 to a credit of £64,950 by December 1944.[72] The proposals gave the party an enormous imaginative and organizational edge, especially since the Conservatives did not form a propaganda committee until March 1945. Whereas Labour's election committee was staffed by the party's professional propagandists, the Conservative committee included only one professional publicist: Elizabeth Neame, an employee of the wartime ministry of information.[73]

Not all of Labour's plans were ultimately realized—principally owing to their impractically in an environment of wartime rationing and government commandeering of resources—but it was nonetheless the most ambitious campaign the party had ever run.[74] An army of commercial illustrators, printing experts, journalists, and campaign strategists were recruited to advise on what was easily the most modern election campaign in Britain to that date. Though they fell short of accepting that the media was the message, the Labour leadership showed an almost fanatical obsession with the design and appearance of party propaganda. The centerpiece of the party's literature campaign was its sixteen-page illustrated election magazine entitled *Straight Left*. Apart from short two- or four-page leaflets, *Straight Left* was the principal exposition of the party's program, and was circulated in larger quantities even than the party manifesto. When the election date was unexpectedly fixed for 5 July after discussions between Churchill and Attlee in April, Will Henderson suggested to the members of the NEC's publicity committee that it might make things easier if the party printed *Straight Left* in black and white, as they were unlikely to be able to secure the facilities for the mass printing of a multicolored pictorial magazine while the war was still ongoing. The committee, however, rebelled against this pragmatic advice. A large part of the appeal of Labour's propaganda magazines was their bright, colorful presentation, and this would be lost if they were printed in black and white. Ultimately, the NEC acquiesced to printing the magazine in two colors (black and red). The now iconic black-and-red production was a compromise solution, and the journal's publication was one of the trickiest aspects of the publicity campaign—the department had to contract with three separate rotary press printers to secure publication of the required two million copies.[75]

The production of *Straight Left* in black and red ultimately gave a chromatic coherence to the Labour election campaign, as the party's text posters were printed in red ink on a white background, and the color

Figure 9.1.   Cover, Labour Party election pamphlet, 1945. (© Labour Party)

played a prominent role in their pictorial posters.[76] The party's use of the color red underscores the change in attitudes that had occurred during the war. In the interwar period Labour posters had largely abjured the use of the color as Conservatives sought to underscore a link between Labour and "Red Russia." By 1945 the socialist implications of red propaganda had lost their threatening aspect. This was partly the result of the public's swing to the left, but it also reflected a surge of sympathy for the Soviet Union during the war.[77] The Labour Party apparently felt that this change in sentiment had gone far enough to allow the party to adopt red as the primary color of its national campaign.[78] Nowhere was this more visible than in the series of posters produced by Philip Zec, a cartoonist for the *Daily Mirror*.[79] The most famous of these posters are his image of a soldier, "This Is Our Chance to Labour for Him," and his composite portrait of the armed forces, "Help Them Finish Their Job" (see Figure I.1 in the Introduction). These two posters explicitly associated the party with the sacrifices of Britain's armed forces, and made it clear that only Labour could guarantee these men the future they deserved. As Morrison recalled in his memoirs, it was an appeal directed primarily at women casting a proxy vote for their loved ones overseas, "and undoubtedly influenced large numbers of women, who had hitherto imagined that politics were of no importance to them, to think about them and to discuss the subject in their letters to their husbands and sons."[80]

Less famous, but no less telling about the scope of Labour's ambitious appeal during the campaign, were Zec's general election posters "Labour for Prosperity" and "Labour for Homes." The first of these associated the party with the "brain workers" whom Morrison saw as the ticket to a Labour majority. The second appealed to women voters, not on the basis of their sympathy for the men in uniform, but on the basis of their own ambitions for the future. The poster underscores the extent to which the issue of housing was conceived in gendered terms during the 1945 campaign. The Zec poster was only one of several housing posters that the party produced for the election.

The language and iconography of Zec's posters paralleled that in the *Daily Mirror* during the campaign. On election day, the paper ran a front page editorial, "Vote for Them," opposite a reproduction of Zec's VE-day cartoon "Don't Lose it Again," in which a battered solider returns "Victory and Peace" to the British people. The similarities were not coincidental. The *Mirror's* election day editorial was part of an ongoing campaign inspired by a letter sent to the paper by an Essex housewife who had declared that "I shall vote for him," in reference to the hopes of her solider husband for a better Britain. The paper's editor discussed the notion of running a campaign around this theme with Herbert Morrison, who strongly supported the idea, and later appropriated it for Labour.[81] Even though the paper's election-day editorial did not specifically mention the Labour Party, the language and imagery would have sent an unmistakable message.

Media scholar James Thomas recently suggested "the need for a re-examination of the [Mirror's] politics," and argued that "the Mirror's coverage was more centrist and anti-Tory than socialist and pro-Labour."[82] While the leftward trajectory of the Mirror's editorial policy over the course of the war may have been more populist than party determined, Labour was quick to exploit the opening that this editorial realignment presented. Morrison began writing for the Mirror in the 1930s, and later cultivated a personal relationship with the paper's editor, Sydney Elliott. Elliot even advised Morrison on the preparation of his 1945 party election broadcast. The home secretary also courted the paper's chairman, Guy Bartholomew. Morrison's biographers describe a meeting that Elliott arranged between the two men at the politician's request shortly after the Mirror had run an editorial particularly sympathetic to Labour: "Morrison bustled in, put his arm round Bartholomew and addressed him as 'you six-ribboned cherub,' and the ice melted. From that point, Bartholomew became a firm friend and Morrison worked closely with the Mirror."[83] Labour also received substantial support from the News Chronicle. As in 1935, the paper officially supported the Liberals, but their election coverage was notably more anti-Tory than pro-Liberal. Together with the Herald, these three papers had a circulation of nearly six million, meaning that for the first time ever, the popular press was equally balanced between right and left.[84]

Discussions of the election campaign have paid particular attention to the two principal parties' negative campaigning.[85] There is certainly an element of truth in such assertions. The Conservative campaign was characterized by the aggressive promotion of Churchill, on the one hand, and an attack on Labour's alleged dictatorial tendencies, on the other.[86] After four decades of "Tory scares," Labour was ready for such an attack. The party's successful deflation of the impact of Churchill's Gestapo broadcast and the Laski Gauleiter affair by preemptively warning the electorate to beware cheap Tory scare tactics has been characterized as "the most brilliant piece of prophylactic medicine ever achieved in electoral history."[87] But the Conservatives were not the only ones to go negative. The Herald's coverage was virulently partisan, and election leaflets such as "Guilty Party" left little question of who was to blame both for the war and for the preceding unemployment. Nonetheless, Labour did not run a primarily negative campaign. "Guilty Party" ranked seventh out of seven among leaflets

HE'S GOT BRAINS, AND DOESN'T WANT THEM WASTED—SO IT'S

LABOUR

FOR PROSPERITY

NATIONAL CONTROL OF INDUSTRY MEANS GREATER SCOPE FOR MANAGERS, TECHNICIANS AND ADMINISTRATORS

LABOUR ☒

Figures 9.2 and 9.3. Two of Philip Zec's series of Labour party election posters appealing to different sectors of the public, 1945. (© Labour Party. Courtesy of the Cambridge University Library)

SHE CAN'T MAKE A HOME TILL SHE GETS ONE ... SO IT'S—

LABOUR

FOR HOMES

A VOTE FOR LABOUR MEANS A FULL NATIONAL EFFORT FOR HOUSING

C.E. 9 PUBLISHED BY THE LABOUR PARTY, TRANSPORT HOUSE, SMITH SQUARE, LONDON, S.W.1.

PRINTED BY J.WEINER LTD., ACTON, W.3.

Figure 9.4. Labour Party election poster emphasizing the crucial issue of housing, 1945. (© Labour Party. Courtesy of the Cambridge University Library)

distributed to local parties from the head office. While over a million copies were printed, only eight hundred thousand were actually dispatched.[88] Conservative policy was frequently critiqued, as in the leaflet "Britain Out of Control," which warned of the economic effects of the rapid deregulation of industry and curtailment of rationing. Yet Labour's literature, posters, and pamphlets predominantly emphasized the party's own plans for a new socialist Britain, conceived in terms of social welfare, national ownership of industry, and state planning. Their ten election broadcasts, which were heard by 44.5 percent of electors, including many middle-class listeners, made a point of justifying nationalization and the maintenance of controls through a language of rationalization and anti-inflation, and emphasized the need for government direction of the country's economic resources to ensure a rapid resolution to the housing crisis.[89]

It will never be possible to know exactly what led 48 percent of voters to choose Labour in 1945. Many doubtless voted Labour simply because "the fashion seemed to be Left."[90] It is clear, however, that the majority did understand what they were voting for (or against). In a Gallup poll conducted after the election, 56 percent answered that they expected the newly elected Attlee government "to introduce sweeping changes such as nationalization," whereas only 30 percent believed that the new government was likely "to govern along existing lines, only more efficiently."[91] This chapter offers an insight into how the public came to appreciate the distinctiveness of Labour's political agenda, even as the party leadership remained publicly wedded to coalition politics. Throughout the war, the party was united around a coherent program of nationalization, planning, and social welfare that had been worked out in detail in the 1930s. Labour's media campaign made sure that that program was effectively and attractively communicated to the public.

CHAPTER TEN

Impacts and Influences

ANY ASSESSMENT OF LABOUR'S interwar media strategy must take into account the impact of that strategy. Yet, it is difficult to establish a direct link between publicity and public opinion, particularly for an era before market research became a regular feature of political campaigns. Little explicit evidence exists on the effectiveness of publicity and propaganda for the period before the Second World War, a circumstance that has led most historians of pre-1945 political culture to focus on "the construction rather than the reception of political discourse."[1] Nonetheless, we can make some inroads into understanding the link between production and reception of interwar publicity and propaganda.

While scholars continue to question the degree of influence that the media has over public opinion, most would agree with Walter Lippmann's 1922 assessment of the agenda-setting power of the news media: in an ever more complex world, people's understanding of their political and social environment is increasingly refracted through the media, to which they look to make sense of the world outside of their immediate experience and understanding.[2] Thus, at a minimum, we can infer that readers of the *Daily Herald*'s international news coverage or of "We Saw in Spain," the Labour pamphlet detailing Clement Attlee's experiences visiting the Republican front in 1937, were unlikely to believe the *Daily Mail*'s characterizations of Spanish government forces as illegitimate architects of "Red Terror."[3] And while reading pro-Labour articles in the daily press, listening to a broadcast from a TUC or party leader, or flipping through the pages of pamphlets such as *Your Britain* did not necessarily result in an elector changing his or her political viewpoint, a positive relationship can be assumed between reading or listening to Labour news and views, and holding a sympathetic view of the party's aims and policies.

As such, we can look at sales figures for party literature, readership figures for the pro-Labour press, and audience figures for Labour or trade union broadcasts as proxy measures for the impact of Labour publicity. In instances where audience figures are not available—as in the audiences for poster propaganda—qualitative evidence from contemporary commentators must take the place of such quantitative measures. Another possible measure of the success of Labour's media strategy is its impact on the coverage of political and industrial issues in the Conservative or Liberal press. This includes both the direct impact of Labour contributions to the "capitalist" press, and, equally importantly, the indirect impact of the *Daily Herald* on the coverage of political and industrial affairs in other popular dailies.

The audience that came into contact with Labour news and publicity increased substantially throughout the interwar period, and in particular from the late 1920s onward. In part this reflected a general rise in the production and distribution of party literature by all three political parties. Postwar leaflets tended to be pithier and less text-heavy than their Edwardian predecessors, and were designed to be accessible to the new democratic electorate created by the 1918 and 1928 franchise reforms. The Conservatives produced thirty-six million leaflets and pamphlets during the 1924 election campaign, and over ninety million in 1929. The Labour Party, which operated on a much tighter campaign budget, nonetheless distributed 21.4 million election leaflets in 1924—more or less one leaflet per eligible voter, and more than twice as many in 1929. A *Daily Express* headline from the October 1924 election referred to the production of "LEAFLETS BY THE TON."[4] Poster production was similarly impressive. While Conservative and Liberal production again outstripped Labour, the party produced 311,000 posters for the 1929 election, about two-thirds the Conservative total, despite operating on a budget less than half the size of their opponents.[5] Despite the ascendance of new forms of political communication in the interwar period, such propaganda remained a pervasive aspect of twentieth-century election campaigns.

The impact of such mass-produced political posters had been fiercely contested since their arrival on the political scene in the late nineteenth century, with both contemporaries and historians divided over whether such forms of propaganda were a waste of money, or an effective—if morally suspect—incorporation of commercial marketing techniques into popular politics. The *Daily Mirror* argued in 1935 that the role of posters was less to educate than to entertain: party posters "enlivened the urban street" and "add[ed] to the fun of the fair." The Liberal political theorist Graham Wallas, in contrast, emphasized the intellectual content of poster arguments, arguing that even if their impact was unconscious, "the mental process which is set in action [may well] be as strictly logical as that which occurs when we correctly solve a mathematical problem during sleep." More recently, the art historian Lisa Tickner has described poster propaganda as capable, through its use of iconographic imagery, of "carry[ing] an impact that written description could never convey." In discussing the visual iconography of the Edwardian suffrage campaign, she argues that poster art combined imagery and argument "in pictorial resources already imbued with political significance and political arguments framed in terms of an appeal to the 'mind's eye.'"[6]

Large-scale posters were, at the very least, hard to ignore—the largest posters were over thirteen feet tall. But how were these massive visual interjections into the political debate read and interpreted? Labour's 1935 poster, "Stop War! Vote Labour," which featured a curly-haired infant in a gas mask, may have been read by some as an indictment of the government's dangerous failure to support a policy of disarmament and collective security, but by others as an unscrupulous piece of scaremongering. Further, the impact of Labour's poster propaganda was arguably limited by the party's failure to match their Liberal and Conservative rivals in terms of size and quantity, particularly before 1929. However, Labour's size disadvantage in this period was partially, if not wholly, offset by its emphasis on quality. Newspaper reports suggest that certain Labour posters were notably successful, such as the Gerald Spencer Pryse series prepared for the 1910 elections, and the posters commissioned by Herbert Morrison for the 1937 LCC campaign. In addition to press reports praising Labour's artistic propaganda, the success of posters such as Pryse's "Forward the Day Is Breaking" can be inferred from the fact that the party repeatedly reissued the poster after its debut in 1910.[7] The NEC records of poster sales to local party organizations further testify to the perceived effectiveness of certain images. The NEC sold twice as many copies of "Poster No. 17," a portrait poster of Ramsay MacDonald, as of any other poster during the 1929 election campaign.[8] Constituency organizations presumably perceived the poster to be an effective counter to the Conservatives' famous "Safety First" portrait poster of Stanley Baldwin. In addition to their merits or demerits in propagandizing Labour's message, party posters also served to alert voters to the party's arrival on the political stage. As historian James Thompson has written of Edwardian postering:

"The proliferating political poster functioned as a means of claiming ownership of contested and symbolically valuable sites."[9] By the 1929 election, Labour was determined to assert its position as a truly national party, running candidates for over 90 percent of seats, and papering the walls and hoardings of the country with evidence of its omnipresence.

Assessing the impact of party literature presents a different set of challenges. For one thing, the link between the distribution of free party literature and its audience is tenuous. Many doubtless did not take the time to read the circulars handed out by canvassers or delivered through the post. The same can be said for those organs of the local Labour press that were distributed gratis. Several such local monthly papers, such as the *Central Southwark News,* the Yardley *Labour Torch,* and the Northwich *Searchlight,* claimed circulations of over 10,000; and the *Labour Organiser* wrote of such publications that they "cause[d] the Capitalist Press instantly to sit up as not even the 'largest circulation' enters every house as the free Labour paper does." However, there was no guarantee of what became of these papers once they entered voters' homes, and local advertisers showed their wariness of such papers' claims to influence by giving a preference to Labour papers that were sold over those given away.[10]

The value of Labour's election newssheets, the mock newspapers advertising the candidate and party that had become a staple of party propaganda by the 1930s, was presumably greater than that of regular gratis newspapers since voters normally pay more attention to party propaganda at election times. The NEC certainly attributed considerable value to election newssheets and strongly encouraged and aided local parties in their production.[11]

An even more persuasive argument about influence can be made by looking at the distribution figures of literature that was offered for sale, as voters were unlikely to pay for something they did not intend to read. *Your Britain* sales, for instance, reached record levels for non-general election year propaganda in 1937, with the first issue selling over two-thirds of a million copies. While those figures represent sales from the NEC to local party organizations and not the ultimate number of copies sold to individual voters, the fact that the publication went through multiple print runs suggests that demand exceeded the NEC's expectations. The 1937 NEC chairman, Hugh Dalton, was unexpectedly impressed by the high sales of *Your Britain* and *Labour's Immediate Programme* that year.[12]

The figures for sales of Labour Party literature are dwarfed by the sales of the *Daily Herald* after its relaunch as a popular daily on 17 March 1930. The paper attained a preeminent circulation shortly after the relaunch, and by the end of 1933 its circulation had passed two million. Of course, not all *Daily Herald* subscribers read the paper for its political views, yet it is hard to argue that the fact that readers took their news from a pro-Labour medium did not, however subtly, improve their opinion of the party. After all, men and women who read the *Herald* for its racing tips or picture page, or women driven to read the *Herald* because their husbands managed the family newspaper subscription, were unlikely to turn to another paper for their news and editorial analysis.[13] According to a 1939 survey, over 75 percent of working-class readers read only one paper. Among *Herald* readers who read multiple daily papers, the most popular second daily was the *Mirror.*[14] Such *Herald* readers, even if not initially predisposed toward Labour, gained a better understanding of and hence presumably developed a more sympathetic attitude toward the party's views and policies than readers of the *Daily Mail* or the *Daily Express.* The high-profile attention that the *Herald* gave to issues such as the iniquities of the means test shaped its readers' consciousness in ways different from those who read the *Daily Express,* which gave little attention to the issues raised by the unemployment assistance board regulations other than to characterize the opposition as "forced and artificial," and to contend that "the country seems largely content with the regulations" and that hardship stories were merely "sob-stuff."[15]

Those who reject the Gramscian model of cultural hegemony tend to argue that newspaper content closely mirrors consumers' pre-existing preferences—that consumers vote with their pocketbooks by purchasing the newspaper with whose views and outlook they most closely agree.[16] The interwar social chroniclers Robert Graves and Alan Hodge argued that interwar readers chose their papers for the prizes, not the content. Mass-Observation, on the other hand, found that "the *Daily Herald* is liked because of its politics to a much greater extent than the average."[17] While the evidence is inconclusive, both the increasingly populist rhetoric of the *Daily Express* in the early 1930s and the leftward shift of the *Daily Mirror* at the end of the decade reflected their proprietors' conviction that the success of the *Herald* stemmed from a hitherto unexposed desire for left-wing news and analysis among the general public.

The first reverberations of the *Herald* relaunch on the existing organs of the popular press were visible in the pages of the *Daily Express.* In September 1932, the *Herald* sent out a circular and questionnaire to local government councillors inquiring into the level of unemployment in their area and what action they believed would best help to alleviate unemployment, and declaring the paper's intention of "conduct[ing] a campaign in its columns designed to compel even this Government to reverse its suicidal 'economy' policy and to set going, through its own agency and that of the municipalities, large-scale schemes of national development."[18] Notably, the TUC filed the papers relating to the unemployment campaign under "*Daily Herald* Schemes," which also contained papers related to the subsidized promotion of the "Wonderland of Knowledge" children's encyclopedia and the gift of a free fountain pen, pencil, and pen knife to those who donated to the Manor House Hospital.[19] The *Express*'s editor, Beverley Baxter, responded to the *Herald* "scheme" by launching a near identical campaign. The week after the *Herald* questionnaire went out, the *Express* sent out a questionnaire of its own, with a covering letter announcing that "The *Daily Express*, believing that it lies within the power of municipal authorities to ease the suffering of thousands of unemployed this winter, intends running a campaign to emphasize that it is their duty to do so by providing work wherever possible."[20] The end result was that the two campaigns ran simultaneously in the rival papers.

The municipal campaign was not the only example of the *Express*'s new-found championship of the working classes. Two months later, the *Express* launched a campaign against wage cuts and sent the following letter to trade union representatives:

Dear Sir,

As you are no doubt aware, the *Daily Express*, under the leadership of Lord Beaverbrook, has consistently attacked the insane policy of wage-cutting.

We propose, with your cooperation to continue the fight with increased intensity.

Hitherto we have attacked each wage-cutting proposal immediately it was made.

This is not enough.

In spite of our opposition and yours, cuts took place in several industries in 1932 and more are threatened in 1933.

We therefore propose to make the question of high wages the most vital and pressing issue in the political and industrial life of the nation.

We propose to mobilize public opinion to fight against every threatened wage-cut.

We will not hesitate to urge men and women to join their appropriate Trade Unions as the best means of fighting this suicidal policy. Nor will we hesitate to urge the public to bring pressure in the constituencies to make this the burning question of the hour.

Each Trade Union can cooperate with us in helping to combat the menace of low wages.

Will you kindly write to the Daily Express *the moment* when a cut in wages is threatened.

Supply us with the facts of the case and we will pledge ourselves to fight the cuts no matter how powerful is the industry involved.[21]

The campaign did not represent a complete reversal for the *Express,* which had periodically come out against the ruinous impact of competition on industrial wages as part of its crusades in favor of imperial preference in international trade agreements.[22] Nonetheless, the supposed cynicism of the *Express* circular incensed Walter Citrine, who viewed it as a maneuver designed to regain the support of former working-class readers who had switched from the *Express* to the *Herald.* In a draft letter to trade union secretaries, Citrine warned that the *Express*'s overtures should be regarded with "not unjustified suspicion" as "the old saying 'Beware the Greeks when they bring you gifts' contains much wisdom." He concluded by emphasizing that it was the *Herald* that had "compelled, by its steady publicity and leading articles, other papers to change or modify their attitudes on this vital question."[23]

While Citrine may have resented what he perceived to be Baxter and Beaverbrook's cynicism and opportunism, the *Express*'s willingness to explore municipal solutions to unemployment and its support for higher wages both redounded to the benefit of the working classes whom Labour sought to assist and, by extension, conferred legitimacy on the political party that had long been advocating such policies. While the *Express*'s attention to working-class issues threatened the *Herald* commercially, it also reflected the success of Labour's efforts to put unemployment and wage issues prominently on the national agenda. The perceived threat of the *Herald* also drove the *Express* to temper its hostility to the Labour Party for fear of the commercial fallout of being branded an "anti-Labour paper."[24] In an October 1936 editorial, the *Express* reiterated that it was "not the enemy of the Socialist Party, though Mr. Bevin and others profess to think so. . . . If Mr. Bevin, or Mr. Morrison, or Sir Walter Citrine came to power here the *Express* would not tremble at those men nor their policies."[25] Two weeks later, the paper urged all working-class readers to "do their duty to themselves" and join their local trade union, if they had not already done so.[26] The *Express* was doing Citrine's work for him.

The follow-on impact of the *Herald*'s success can also be seen in the transformation of the *Mirror* from a broadsheet with a lagging circulation and a largely female readership to a mass-market populist and left-leaning tabloid that, by 1939, had become the second most popular national daily among younger readers. In the four years leading up to the war, the *Mirror* moved progressively to the left, projecting an "irreverent, populist and patriotic brand of politics," which, while never explicitly pro-Labour, became increasingly anti-government after 1935. The shift in the paper's politics was largely contingent on the changes in editorial leadership after Lord Rothermere relinquished his ownership stake and the new board appointed W. M. Bartholomew as editorial director.[27] Yet, while the personal convictions of the editorial staff were critical to the *Mirror*'s political realignment, the shift would have been highly unlikely but for the success of the *Herald* in convincing advertisers of the wisdom of investing in a popular, left-leaning daily with a predominantly working-class readership.

In the 1910s and 1920s the *Herald* had been handicapped in securing advertisements by manufacturers and retailers' prejudices against advertising in publications directed at working-class readers. An article in the industry publication *Newspaper World* stated in 1919: "Obviously its readers cannot be described as moneyed nor possessed of the virtues or vices of the middle-class. However large the constituency may become, the advertisers in the *Daily Herald* will never hope to reach readers with the opportunity to respond to their appeals as, for instance, the clientele of the *Daily Mail* or the *Daily News*. The fact creates one of the greatest difficulties of a Labour daily and handicaps it in the attempt to create a paying proposition."[28] The *Herald*'s advertising department had frequently reported companies' anxieties about placing advertisements in a publication with socialist and progressive sympathies. A 1923 report noted that "May-Day Labour processions cause our advertisement revenue to slump for a month (advertisers not being impressed with what they term 'a procession of *Daily Herald* readers with not a shilling amongst them.') The Labour Party's Capital Levy programme of last Autumn aroused advertisers to furious resentment against us, and it took them six months to get over it and to begin to be a bit reasonable."[29]

For the first several decades of the twentieth century, manufacturing and agency executives consistently underestimated the importance of the working classes to the growing consumer market. It was not until the advent of new techniques of market analysis in the late 1920s that producers began to appreciate the importance of working-class shoppers, and hence the value of advertising in media aimed at a working-class audience. Once this appreciation dawned, papers with large working-class readerships, such as the *Daily Herald,* began to attract greater interest from advertisers.[30] Yet, even after his company committed to purchasing the *Herald* in 1929, J. S. Elias, the chairman of Odhams Ltd, continued to worry that "the big advertisers, who thrived under the prevailing system of capitalist opportunity, [would not] support a paper advocating Socialism and the destruction of the capitalist system."[31] The paper did in fact face greater difficulties in securing advertisements than its conservative competitors, even after its commercial relaunch. During the month of May 1930, the *Herald* carried only 776 columns of display advertising and 94 columns of smalls compared to 1,595 and 317, respectively, in the *Express* and 1,928 and 42 in the *Mail*.[32] Despite its preeminent circulation, the Daily Herald (1929) Ltd only issued its first dividend in 1942.[33] Nonetheless, the financial position of Odhams' *Daily Herald* was much stronger than that of its predecessor, and showed that a left-wing daily could compete successfully in the modern commercial marketplace.

The importance of the example of the *Herald*—and of the success of the Hearst and Pulitzer papers in America—to the decision of the *Mirror* executives to realign the paper's politics should not be underestimated. In 1934, Bartholomew called in consultants from the advertising firm J. Walter Thompson to advise on methods of reviving the paper's ailing circulation. The firm suggested to Bartholomew that the paper could profit from a reorientation "down market."[34] This reorientation was embodied in the shift from a broadsheet to a tabloid format and the conspicuous launch of a series of strip cartoons and advice columns. J. Walter Thompson's market research also helped legitimize the decision to realign the paper's politics, as the "downmarket" working classes were assumed to have a greater sympathy for Labour politics. It has been suggested that the *Daily Mirror*, and not the *Daily Herald*, played the dominant role in shifting public opinion leftward in the 1930s;[35] yet without the example of the *Daily Herald*'s success, it is not clear that the *Mirror* would have followed the course it did.

Labour's media policy was not limited to support for the *Herald*. Labour and trade union publicists and individual members of the Labour movement actively courted publicity for issues of importance to the movement both in the print press and on the airwaves and, occasionally, through the newsreels in the 1930s. The success of Labour's attempts to publicize its policies in the 1930s was of course impacted by the actual content of Labour's program in this period. On issues where Labour remained confused or divided—particularly on rearmament in 1935 and nonintervention in Spain in 1936—Labour publicists faced considerable challenges. Attempts to square the many contradictions of Labour's foreign policy in the mid-1930s often led to bizarre outcomes, as when the *Daily Herald* distinguished itself as the only paper *not* to include any coverage of the Labour Party conference on either its front page or pages 2 or 3 the morning after the party voted against intervention in the Spanish conflict, relegating discussion of the resolution to page 18.[36] Such gaffes allowed the party's enemies to score several easy points at their expense. However, an overemphasis on such events can be misleading, as similar embarrassments beset Conservative publicists in the 1930s, particularly over the India round table discussions.[37] Labour did prove remarkably successful in the 1930s at keeping public attention focused on domestic issues even in the face of international upheaval, and from late 1936 onward it reaped the benefits of anti-fascist dissatisfaction with the National Government.

Professional publicists began to play an increasingly important role in setting news agendas after the First World War, though Whitehall did not enter the public relations arena in a serious capacity until the Second World War.[38] But while government agencies were slow to get in on the act, public relations became an important aspect of party organization in the interwar period, so much so that, as the *Daily Mirror* noted in 1935: "Politics, like every other popular commodity, cannot exist today without advertising, and advertising improves in all its various techniques."[39]

The dividends of the successful courtship of the industrial correspondents for the major papers were visible in the expanded and increasingly objective coverage of the trade union affairs throughout the 1930s. TUC press officer Herbert Tracey kept his preferred reporters so close that Hugh Dalton in 1936 allegedly mistakenly assumed that the *Express*'s industrial correspondent was a member of the TUC General Council.[40] Relations between the party publicity department and the media similarly improved. While individual Labour leaders still railed against the iniquities of the anti-socialist media, the NEC made a point of thanking the press at the end of each party conference and assuring the "capitalist hacks in the orchestra stalls" that Labour thought them "fine fellows after all."[41] The mutually respectful relationship that developed between Labour leaders and reporters from the late-1920s helped assure that even the most hostile papers no longer filed reports in which they characterized conference speakers as "threaten[ing] this country with insurrection and revolution."[42]

In addition to day-to-day public relations management, Labour leaders in the 1930s also orchestrated several high profile media events, such as the Jarrow Hunger March. Gauging the impact of such multimedia spectacles entails many of the same difficulties encountered in attempting to gauge the impact of leaflet or poster campaigns. Moviegoers did not choose the Majestic on Tottenham Court Road over the Odeon in Leicester Square because the former was showing the *Pathé Gazette* newsreel of the Jarrow crusade. Many doubtless paid little or no attention to the newsreels at all.[43] Further, did a viewer watching Attlee's first newsreel appearance as opposition leader hear his message that "Labour's policy is the true national policy. They will organize the resources of the nation in the interests of all," and take that message at face value? Or did he or she recoil at the image of the new leader of the Labour movement as a nervous, middle-class politician with the manner of a school teacher and the appearance of a "little mouse"?[44] Newsreels introduced a plethora of considerations about the importance of "telegenic" party leaders that would become increasingly important with the expansion of television after the war.[45]

While similar limitations attend an analysis of the impact of radio broadcasts, it is possible to draw more confident conclusions about the reach of political broadcasting through an analysis of listening figures. Radio may still have been a novelty of sorts for many families in 1930s Britain; nonetheless, listeners did not tune in uncritically to whatever was on. Listening levels for specific programs could vary widely from one night or week to the next, depending on who was speaking or what was being discussed. During World War II, audiences for the 9:15 PM "topical talks" series were higher for talks on the war than for general political commentary, and significantly higher for political subjects than for broadcasts on "more esoteric" themes such as "The Artist in the Witness Box." Audiences for the "Postscripts to the News" program, the famous Sunday evening "'lay sermons' on aspects of the war and its meaning," diverged depending on the speaker, with audience ratings for J. B. Priestley's broadcasts occasionally exceeding 40 percent, while other speakers garnered ratings at about half that number. The BBC Listener Research Department attributed this variation in part to the size of the audience for the 9 o'clock news, which preceded the talks. However, the variation also clearly indicated audience preferences for certain speakers, of which Priestley was only the most popular. If a broadcast were not of interest to listeners, they would simply tune out.[46] As such, a survey of audience figures for Labour broadcasts can arguably give us a plausible sense of the number of people who made time for Labour's arguments.

On such a measure, Labour was remarkably successful at communicating its views over the airwaves. The BBC did not begin collecting data on audience figures until just before the outbreak of the Second World War, so evidence for the 1930s is scarce and largely anecdotal. Informal polls conducted by the *Daily Telegraph* and the *Daily Express* during the 1935 election campaign suggested that Morrison's broadcast was heard by between 30 and 40 percent of electors. The *Daily Express* poll, which yielded the lower estimate, was conducted largely by telephone, and hence its sample can be assumed to have contained a larger proportion of middle-class listeners than a more scientifically selected random sample would have done.[47] That Morrison's audience figures were nonetheless so high suggests the party's success at gaining a hearing from an upper-middle-class audience through the airwaves.

During the war, certain Labour leaders, particularly Morrison and Arthur Greenwood, rated consistently large audiences for their "Postscript" broadcasts.[48] The talks series "Trade Unions in Wartime," which ran on Mondays at 9:15 PM in March and April 1940, "had a considerable audience who greatly welcomed hearing their Trade Union leaders over the air." "Trade Unions in Wartime" marked the microphone debut of George Hicks, MP, the president of the amalgamated union of building trade workers. The BBC producers felt that Hicks was a naturally gifted broadcaster, who "could well become a microphone personality," and subsequently recruited him to give a series of Postscripts, the audience for which was nearly as high as that for the concurrent series of talks by Priestley.[49] Audience interest was exceptionally high for BBC programs on reconstruction from December 1942 onward, many of which featured Labour speakers or speakers sympathetic to the party's program.[50] In June 1945, audiences for Labour election broadcasts were nearly identical to those for the Conservatives (44.5 percent versus 45.4 percent). The *News Chronicle* characterized the Co-operative Party leader A. V. Alexander, who had served as first lord of the admiralty in the 1929–1931 and 1940–1945 governments and who delivered one of the Labour Party's ten broadcasts, as among the best broadcasters of the campaign. By 1951, middle-class listeners showed a distinct preference for listening to Conservative election broadcasts over Labour, but this was not the case in 1945 or 1950, when middle-class listeners tuned-in in large numbers to hear Labour speakers.[51]

Labour recognized the unique opportunity that the radio afforded to reach an audience that might otherwise remain deaf to its arguments, and the party repeatedly sought to leverage its constitutional position as the official opposition in its dealings with the BBC. While Labour did not succeed in obtaining an automatic "right-of-reply" to all government broadcasts, it did secure a more equitable distribution of government and opposition speakers in talks series throughout the 1930s;[52] and, significantly, it did establish the right to respond over the air to the chancellor's annual budget broadcast (although the budget broadcasts themselves drew a bigger crowd than these rejoinders). Nonetheless, in April 1940 Labour's critique of Sir John Simon's final budget attracted a quarter of the public.[53]

Your Britain sales or BBC audience figures alone cannot definitively prove that interwar voters were influenced by Labour's media campaign.

However, taken together the quantitative evidence demonstrates that Labour's publicity efforts were successful in reaching a large number of potential voters. And, combined with qualitative reports, such evidence supports the link between publicity and public opinion. While the media was not the only cause of Labour's success in 1945, it was an important and too often discounted component.

Conclusion

I N 1975, Paul Addison published his seminal study of the Second World War, *The Road to 1945,* in which he argued that the experience of the war, both on the home front and in the army, caused a shift to the left in public opinion in the early 1940s, and that the Labour Party was essentially the passive beneficiary of this realignment.[1] In his opinion, the experience of the war, and not Labour policy, made the party's fortunes in 1945. In the decades that followed, historians have tended to support Addison's interpretation of the wartime "swing to the left," even as they questioned the mechanisms or permanency of this social transformation. The work of political scientists has buttressed such a view by highlighting the limits of Labour's electoral revival after 1931. In the first major study of interwar voting, David Butler dismissed Labour's success in winning thirteen seats from the government between 1935 and 1939 by emphasizing that by-elections tend to be more "agin' the Government" than general elections.[2] More recently, John Stevenson and Chris Cook concluded that Labour's significant municipal gains in 1932 reflected "the return of the Labour faithful and the recovery of Labour confidence and morale at this local level, especially in areas where the issues of unemployment and the means test were most explosive," but that Labour never really secured gains in middle-class seats from 1931 to 1935.[3]

Such studies illustrate the limits of the pre-war shift to Labour, but they also obscure the party's significant regional gains throughout the period. Individual party membership rose substantially in the 1930s, particularly in the southeast. In suburban London, in particular, constituency Labour parties blossomed in former Conservative strongholds such as Greenwich, West Woolwich, Henden, and Harrow.[4] The *Times* expressed alarm at the growth of Labour support in suburban districts such as Twickenham, where the party rebounded from its 1931 setback to raise its poll from a previous high of 14,202 in 1929, to 16,881 in 1932, and to 19,890 in 1934, or in Putney, where the party's 1934 by-election poll exceeded its previous 1929 high by nearly 2,000 and the Conservative vote collapsed to just over half its 1929 level. The paper attributed the 1934 Twickenham result to the construction of new municipal housing estates and to the "Socialist manipulation" of the Conservative candidate's message in the local media. The Putney result was put down to the "nauseous and lying" propaganda of the Labour Party.[5] Clearly a swing too small to effect a turnover could still cause consternation and panic in the Conservative ranks. Assessments that point to the government's ability to hold onto seats at by-elections without considering the swing away from the party in power can mask significant shifts in electoral support.[6]

Recent analyses of interwar county borough elections also reveal a surge in Labour support in the early 1930s, which was not limited to working-class areas such as Burnley, where the party secured twelve net gains between 1932 and 1934.[7] Even in Canterbury, a relatively small town in Kent with a "small and poorly organized working-class," the Labour Party saw a significant growth in support after 1931, obtaining over one third of the vote in 1933 and securing the return of "one solitary [Labour] councillor."[8] It is risky to extrapolate attitudes about national politics from local results, and notably Labour's local electoral performance stagnated in the latter half of the 1930s, yet the geographical distribution of Labour gains between 1932 and 1934 suggest more than simply a recovery of confidence and morale among previous supporters.[9]

Even such evidence arguably understates the degree of Labour's success. Voting patterns can be misleading, particularly in gauging attitudes about political parties. It is impossible to discern whether an elector who voted for the National candidate in 1935 did so because he or she positively supported the government, or because he or she believed that Labour was incompetent and unsuitable for office. Given that a key argument of this book is that the post-1931 Labour Party worked effectively to reestablish its reputation as a legitimate alternative to the National Government, the distinction is important. Much of the emphasis of Labour propaganda in the interwar period was on the party's constitutionality and respectability. As historian Kenneth O. Morgan has noted, "by the end of the 1930s, Labour looked credible as a party of government as it had never done before."[10] By 1939, such propaganda had had a significant impact on public perceptions of the movement, and during the war the party made effective use of the mass media to consolidate and build on those gains.

The significance of the shift in Labour's media policy goes beyond the impact of Labour propaganda on voting intentions. Labour's embrace of a national media strategy reflected its commitment to winning over a broad coalition of British voters, including women, clerks and service workers, the professional classes, and even agricultural laborers.[11] This commitment was underscored in the wording of Clause Four of the 1918 Labour Party constitution in which the party committed itself to securing for "*the workers by hand or by brain* the full fruits of their industry."[12] Labour's political strategy was premised not only on working-class mobilization but on "persuading the community that [Labour's] views of affairs are right."[13] Despite a brief radicalization in 1931, the party leadership's commitment to achieving gradual social reform through national consensus persisted. This commitment was embodied in the ideology of "democratic socialism" espoused by the National Council of Labour in the 1930s. Scholars of Labour politics have tended to conflate the turn toward democratic socialism with the continental movement toward social democracy.[14] But while Labour's pursuit of a democratic socialist majority ultimately led it to embrace social democratic policies such as state-sponsored social welfare and a mixed economy, the distinction between the two terms is significant. First, democratic socialism had as its professed end goal the establishment of a socialist state. While social democratic reforms were a step in this direction, many on the left-wing of the party believed that such reforms represented the beginning not the end goal of democratic socialism. Second, and most pertinent to this study, democratic socialism focused on the means of social transformation, even more than on the ends. As the economist and Labour Party theorist Evan Durbin wrote in 1940: "Democracy is a *method* of taking political decisions, of compromising and reconciling conflicting interests. The method is more important, more formative of the resulting order, than the disputes so resolved."[15] The party's commitment to a national democratic vision led it to pursue a particular electoral strategy and to embrace a particular style of political communication.

This strategy was not predetermined. The party would arguably have done better to focus its attention on winning working-class seats in areas such as Birmingham and Liverpool, both of which remained bastions of working-class conservatism throughout the interwar period. Yet, such a course of action would have conflicted with Labour's self-conception as a party which could and should speak for the broad majority of Britons against "the small minority (less than 10 percent of the population) who own the great part of the land, the plant and the equipment without access to which their fellow-countrymen can neither work nor live."[16] Having determined on a strategy of winning suburban London as well as the Welsh mining country, the Labour Party set about prioritizing policies that could attract a lower-middle-class and professional audience, and broadening its political tactics to include not only grassroots activism, but innovative approaches aimed toward an audience disinclined to attend political meetings and potentially hostile to household canvassing by party activists whose enthusiasm they were not likely to share. In an era in which many Britons were arguably wary of overtly partisan appeals, Labour sought to use the mass media to present itself as the natural representative of the British nation.[17] The popular press, the radio, and publications such as *Your Britain* served to normalize Labour politics, and bring them to the breakfast table or sitting room of homes that Labour had failed to penetrate through more traditional modes of political outreach.

Measured in such terms, Labour's media strategy was a success, and even those party supporters who remained wary of the mass media and commercial culture came to appreciate the benefits of such new communication techniques in selling socialism to the masses. All of which is certainly not to say that Labour politicians had no reservations about embracing this new style of mass politics. In 1937, the future party leader Hugh Gaitskell excused his support for importing commercial techniques into Labour politics by noting that the new techniques of political advertising, however bereft of educational value, at least had the benefit of success. Yet, Morrison and other advocates of mediated politics justified their position on the grounds that propaganda and political education were not necessarily incompatible. Rather than rejecting the goal of "making socialists" for the more cynical project of "selling socialism," the Labour leadership came to accept the argument that traditional methods of educationalist propaganda would have to be supplemented by new forms of political communication. By the 1930s, the party and trade union leadership were determined that, if they could not change the system, they would at least be as successful at it as their rivals. To quote TUC leader Ernest Bevin, Labour was determined to "pla[y] Lord Beaverbrook at his own game," and to play to win.[18] The party's ability to compete successfully in the new arena of mass media politics played a crucial role in its political recovery after 1931 and its landslide victory fourteen years later.

To a degree, Labour's media revolution was the product of political desperation. The Conservative Party had proved itself remarkably successful in navigating the waters of mass democracy in the decade after the First World War, and had itself pioneered many new techniques in political communication. Crucially, the experience of the 1926 general strike convinced many within the industrial wing of the movement of the importance of effectively communicating Labour's ideals and ambitions to the democratic public. In an environment in which Labour's leaders increasingly perceived their backs to be up against the wall, those who most vocally opposed the new style of mass political communication were outnumbered by advocates for change. Similarly, those who advocated a more polarizing and class-based approach to politics were sidelined by advocates of a moderate message capable of attracting a broad coalition of support.

Once Labour achieved power, the perceived necessity for such a "compromise" with capitalist culture was less self-evident. In the 1950s and 1960s, the left wing of the party became increasingly vocal in its opposition to the "national" approach that the Labour had hitherto pursued and that the Gaitskellite/revisionist wing continued to advocate. As New Left theorist Ralph Miliband would write in 1962: "In fact, it was not a monstrous falsehood of the Tories to claim that the Labour party is a class party. . . . But the Labour Party is also a party whose leaders have always sought to escape from the implications of its class character by pursuing what they deemed to be 'national' politics: these policies have regularly turned to the detriment of the working classes and to the advantage of Conservatism. Nor can it be otherwise in a society whose essential characteristic remains class division."[19] New Left critics took a particular interest in the role of the mass media in national culture. The propagation of a new school of cultural theory, heavily influenced by Antonio Gramsci, questioned whether real social reform could be achieved under the conditions of capitalist media domination.[20] Such critiques had been foreshadowed in the political realm by the Royal Commission on the Press, convened by the Labour government in 1947, and were reinforced in the report of the Labour Party's Committee on Advertising issued in 1966. Their impact was also felt in Labour's disassociation from new methods of political research and marketing in the 1970s and 1980s.[21] Yet post–Second World War debates over the direction of Labour politics and the role of the mass media in British political life should not overshadow the extent of the cohesion achieved within the party in the 1930s and 1940s. Similarly, the differences between New Labour's policies and the program of the postwar administration should not disguise the strategic similarities between Peter Mandelson and Tony Blair and Herbert Morrison and Clement Attlee. We cannot understand Labour's long road to 1945 without understanding the party's commitment both to constructing a cohesive political program that could appeal to a broad national coalition and to selling that vision of politics to the public through the new media of mass democracy.

ARCHIVES CONSULTED / NOTES / INDEX

Archives Consulted

MSS Attlee	Attlee papers, Bodleian Library, Oxford
BBC WAC	BBC Written Archives Centre, Caversham Park, Reading
BBK	Beaverbrook papers, House of Lords Record Office, London
BEVN	Bevin papers, Churchill Archives Centre, Cambridge
	Bevin papers, Modern Records Centre, Warwick
CAB	Cabinet papers, National Archive, London
MSS Castle	Castle papers, Bodleian Library, Oxford
	Lord Citrine papers, London School of Economics
CPA	Conservative Party Archive, Bodleian Library, Oxford
	Hugh Dalton diaries, London School of Economics
FO	Foreign Office papers, National Archives, London
	Hugh Gaitskell papers, University College London
HO	Home Office papers, National Archives, London
	John Johnson Collection, Bodleian Library, Oxford.
LAB	Department of Labour papers, National Archives, London
LPA	Labour Party Archives, Manchester (NEC minutes held at the LPA)
NLW	Lloyd George papers, National Library of Wales, Aberystwyth
LLP	London Labour Party archives, London Metropolitan Archives
	Lloyd George papers, House of Lords Record Office, London
PRO	Ramsay MacDonald diary, National Archives, London
RMD	Ramsay MacDonald papers, Johns Rylands Library, Manchester

M-O	Mass-Observation archive, University of Sussex, Brighton
INF	Ministry of Information papers, National Archives, London
	Herbert Morrison papers, London School of Economics
NBKR	Philip Noel-Baker papers, Churchill Archives Centre, Cambridge
	Northcliffe papers, British Library, London
	Pathé Gazette online archive, available at www.britishpathe.com
	Political Poster Collection, Cambridge University Library (CUL)
PREM	Prime Ministers' papers, National Archives, London
	John Reith diary, held at BBC WAC, Caversham Park, Reading
CPS	C. P. Scott papers, John Rylands Library, Manchester
TUC	Trades Union Congress Archives, Modern Records Centre, University of Warwick
TUCL	Trades Union Congress Library, London
T	Treasury papers, National Archives, London
	A. P. Wadsworth papers, John Rylands Library, Manchester
	Beatrice Webb diaries, London School of Economics

Notes

Introduction

1. LPA, "His Own," 1903; Labour Party election manifesto, 1906. On 12 February 1906, the LRC rechristened itself the Labour Party of Great Britain.
2. R. B. McCallum and Alison Readman, *The British General Election of 1945* (Oxford, 1947), 265–266.
3. Although Labour's 1945 campaign was unprecedented in its scale and scope, professional consultants had been a feature of British politics since the Conservatives employed the advertising firm S. H. Benson's to advise on their ill-fated Safety First campaign in 1929; see John Ramsden, *The Age of Balfour and Baldwin, 1902–1940* (London, 1978), 232.
4. Labour Party press and publicity department, "General Election, July, 1945: Report on Campaign Publicity Services" (filed in National Executive Committee [NEC] minutes); Harold Croft, *The Conduct of Parliamentary Elections* (London, 1945), 578; BBC WAC R9/1/5: Audience Research Bulletins: General Bulletin no. 251, July 1945.
5. Clement Attlee, party election broadcast (PEB), 5 June 1945, reported in *The Listener,* 14 June 1945, 660.
6. Philip Williamson, *Stanley Baldwin: Conservative Leadership and National Values* (New York, 1999), chap. 3; Sian Nicholas, "The Construction of a National Identity: Stanley Baldwin, 'Englishness' and the Mass Media in Inter-War Britain," in *The Conservatives and British Society, 1880–1990,* ed. Martin Francis and Ina Zweiniger-Bargielowska (Cardiff, 1996), 127–146; David Jarvis, "British Conservatism and Class Politics in the 1920s," *English Historical Review* 111 (1996): 58–84. For an earlier treatment of this theme, see Ramsden, *Balfour and Baldwin.*
7. For two exceptions to this trend, see Duncan Tanner, "Class Voting and Radical Politics: The Liberal and Labour Parties, 1910–1931," in *Party, State and Society: Electoral Behavior in Britain since 1820,* ed. Jon Lawrence and Miles

Taylor (Brookfield, VT, 1997), 106–130; and Matthew Worley, *Labour inside the Gate: A History of the British Labour Party between the Wars* (London, 2005).

8. H. C. G. Matthew, R. I. McKibbin, and J. A. Kay, "The Franchise Factor and the Rise of the Labour Party," *English Historical Review* 91 (1976): 723–752; George Dangerfield, *Strange Death of Liberal England* (New York, 1961 [1935]); Maurice Cowling, *The Impact of Labour, 1920–1924* (Cambridge, 1971); Peter Clarke, *Lancashire and the New Liberalism* (Cambridge, 1971); Ross McKibbin, *The Evolution of the Labour Party, 1910–1924* (Oxford, 1974).

9. Paul Addison, *The Road to 1945: British Politics and the Second World War* (London, 1975). See also Sonya Rose, *Which People's War? National Identity and Citizenship in Britain, 1939–1945* (Oxford, 2004), 69–70. For a critique of this view, see Steven Fielding et al., *"England Arise!": The Labour Party and Popular Politics in 1940s Britain* (Manchester, 1995).

10. Michael Savage, *The Dynamics of Working-Class Politics: The Labour Movement in Preston, 1880–1940* (Cambridge, 1987); Jack Reynolds and Keith Laybourn, *Labour Heartland: The History of the Labour Party in West Yorkshire during the Inter-war Years, 1918–1939* (Bradford, 1987); Sue Goss, *Local Labour and Local Government: A Study of Changing Interests, Politics, and Policy in Southwark from 1919 to 1982* (Edinburgh, 1988). More recent works on the local origins of Labour politics include Worley, *Labour inside the Gate,* and Michael Worley (ed.), *Labour's Grass Roots: Essays on the Activities and Experiences of Local Labour Parties and Members, 1918–1945* (Aldershot, 2005). For an up-to-date survey of this literature, see Matthew Worley, "Building the Party: Labour Party Activism in Five British Counties between the Wars," *Labour History Review* 70, 1 (2005): 92.

11. Ralph Miliband, *Parliamentary Socialism: A Study in the Politics of Labour* (London, 1961). For an earlier exposition of this view, see Allen Hutt, *The Post-war History of the British Working Class* (London, 1937). Studies of local Labour politics have similarly posited an "organic" history of the rise of Labour which diminishes the role of national politics in the party's development.

12. D. L. LeMahieu, *A Culture for Democracy: Mass Communication and the Cultivated Mind in Britain between the Wars* (Oxford, 1998); Victoria de Grazia, *Irresistible Empire: America's Advance through Twentieth-Century Europe* (Cambridge, MA, 2005). On the persistent importance of class in defining British identity, see McKibbin, *Classes and Cultures,* and David Cannadine, *The Rise and Fall of Class in Britain* (New York, 1999). Of the local political studies discussed in note 10 above, Savage, *Dynamics of Working-Class Politics,* and Reynolds and Laybourn, *Labour Heartland,* in particular emphasize the continued importance of local difference in shaping interwar culture. For an insightful consideration of the evolving concept of a "mass public" and "average" public opinion in the twentieth century, see Sarah Igo, *Averaged American: Surveys, Citizens, and the Making of a Mass Public* (Cambridge, MA, 2007).

13. Advocates of this view have been a constant presence within the Labour movement. See Chris Waters, *British Socialists and the Politics of Popular Culture, 1884–1914* (Manchester, 1990); Lawrence Black, *The Political Culture of the Left in Affluent Britain, 1951–1964: Old Labour, New Britain?* (Basingstoke, 2003).

14. David Howell, *MacDonald's Party: Labour Identities and Crisis, 1922–1931* (Oxford, 2002).

15. On the attitude of left-wing and communist activists in the 1930s, see Roderick Martin, *Communism and the British Trade Unions, 1924–1933: A Study of the National Minority Movement* (Oxford, 1977); Andrew Thorpe, *The British Communist Party and Moscow, 1920–1943* (Manchester, 2000), chaps. 6–7. On the Labour leadership's opposition to this view, see Ben Pimlott, *Labour and the Left in the 1930s* (Cambridge, 1977).

16. The term *new political history* encompasses an increasingly wide body of scholarship. Among the more noted works focusing specifically on political language are Gareth Stedman Jones, "Rethinking Chartism," in *Languages of Class: Studies in English Working-Class History, 1832–1982* (Cambridge, 1983), 90–178; Patrick Joyce, *Visions of the People: Industrial England and the Question of Class, 1848–1914* (Cambridge, 1991); Eugenio Biagini, *Liberty, Retrenchment and Reform: Popular Liberalism in the Age of Gladstone, 1860–1880* (Cambridge, 1992); David Jarvis, "Mrs. Maggs and Betty: The Conservative Appeal to Women Voters in the 1920s," *Twentieth Century British History* 5, 2 (1994): 129–152; Jon Lawrence, *Speaking for the People: Party, Language and Popular Politics in England, 1867–1914* (Cambridge, 1998); and E. H. H. Green, *Ideologies of Conservatism: Conservative Political Ideas in the Twentieth Century* (Oxford, 2002).

17. Ross McKibbin, "Class and Conventional Wisdom: The Conservative Party and the 'Public' in Interwar Britain," in *Ideologies of Class: Social Relations in Britain, 1880–1950* (Oxford, 1990), 272, 282, 285.

18. Williamson, *Stanley Baldwin,* chap. 3; Nicholas, "Construction of a National Identity." For an earlier treatment of this theme, see Ramsden, *Balfour and Baldwin.*

19. Laura Beers, "Counter-Toryism: Labour's Response to Anti-socialist Propaganda, 1918–1939," in *Foundations of the British Labour Party: Identities, Cultures, and Perspectives, 1900–1939,* ed. Matthew Worley (Farnham, Surrey, 2009), 231–268.

20. Stephen Brooke, "Labour and the 'Nation,' 1945 to the Present," in *Party, State and Society: Electoral Behavior in Britain since 1820,* ed. Jon Lawrence and Miles Taylor (Brookfield, VT, 1997), 153–154.

21. E.g., Linda Colley, *Britons: Forging the Nation, 1707–1837* (New Haven, 1992), 237–282; James Vernon, *Politics and the People: A Study in English Political Culture, c. 1815–1867* (Cambridge, 1993), chap. 6; Anna Clark, *The Struggle for the Breeches: Gender and the Making of the British Working Class* (Berkeley, CA, 1997); Julia Bush, *Women against the Vote: Female Anti-suffragism in Britain* (Oxford, 2007). Scholars who have examined the impact of female enfranchisement on party politics include Martin Pugh,

The Tories and the People: 1880–1935 (Oxford, 1985); and Martin Pugh, *Women and the Women's Movement in Britain, 1914–1999,* 2nd ed. (Basingstoke, 2000); Ina Zweiniger-Bargielowska, *Austerity in Britain: Rationing Controls and Consumption, 1939–1955* (Oxford, 2000); and Jarvis, "Mrs. Maggs and Betty" and "British Conservatism and Class Politics in the 1920s."

22. A large literature has developed on the centrality of consumerism to Western politics, much of which has focused on the comparative appeal to women voters of consumerist over productivist appeals. On the British case, see Zweiniger-Bargielowska, *Austerity in Britain;* Stephen Brooke and Amy Black, "The Labour Party, Women and the Problem of Gender, 1951–1966," *Journal of British Studies* 36 (1997): 419–452; Matthew Hilton, "The Female Consumer and the Politics of Consumption in Twentieth-Century Britain," *Historical Journal* 45 (2002): 103–128. International studies include de Grazia, *Irresistible Empire,* chap. 8; Lizabeth Cohen, *A Consumers' Republic: The Politics of Mass Consumption in Postwar America* (New York, 2003), esp. parts I and IV; Meg Jacobs, "Pocketbook Politics: Democracy and the Market in Twentieth-Century America," in *The Democratic Experiment: New Directions in American Political History,* ed. Meg Jacobs, W. J. Novak, and J. E. Zelizer (Princeton, 2003), 250–275.

23. Savage, *The Dynamics of Working-Class Politics;* Reynolds and Laybourn, *Labour Heartland;* Goss, *Local Labour;* Worley, *Labour Inside the Gate;* and Worley, "Building the Party," p. 92.

24. Goss, *Local Labour.*

25. On the perceived relationship between national politics and local political fortunes in the interwar period, see NEC, "Report of the Campaign Activities, Municipal Election Campaign," n.d. Nov 1938, and "Memorandum on Municipal Elections," n.d. Nov 1938 (filed in NEC minutes).

26. Howell's *MacDonald's Party* is a refreshing exception to this, analyzing the two-way relationship between the national leadership and local organizations. See also Andrew Thorpe, *Parties at War: Political Organization in Second World War Britain* (Oxford, 2009).

27. Ramsden, *Balfour and Baldwin,* 232; "Leaflets by the Ton: Conservatives Break All Records," *Daily Express,* 18 October 1924.

28. Jon Lawrence, "The Transformation of British Public Politics after the First World War," *Past and Present* 190 (2006): 185–216; and Jon Lawrence, *Electing Our Masters: The Hustings in British Politics from Hogarth to Blair* (Oxford, 2009), chap. 4.

29. John Lewis, *The Left Book Club: An Historical Record* (London, 1970); E. H. H. Green, "The Battle of the Books," in *Ideologies of Conservatism,* 135–156; Pugh, *The Tories and the People,* 183; Selina Todd, "Pleasure, Politics and Co-operative Youth: The Interwar Co-operative Comrades' Circles," *Journal of Co-operative Studies* 32, 2 (1999): 129–145. On lotteries and other forms of gambling, see "To Run a Draw and Keep the Law! The Betting and Lotteries Act, 1933," *Labour Organiser,* May 1935, 88–89, and subsequent correspondence. On civic organizations, see Helen McCarthy, "Parties,

Voluntary Associations and Democratic Politics in Interwar Britain," *Historical Journal* 50, 4 (2007): 891–912. On literature, see McKibbin, "Class and Conventional Wisdom," 272–275, 291; and Alison Light, *Forever England: Femininity, Literature and Conservatism between the Wars* (London, 1991).

30. Norman Angell, *The Press and the Organisation of Society* (London, 1922), 1.

31. "Selling Socialism" was the title given to a conference on political communication sponsored by the New Fabian Research Bureau on 23–24 October 1937. See LSE Fabian Society J14/7.

32. Dominic Wring, *The Politics of Marketing the Labour Party* (Basingstoke, 2005); James Thomas, *Popular Newspapers, The Labour Party and British Politics: From Beaverbrook to Blair* (Abingdon, 2005), esp. chaps. 2 and 5. On the fraught relationship between the Left and the media in the 1950s, see Lawrence Black, *Political Culture of the Left,* chap. 7. On the first Attlee government's successful attention to political communication, see Martin Moore, *The Origins of Modern Spin: Democratic Government and the Media in Britain, 1945–51* (Basingstoke, 2006).

1. The Rise of a Mass Media Culture

1. See Bernard Donoughue and G. W. Jones, *Herbert Morrison: Portrait of a Politician,* 2nd ed. (London, 2001).

2. Asa Briggs, *The History of Broadcasting in the United Kingdom,* vol. 1, *The Birth of Broadcasting* (London, 1961), 141; *Daily Express,* 11 November 1935. The *Daily Express* telephone poll, which was skewed to a middle-class audience, found that 29.5 percent of those polled had listened to Morrison's broadcast.

3. Herbert Morrison, Party Election Broadcast (PEB), reported in *The Listener,* 13 November 1935, 882.

4. See the list of MPs complied by the Labour Party Research Department, 21 March 1944. Filed in BEVN II 812.

5. Jose Harris, "The Transition to High Politics in English Social Policy, 1880–1914," in *High and Low Politics in Modern Britain,* ed. Michael Bentley and John Stevenson (Oxford, 1983); E. H. H. Green, *Crisis of Conservatism: The Politics, Economics and Ideology of the British Conservative Party, 1880–1914* (Oxford, 1995); James Thompson, "The Genesis of the 1906 Trades Disputes Act: Liberalism, Trade Unions and the Law," *Twentieth Century British History* 9, 2 (1998): 175–200.

6. David Jarvis, "The Conservative Party and the Politics of Gender 1900–1939," in *Conservatives and British Society,* ed. Martin Francis and Ina Zweiniger-Bargielowska (Cardiff, 1996); Ina Zweiniger-Bargielowska, *Women in Twentieth-Century Britain: Economic, Social and Cultural Change* (London, 1991); Martin Pugh, *Women and the Women's Movement in Britain, 1914–1959* (Basingstoke, 1992).

7. For an early reference to the floating voter, see " 'Floating Vote' Will Decide," *Daily Express,* 28 October 1935.

8. Mark Abrams, ed., *The Home Market: 1939* (London, 1939), 106.

9. Graham Wallas, *Human Nature in Politics* (London, 1948 [1908]), 87–91; Martin Rosenbaum, *From Soapbox to Soundbite* (London, 1997), introduction; Dominic Wring, *The Politics of Marketing the Labour Party* (Basingstoke, 2005), chap. 1. On the United States, see Sarah Igo, *The Averaged American: Surveys, Citizens and the Making of a Mass Public* (Cambridge, MA, 2007).

10. George Orwell, "A Farthing Newspaper," in *The Collective Essays: Journalism and Letters of George Orwell*, vol. 1, ed. Sonya Orwell and Ian Angus (London: 1968 [1928]). On the United States, see Paul Starr, *The Creation of the Media: Political Origins of Modern Communications* (New York, 2004).

11. Herbert Morrison, "Can Labour Win London without the Middle Classes?" *Labour Organiser*, October 1923, 19 (reprinted from the *London Labour Chronicle*).

12. BBC WAC, Talks Department Index cards: Morrison PEB, 21 October 1951.

13. Ross McKibbin, *Classes and Cultures: England 1918–1951* (Oxford, 1998), 527, contends that D. H. LeMahieu overstates this phenomenon in his *Culture for Democracy: Mass Communication and the Cultivated Mind in Britain between the Wars* (Oxford, 1988).

14. Juliet Nicholson, *The Perfect Summer: Dancing into Shadow in 1911* (London, 2006), plate 22.

15. Lynda Nead, *Victorian Babylon: People, Streets and Images in Nineteenth-Century London* (New Haven, 2000), 59.

16. G. R. Searle, *New England? Peace and War, 1886–1918* (Oxford, 2004), 111.

17. James Thompson, "'Pictorial Lies?'—Posters and Politics in Britain, c. 1880–1914," *Past and Present* 197 (2007): 177–210.

18. The middle classes were more likely to see British-produced films, especially in the 1920s; however, all classes preferred American-produced features. Andrew August, *The British Working Class, 1832–1940* (Harlow, Eng., 2007), 213.

19. Jeffrey Richards, *The Age of the Dream Palace: Cinema and Society in Britain, 1930–1939* (London, 1984), 11–17.

20. Evelyn Waugh, *Put Out More Flags* (London, 2000 [1942]), 153. On such cinema stratification, see also, Claire Langhamer, *Women's Leisure in England, 1920–1960* (Manchester, 2000), 59–62.

21. On the export of the American star system, see Victoria de Grazia, *Irresistible Empire: America's Advance through Twentieth-Century Europe* (Cambridge, MA, 2005), chap. 6. On British government efforts to curb Britons' obsession with American cinema, see LeMahieu, *Culture for Democracy*, chap. 6, and McKibbin, *Classes and Cultures*, chap. 11.

22. Sally Alexander, "Becoming a Woman in London in the 1920s and 1930s," in *Metropolis/London: Histories and Representations since 1800*, ed. David Feldman and Gareth Stedman Jones (London, 1989), 264.

23. Ina Zweingier-Bargielowska, "The Body and Consumer Culture," in *Women in Twentieth-Century Britain* (Harlow, Eng., 2001), 187.

24. J. B. Priestley, *English Journey: Being a Rambling but Truthful Account of What One Man Saw and Heard and Felt and Thought during a Journey through England during the Autumn of the Year 1933* (London, 1934), 320.

25. Martin Pugh, "The *Daily Mirror* and the Revival of Labour, 1935–1945," *Twentieth Century British History* 9, 3 (1998): 432.

26. See, e.g., Agatha Christie, "The Affair at the Victory Ball," first published in *The Sketch*, 7 March 1923, wherein Poirot and Hastings read the *"Daily Newsmonger"* over breakfast.

27. Evelyn Waugh, *Scoop!* (London, 1937). Mrs. Stitch was a parody of Waugh's friend Lady Diana Cooper.

28. International Institute of Practitioners of Advertising (IIPA), *Survey of Press Readership*, vol. 1 (London, 1939), table 2. The figures in the table sum to more than 100 percent due to duplicate readership, outlined in table 8 of that volume.

29. On the national appeal of these sports, cricket in particular, see McKibbin, *Classes and Cultures*, 332ff.

30. See Sian Nicholas, "All the News That's Fit to Broadcast: The Popular Press versus the BBC, 1922–45," in *Northcliffe's Legacy: Aspects of the British Popular Press, 1896–1006*, ed. Peter Catterall, Colin Seymour-Ure, and Adrian Smith (London, 2000), 121–148.

31. LeMahieu, *Culture for Democracy,* chap. 6; McKibbin, *Classes and Cultures,* 462–467.

32. McKibbin, *Classes and Cultures,* 457.

33. Political and Economic Planning (PEP), *Report on the British Press: A Survey of Its Current Operations and Problems with Special Reference to National Newspapers and Their Part in Public Affairs* (London, 1938), 232.

34. McKibbin, *Classes and Cultures,* 466.

35. PEP, *Report on the British Press,* 248–249.

36. Tom Jeffrey, "The Suburban Nation: Politics and Class in Lewisham," in *Metropolis/London,* 201; Paul Addison, *The Road to 1945: British Politics and the Second World War* (London, 1975), 153–154; Helen MacCarthy, "Democratic Politics, Parties, and Voluntary Associations in Interwar Britain," *Historical Journal* 50 (2007): 891–912.

37. Addison, *The Road to 1945,* 154.

38. M-O File Report 126: Report on the Press, May 1940.

39. PEP, *Report on the British Press,* 264.

40. A. P. Wadsworth, "Newspaper Circulations, 1800–1954," *Report of the Manchester Statistical Society* March (1955), 28; Abrams, *Home Market,* 109, 113; Mark Abrams, *The Condition of the British People, 1911–1945* (London, 1945), 85; Adrian Bingham, *Gender, Modernity and the Popular Press in Interwar Britain* (Oxford, 2004), 3.

41. IIPA, *Survey of Press Readership,* vol. 1, table 2.

42. Colin Seymour-Ure, "The Press and the Party System between the Wars," in *The Politics of Reappraisal, 1918–1939,* ed. Gillian Peele and Chris Cooke (London, 1975), 235, 238; Abrams, *Home Market,* 109.

43. Michael Dawson, "Party Politics and the Provincial Press in Early Twentieth Century England: The Case of the South West," *Twentieth Century British History* 9, 2 (1998): 212.

44. Seymour-Ure, "The Press and the Party System," 235–236; PEP, *Report on the British Press,* 9–11.

45. Paul Giddon, "The Political Importance of Provincial Newspapers, 1903–1945: The Rowntrees and the Liberal Press," *Twentieth Century British History* 14, 1 (2003): 24–42; Dawson, "The Provincial Press," 202.

46. Stephen Koss, *The Rise and Fall of the Political Press in Britain,* vol. 1 (London, 1981), introduction; Mark Hampton, *Visions of the Press in Britain, 1850–1950* (Urbana, IL, 2004), chap. 1.

47. Walter Lippmann, *Public Opinion* (Mineola, NY, 2004 [1922]), 186–187; PEP, *Report on the British Press,* 263–265.

48. *Daily Express,* 2 November 1922.

49. PEP, *Report on the British Press,* 254. Of course, their newspaper consumption was not the only factor likely to cause these two men to hold divergent world views.

50. Colin Seymour-Ure, "Northcliffe's Legacy," in *Northcliffe's Legacy,* 9–16.

51. Tom Jeffrey and Keith McClelland, "A World Fit to Live In: The *Daily Mail* and the Middle Classes, 1918–39," in *Impacts and Influences: Essays on Media Power in the Twentieth Century,* ed. James Curran, Anthony Smith, and Pauline Wingate (London, 1987), 27–52.

52. Maurice Cowling, *The Impact of Labour, 1920–1924* (Cambridge, 1971), chap. 2.

53. For a more detailed history of the politics of the Harmsworth family and of the *Daily Mail* and the *Daily Mirror,* see Reginald Pound and Geoffrey Harmsworth, *Northcliffe* (London, 1969); J. Lee Thompson, *Northcliffe: Press Baron in Politics* (London, 2000); Sally Taylor, *The Great Outsiders: Northcliffe, Rothermere and the Daily Mail* (London, 1996); Maurice Edelman, *The Mirror: A Political History* (London, 1966).

54. BBK/H/37: Minutes of Evidence taken before the Royal Commission on the Press, 18 March 1948.

55. D. G. Boyce, "Crusaders without Chains: Power and the Press Barons, 1896–1951," in *Impacts and Influences* (London, 1987), 106–108.

56. Quoted in Stephen Koss, *The Rise and Fall of the Political Press in Britain,* vol. 2 (London, 1984), 504.

57. John Ferris and Uri Bar-Joseph, "Getting Marlowe to Hold His Tongue: The Conservative Party, the Intelligence Services and the Zinoviev Letter," *Intelligence and National Security* 8, 4 (1993): 100–137.

58. A. J. Cummings, *The Press and a Changing Civilisation* (London, 1936), 79–80.

59. Richard Cockett, "The Party, Publicity and the Media," in *Conservative Century: The Conservative Party since 1900,* ed. Anthony Seldon and Stuart Ball (Oxford, 1994), 551; Sian Nicholas, "The Construction of a National Identity: Stanley Baldwin, 'Englishness' and the Mass Media in Inter-war Britain,"

in *The Conservatives and British Society, 1880–1990*, ed. Martin Francis and Ina Zweiniger-Bargielowska (Cardiff, 1996), 132–133.

60. CPA, CCO 4/1/22: Davidson to Patrick Gower, 23 May 1928.

61. Koss, *Rise and Fall*, vol. 2, 504.

62. A. J. A. Morris, "Sir Robert Donald," *Oxford Dictionary of National Biography*, ed. H. C. G. Matthew and Brian Harrison (Oxford, 2004). CD-ROM.

63. On the relationship between Lloyd George and the syndicate owning the *Daily Chronicle*, see Koss, *Rise and Fall*, vol. 2, 446–447; Henry Dalziel, MP, to the House of Commons, 15 October 1918, *Parliamentary Debates*, 5th series, vol. 110, cols. 82–94; David Lloyd George to Margaret Lloyd George, 22 September 1926 and 3 January 1930, in *Lloyd George Family Letters, 1885–1936*, ed. K. O. Morgan (Cardiff, 1973), 206–207, 210.

64. For the role of the press in prewar progressive politics in Lancashire, see Peter Clarke, *Lancashire and the New Liberalism* (Cambridge, 1971), chap. 7. For the desire of the *Daily News* editor and publisher to revive this progressive coalition after the war, see Stephen Koss, *Fleet Street Radical: A. G. Gardiner and the Daily News* (London, 1973), 243, 247, 250–251.

65. *Report of the Trades Union Congress (TUC)* (London, 1869), 206–212.

66. *Report of the TUC* (London, 1903), 92.

67. Ibid.

68. LPA LP/DH: Minutes of the meeting of trade union representatives at Caxton Hall, Westminster, 26 February 1908.

69. On the wider implications of the Osborne judgment, see Michael J. Klarman, "Parliamentary Reversal of the Osborne Judgement," *Historical Journal*, 32, 4 (1989): 893–924.

70. *Labour Party Annual Conference (LPAC) Report* (1910), 93.

71. LPA LP/DH: *Daily Citizen* Prospectus; "Fabian Fund for the Daily Citizen," circular, n.d. (1912), available through the Robert Dudley Howland Fabian Society Collection digitization project at Brandon University Library, Manitoba, CA.

72. Alastair Hatchett, "The Role of the Daily Herald with Particular Reference to Direct Action, 1919–1921" (master's thesis, University of Warwick, 1971).

73. R. J. Holton, "Daily Herald v. Daily Citizen, 1912–15," *International Review of Social History* 19, 3 (1974): 347–376.

74. Hatchett, "The Role of the Daily Herald"; Ross McKibbin, *The Evolution of the Labour Party, 1910–1924* (Oxford, 1974), 125. In 1914, Thomas sued Lansbury's paper for libel, and his personal dislike of the *Herald* editor was evident in his denunciations of the Poplar Rates Rebellion six years later. See John Shepherd, *George Lansbury: At the Heart of Old Labour* (Oxford, 2002), 145, 196.

75. McKibbin, *Evolution*, 221–234; Huw Richards, *The Bloody Circus: The Daily Herald and the Left* (London, 1997), 32–64.

2. Speaking to the People

1. David Marquand, *Ramsay MacDonald* (London, 1997).
2. F. M. Leventhal, *Arthur Henderson* (Manchester, 1989).
3. As MacDonald's diary entry for 20 October 1935 makes clear, his dislike of Henderson was not even softened by the news of the older man's death (PRO 30/69/1753/3).
4. 22 February 1906. *Parliamentary Debates*, 4th series, vol. 62, col. 600. For a discussion of pictorial propaganda during the 1906 election, see James Thompson, "'Pictorial Lies'?—Posters and Politics in Britain, c. 1880–1914," *Past and Present* 197 (2007): 177–211. On Liberal and Labour exploitation of the "Chinese slavery" issue during the 1906 election, see Kevin Grant, *A Civilised Savagery: Britain and the New Slaveries in Africa, 1884–1926* (London, 2005), chap. 2.
5. Thompson, "'Pictorial Lies,'" 186, 206.
6. Timothy Hollins, "The Presentation of Politics" (PhD diss., University of Leeds, 1981), 118, 122.
7. On Morrison and the media, see Martin Moore, *The Origins of Modern Spin, 1945–51* (Basingstoke, 2006).
8. NEC, *Annual Report to the Labour Party Conference* (1904), 21.
9. Report of the Political Committee to the NEC, 18 June 1903 (filed in NEC minutes).
10. Thompson, "'Pictorial Lies,'" 185.
11. NEC, *Annual Report* (1904), 21.
12. NEC, *Annual Report* (1907), 4, 11.
13. NEC, *Annual Report* (1910), 12.
14. NEC minutes, 27 July 1907. For more on poster designs see, e.g., NEC minutes, 8 July 1909.
15. NEC minutes, 17 December 1903; 6 October 1909.
16. NEC, *Annual Report* (1910), 12. The sales figures given are 7,000 large to 44,000 small.
17. *Times*, 23 April 1910.
18. In 1900, the largest poster was a 60" by 40" representation of "Kruger and His Supporters" produced by the Liberal Unionist Association. James Thompson, "Visual Culture and the Boundaries of the Political: Revisiting the 1907 LCC Election" (paper presented at the New Directions in Modern Political History Conference, Institute for History Research, London, April 2005).
19. "The Poster Election," *Pall Mall Magazine*, February 1910, 211.
20. *Manchester Guardian*, 8 January 1910.
21. The bulk of these display posters were the same size as Labour's larger posters. However, some were even larger, as in the December 1910 contest in Hackney South, where Horatio Bottomley made extensive use of giant 12' by 10.5' posters in his successful three-way reelection contest. *Times*, 6 December 1910.
22. *Manchester Guardian*, 1 January 1910.

23. "The Poster Election," 217.
24. *Times*, 1 December 1910.
25. *Times*, 21 November 1928.
26. See NEC minutes, 10 and 17 November 1920, 8 February 1921, 24 November 1921.
27. NEC minutes, 24 November 1921.
28. Political poster collection, Cambridge University Library.
29. See discussion of *Daily Herald* in this volume, Chapters 1, 5, and 7.
30. Ross McKibbin, *The Evolution of the Labour Party, 1910–1924* (Oxford, 1974), 206–214.
31. Memorandum presented to the NEC, 27 September 1917 (filed in NEC minutes).
32. NEC, *Annual Report* (1920), 41.
33. TUC MSS 292/30/4: Memorandum on the formation and objectives of the Joint Press and Publicity Committee, n.d. October 1921.
34. TUC MSS 292/30/4: Joint Press and Publicity Committee, October 1921.
35. McKibbin, *Evolution*, 209.
36. Sidney Webb and Herbert Tracey, Memorandum presented to the NEC, 17 April 1918 (filed in NEC minutes).
37. Both Webb and Morrison were early advocates of a cross-class electoral strategy, which was almost certainly influenced by their experiences on the LCC. In 1922–1923, the two contributed articles to a series in the *London Labour Chronicle* (August 1922, September 1923) on the importance of the middle -class.
38. Sidney Webb, *London Labour Chronicle,* December 1922.
39. See reports of Bonar Law and Winston S. Churchill's speeches in *Manchester Guardian*, 21 March and 30 May 1919. For a general discussion of this period see K. O. Morgan, *Consensus and Disunity: The Lloyd George Coalition Government, 1918–1922* (Oxford, 1979); John Turner, *British Politics and the Great War: Coalition and Conflict, 1915–1918* (Yale 1992).
40. *Daily Mail*, 30 November 1918.
41. Northcliffe papers, Add 62206, vol. LIV ff. 68–211: Fyfe to Northcliffe, 27 November 1918.
42. *Daily Citizen*, 8 October 1912. Cited in R. J. Holton, "Daily Herald v. Daily Citizen, 1912–15," *International Review of Social History* 19, 3 (1974): 360–361.
43. *Daily Mail*, 2 December 1918.
44. NEC, *Annual Report* (1919), 47.
45. *Daily Mail*, 2 December 1918; emphasis added.
46. Testimonials by Major H. J. Gillespie, D.S.O., and Ernest Barker, M.A., *Daily Mail*, 3 December 1918.
47. *Daily Mail*, 4 December 1918.
48. *Daily Mail*, 5, 7, and 9 December 1918.
49. *Daily Mail*, 6 December 1918.
50. *Daily Mail*, 9 December 1918.
51. *Daily Mail*, 6 December 1918.

52. NEC, *Annual Report* (1919), 29.
53. *Daily Mail*, 4 December 1918.
54. NEC, *Annual Report* (1919), 29. See also letter of thanks from Henderson to C. P. Scott, 3 January 1919, CPS 335/72.
55. *Daily Express*, 31 October 1918.
56. *Daily Express*, 15 and 16 November 1918.
57. *Daily Express*, 5 and 10 December 1918.
58. *Times*, 3, 5, 10, and 12 December 1918.
59. *Daily Express*, 30 December 1918; *Times*, 30 December 1918.
60. NEC, *Annual Report* (1919), 46.
61. *Daily News*, 29 September 1919.
62. R. Page Arnot, *History of the Labour Research Department* (London, 1926), 45.
63. *Daily News*, 29 September 1919.
64. Arnot, *History of the LRD*, 45.
65. Reported in *Railway Review*, 3 October 1919, and in most of the daily press.
66. *Daily Express*, 1 October 1919.
67. *Manchester Guardian*, 2 October 1919.
68. The initial figure mooted was £2,000 per day (Arnot, *History of the LRD*, 47). The total expenditure on all forms of publicity during the nine days was £16,355, NUR Report and Financial Statement for 1919, cited in Philip Bagwell, *The Railwaymen: A History of the National Union of Railwaymen* (London, 1963), 396.
69. *Railway Review*, 10 October 1919.
70. See advertisements in the *Times*, 2 and 3 October 1919; and *Manchester Guardian*, 2, 3, and 4 October 1919.
71. *Daily Chronicle*, 3 and 4 October 1919; *Daily News*, 4 October 1919.
72. For footage of the posters, see Pathé Gazette, "The National Railway Strike" (1919), available at www.britishpathe.com. On trade unionism and popular numeracy in the early twentieth century, see James Thompson, "Statistics and the Public Sphere, 1880–1914: Numbers, Numeracy and Political Culture" (unpublished paper, Bristol University, 2008).
73. See press reports of the prime minister's Caernarfon telegram, 29 October 1919.
74. "The National Railway Strike" newsreel shows several of the press advertisements blown up as wall posters.
75. *Railway Review*, 10 October 1919; Rodney Mace, *British Trade Union Posters* (Thrupp, Gloucestershire, 1999), 63–75.
76. *Times*, 3 October 1919.
77. It is unclear whether or not Lloyd George's message was also accompanied by film footage. According to Arnot, *History of the LRD*, 49, "as far as can be ascertained" there was "no preliminary filming of the Premier." However, according to one of Thomas's biographers, Lloyd George himself appeared on screen "jerking about and mouthing a message, shown in print below" (Gregory Blaxland, *J H Thomas: A Life for Unity* [London, 1965], 34). In the Pathé Gazette on the strike, neither leader is shown—only their messages.

78. *Railway Review,* 10 October 1919.
79. *Times,* 6 October 1919.
80. *Railway Review,* 10 October 1919.
81. *Daily Express,* 29 Sept 1919.
82. *Daily Herald,* 3 October 1919.
83. Arnot, *History of the LRD,* 46.
84. *Times,* 6 October 1919.
85. Quoted in Arnot, *History of the LRD,* 50.
86. Allen Hutt, *The Post-war History of the British Working-Class* (London, 1937), 28. The NEC's *Annual Report* for 1920 (p. 59) notes an expenditure on "cinema propaganda" as part of the joint NEC-TUC "Mines for the Nation" publicity campaign.
87. For a fuller discussion of industrial relations and the media in the interwar period, see Laura Beers, "'Is This Man an Anarchist?': Industrial Action, Publicity and Public Opinion in Britain, 1919–1926," *Journal of Modern History* 82, 1 (forthcoming).

3. The Anti-Labour Turn

1. *Daily Mail,* 14 November 1923; emphasis in original.
2. For the leader of the Conservative Central Office's assessment of press impact, see CPA CCO 4/1/22: Davidson to Patrick Gower, 23 May 1928.
3. Historians have tended to share contemporaries' views of press power. See, e.g., Jean Seaton and James Curran, *Power without Responsibility: The Press and Broadcasting in Britain* (London, 1981), 42–58; James Curran, "Advertising as a Patronage System," in *The Sociology of Journalism and the Press,* ed. Harry Christian (Keele, 1980), esp. 90–91; Richard Cockett, "The Conservative Party and the Media," in *Conservative Century: The Conservative Party since 1900,* ed. Anthony Seldon and Stuart Ball (Oxford, 1994), 547–577. Colin Seymour-Ure is comparatively skeptical about the impact of press propaganda, but even he admits that hostile press coverage hurt Labour politically; see his "The Press and the Party System between the Wars," in *The Politics of Reappraisal, 1918–1939,* ed. Gillian Peele and Chris Cook (London, 1975), 240.
4. Ross McKibbin, "Class and Conventional Wisdom: The Conservative Party and the 'Public' in Interwar Britain," in *Ideologies of Class: Social Relations in Britain, 1880–1950* (Oxford, 1990), 270, 271, 275.
5. Ross McKibbin, *The Evolution of the Labour Party, 1918–1924* (Oxford, 1974).
6. On this tendency, see Adrian Bingham, *Gender, Modernity and the Popular Press in Interwar Britain* (Oxford, 2004), 5–6. Notably, James Thomas, *Popular Newspapers, the Labour Party and British Politics* (London, 2005), recognizes the change in tone within the popular press in the 1930s.
7. Herbert Morrison, "On the Fighting of a Municipal Election," in *The Labour Party Handbook of Local Government* (London, 1920), 202; and Frank Edwards, "Propaganda Articles for the Local Press," *Labour Organiser*

(September 1925). For a contrary view, see Herbert Drinkwater, "The Organisation of Propaganda," *Labour Organiser* (July 1924).

8. *Newspaper World,* 12 February 1919, 12.

9. *Daily Express,* 2 November 1922.

10. *Daily Express,* 1 November 1922.

11. *Daily Mail,* 1 November 1922; emphasis in original.

12. *Daily Mail,* 15 November 1922; 3 November 1922; emphasis in original.

13. Hugh Dalton diaries, entry for 29 December 1922.

14. A. J. Cummings, *The Press and a Changing Civilisation* (London, 1936), 80.

15. Northcliffe to H. G. Price, 12 April 1921 (telegram), quoted in Stephen Koss, *The Rise and Fall of the Political Press in Britain,* vol. 2 (London, 1984), 368. See also Northcliffe Papers, Add 62206, vol. 54: Northcliffe to Price, 8 January 1921.

16. Koss, *Rise and Fall,* vol. 2, 396.

17. See Northcliffe to Price, 8 January 1921, and BBK/H/37: Beaverbrook testimony before the Royal Commission on the Press, 18 March 1948.

18. The Spen Valley by-election was actually held in the first week of 1920, but the campaign took place in December 1919. In the twelve by-elections that the party contested in 1919, the party polled 113,783 votes against 104,485 for their coalition opponents. *Times,* 9 January 1920.

19. The party gained control of twelve London boroughs, and the LLP candidates won a plurality of votes cast.

20. *Times,* 6 January 1920.

21. Laura Beers, "Punting on the Thames: Stock Market Electoral Betting in Interwar Britain," *Journal of Contemporary History* 45, 2 (forthcoming).

22. McKibbin, *Evolution,* 91. Ralph Miliband has described the 1918 constitution as the apotheosis of "Labourism" in *Parliamentary Socialism: A Study in the Politics of Labour* (London, 1961), 61.

23. John Shepherd, *George Lansbury: At the Heart of Old Labour* (Oxford, 2002), 189.

24. K. O. Morgan has emphasized the limits of McKibbin's analysis of the fundamental constitutionalism of pre-1924 Labour, with particular reference to the trade unions. See his "The High and Low Politics of Labour: Keir Hardie to Michael Foot," in *High and Low Politics in Modern Britain,* ed. Michael Bentley and John Stevenson (Oxford, 1983), 291–292.

25. *Daily Mail,* 31 August 1921.

26. *Daily Mail,* 2 September 1921.

27. *Daily Chronicle,* 11 December 1919.

28. *Daily Chronicle,* 4 November 1919; 14 November 1919; 27 February 1920. The 1920 railway strike also saw an escalation of rhetoric within the French press. See Charles Maier, *Recasting Bourgeois Europe: Stabilization in France, Germany and Italy in the Decade after World War I* (Princeton, NJ, 1975), 156.

29. John Turner, *British Politics and the Great War: Coalition and Conflict, 1915– 1918* (New Haven, 1992), 387; *Daily Chronicle,* 5 September 1921.

30. *Daily News,* 2 September 1921; 3 September 1921.

31. *Daily News,* 3 November 1919. In a 10 November 1924 letter to C. P. Scott (CPS 336/133), the former prime minister chided the *Manchester Guardian* editor for believing that such a fusion could still potentially be achieved.

32. *Star,* 2 March 1922.

33. CPS 336/35: Lloyd George to Scott, 14 December 1922.

34. Beatrice Webb diaries, 19 November 1923.

35. Maurice Cowling, *The Impact of Labour* (Cambridge, 1971), passim, esp. chaps. 18 and 19.

36. *Daily Mail,* 14 November 1923.

37. *Daily Chronicle,* 4 November 1922.

38. Matthew Worley, *Labour inside the Gate: A History of the British Labour Party between the Wars* (London, 2005), 150.

39. Laura Beers, "Counter-Toryism: Labour's Response to Anti-socialist Propaganda, 1918–1939," in *Foundations of the British Labour Party: Identities, Cultures, and Perspectives, 1900–1939,* ed. Matthew Worley (Farnham, Surrey, 2009), 234–235.

40. On the use of stereotypes by the American press in this period, see Walter Lippmann, *Public Opinion* (New York, 2004 [1922]), 192.

41. *Daily Express,* 24 May 1929.

42. Neil Riddell, "The Catholic Church and the Labour Party, 1918–1931," *Twentieth Century British History* 8, 2 (1997): 165–193.

43. *Times,* 2 November 1922.

44. *Daily Mail,* 11 November 1922.

45. *Daily Mail,* 20 November 1923.

46. *Daily Mail,* 25 October 1924.

47. The question over whether the publication of the letter can be considered a scoop or merely a journalistic stunt continues to be debated. While few doubt the letter to be a forgery, it remains unclear whether the *Mail*'s editor, Thomas Marlowe, knew it to be at the time. See John Ferris and Uri Bar-Joseph, "Getting Marlowe to Hold His Tongue: The Conservative Party, the Intelligence Services and the Zinoviev Letter," *Intelligence and National Security* 8, 4 (1993): 100–137.

48. See MacDonald's diary entries in David Marquand, *Ramsay MacDonald* (London, 1997), 373–377.

49. "A World Fit to Live In: The *Daily Mail* and the Middle Class, 1918–39," in *Impacts and Influences: Essays on Media Power in the Twentieth Century,* ed. James Curran, Anthony Smith, and Pauline Wingate (London, 1987), 29.

50. E. H. H. Green, "Conservatism, Anti-Socialism and the End of the Lloyd George Coalition," in *Ideologies of Conservatism: The Politics, Economics and Ideology of the British Conservative Party, 1880–1914* (Oxford, 2002), 132.

51. *Daily Mail,* 17 October 1924.

52. This line of reasoning was made explicit in several of the *Express*'s editorials, including "A Word of Warning," 23 October 1924, and "The Red Left: Vote against It All along the Line," 29 October 1924.

53. *Daily Mail,* 15 October 1924.

54. *Daily Mail,* 2 November 1922; 24 November 1923.

55. On Hugh Dalton's agent's attempts to suppress discussion of the capital levy in his campaign, see his diary entry for 20 May 1922.
56. *Daily Mail*, 25 October 1924.
57. *Daily Mail*, 15 October 1924.
58. John Ramsden, *The Age of Balfour and Baldwin, 1902–1940* (London, 1978), 203.
59. Political Poster Collection, Cambridge University Library.
60. James Thompson, "Visual Culture and the Boundaries of the Political: Revisiting the 1907 LCC Elections" (unpublished paper, Bristol University).
61. On cabinet members' response to the scandal, see Lloyd George papers, NLW 22528E, ff. 1–3: A. J. Sylvester memorandum to D. Lloyd George, 15 September 1924.
62. On posters and the interplay between conscious and subconscious, and particularly the efficacy of the subconscious connections triggered by the "It's Your Money We Want" poster, see Graham Wallas, *Human Nature in Politics* (London, 1948 [1908]), 109–110.
63. *Daily Mail*, 15 and 16 October 1924. On the coverage of "women's issues," see Bingham, *Gender, Modernity and the Popular Press*, 125.
64. *Daily Mail*, 9, 11, 13, and 15 October 1924.
65. Jon Lawrence, "Class and Gender in the Making of Urban Toryism, 1880–1914," *English Historical Review* 108, 428 (1993): 649. See also David Jarvis, "Mrs. Maggs and Betty: The Conservative Appeal to Women Voters in the 1920s," *Twentieth Century British History* 5, 2 (1994): 144–145, 149–151.
66. Jon Lawrence, "The Transformation of British Public Politics after the First World War," *Past & Present* 190 (2006): 207–208; Jarvis, "Mrs. Maggs and Betty," 145–148.
67. *Daily Express*, 24 October 1924.
68. *Daily Mail*, 25 October 1924.
69. Lawrence, "Transformation," 199.
70. For the close links between Conservative propaganda publications such as *Home and Politics* and the rhetoric of the anti-socialist press, see Jarvis, "Mrs. Maggs and Betty"; Jarvis, "British Conservatism and Class Politics in the 1920s," *English Historical Review* 111 (1996): 63–64.
71. S. J. Taylor, *Northcliffe, Rothermere and the Daily Mail* (London, 1996), 249.
72. Bernard Donoughue and G. W. Jones, *Herbert Morrison* (London, 2001), 110.
73. Robert Graves and Alan Hodge, *The Long Week-End: A Social History of Great Britain, 1918–1939* (New York, 1963), 157; Kingsley Martin, "The Influence of the Press," *Political Quarterly* 1, 2 (1930): 163.
74. Seaton and Curran, *Power without Responsibility*, 52. S. J. Taylor attributes the Labour Party's defeat primarily to the letter's publication (*Northcliffe*, 248–249). Recently, Matthew Worley has broken with the conventional wisdom and argued that the letter's publication probably had little effect on the election outcome (*Labour inside the Gate*, 81).
75. The Liberal vote fell 1.3 million between 1923 and 1924.

76. D. G. Boyce, a profound skeptic of the power of the interwar press barons, has argued that the failure of the Empire Crusaders proves the inability of the *Mail* or the *Express* to lead public opinion. See Boyce, "Crusaders without Chains: Power and the Press Barons, 1896–1951," in *Impacts and Influences,* 97–112.

77. Jon Lawrence, *Speaking for the People* (Cambridge, 1998), esp. 52–53.

78. Seaton and Curran, *Power without Responsibility,* 52–53.

79. Duncan Tanner, "Class Voting and Radical Politics: The Liberal and Labour Parties, 1910–1931," in *Party, State and Society: Electoral Behavior in Britain since 1820,* ed. Jon Lawrence and Miles Taylor (Brookfield, VT, 1997), 122.

80. Gareth Stedman Jones, "Why Is the Labour Party in a Mess?," in *Languages of Class: Studies in English Working-Class History, 1832–1982* (Cambridge, 1983), 242.

81. McKibbin, "Class and Conventional Wisdom."

82. Gareth Stedman Jones, "Rethinking Chartism," in *Languages of Class,* 107.

4. Changing Attitudes in the 1920s

1. W. W. Henderson, "The Press and Labour," *Labour Organiser,* April 1922, 7.

2. H. H. Fyfe, "The Poison Gas Press," *Labour Magazine,* January 1924, 397; Beatrice Webb diaries, 2 June 1924.

3. On the Fabian strategy of "permeation," see R. C. K. Ensor, "Permeation," in *The Webbs and Their Work,* ed. Margaret Cole (London, 1974), 57–71.

4. The Conservative politician Lord Elton complained to Reith in 1935 that BBC debates invariably featured "four or five advocates of change, of one brand or another, against one defender of the status quo." BBC WAC R/71/1: Elton to Reith, 24 September 1935.

5. *Report of the Trades Union Congress (TUC)* (1869), 206–212. See also Deian Hopkin, "The Socialist Press in Britain, 1890–1910," in *Newspaper History from the Seventeenth Century to the Present Day,* ed. George Boyce, James Curran, and Pauline Wingate (London, 1978), 294.

6. Upton Sinclair, *The Brass Check: A Study of American Journalism* (Urbana, IL, 2003 [1919]), 224, 282.

7. Hilaire Belloc, *The Free Press* (London, 1918), 18.

8. Kingsley Martin, *The British Public and the General Strike* (London, 1926), 50–51; emphasis in original.

9. Walter Lippmann, *Public Opinion* (Mineola, NY, 2004 [1922]), 186–187.

10. Ibid., 188.

11. Northcliffe papers, Add 62216, vol. LCIV: Angell to Northcliffe, 15 May 1911.

12. Norman Angell, *The Press and the Organisation of Society* (London, 1922), 1, 17, 51–52.

13. A. J. Cummings, *The Press and a Changing Civilisation* (London, 1936), 41.

14. Angell, *The Press,* 38. This view of the incompatibility of press ownership and political leftism was still popular forty-five years later. See Ian

Waller, "The Left-Wing Press," in *The Left*, ed. Gerald Kaufman (London, 1966), 79.

15. Gordon Hosking, "Labour and Advertising," *Labour Organiser*, July 1924; Gerald Gould, "Labour and the Press," *Labour Magazine*, July 1923; emphasis in original; H. M. Richardson, "The Press Problem," *Labour Magazine*, July 1923, 102–103; Herbert Tracey, "The Newspaper Trust and Freedom of the Press," *Labour Organiser*, November 1926, 180. See also Hamilton Fyfe, "The Poison-Gas Press," *Labour Magazine*, January 1924, 397–399; LPA LP/DH: *Daily Herald* circular, 21 November 1921.

16. George Orwell, "A Farthing Newspaper," *G.K.'s Weekly*, 29 December 1928.

17. Resolution tabled by the Hammersmith North LP, *LPAC Report* (1925), 277. The resolution was not ultimately put to a vote.

18. *LPAC Report* (1926), 209.

19. *Daily Express*, 15 April 1929. For Wilkinson's enthusiasm for publicity, see Ellen Wilkinson, "Ways of Winning the Women," *Daily Herald*, 3 October 1928.

20. Ellen Wilkinson, *Peeps at Politicians* (London, 1930), 5.

21. W. W. Henderson, "The Press and Labour," *Labour Organiser*, April 1922; LPA LP/DH: Circular to trade unionists from the *Daily Herald* Trade Union Committee, 20 January 1920.

22. "Shall We Canvass?" *Labour Organiser*, March 1922, 8.

23. Fyfe, "The Poison-Gas Press," 398.

24. *Daily Herald*, 24 December 1919.

25. *Report of the TUC* (1869), 206.

26. *Daily Herald*, 5 January 1920.

27. Ibid.

28. *Daily Herald*, 4 March 1922.

29. E.g., "Mod.-Progs. Flounder in Local Currents," *Daily Herald*, 1 March 1922.

30. *Star*, 2 March 1922. By 1928, however, the *Star* was no longer encouraging voters to "return sound, sane, and thoughtful Labour candidates" in "constituencies where there are no Progressives in the field."

31. Fyfe, "Poison-Gas Press," 398.

32. *Daily Express*, 5 December 1923.

33. *Daily Express*, 14 October 1924.

34. *Daily Express*, 26 April 1929.

35. The use of film was discussed by the NEC in 1918 (17 April, 10 July), in 1919–1920 (7 October, 11 November, 9 February, 18 March), and again in 1928 (25 June, 25 September). On unofficial experiments with film by groups sympathetic to the Labour movement, see Stephen Jones, *The British Labour Movement and Film, 1918–1939* (London, 1987).

36. The British Broadcasting Company's initial charter from the Post Office listed "Lectures" and "Education" second and third, respectively, in its catalogue of permissible broadcast content, Cmd. 1882 (1922).

37. BBC WAC R4/27/1: John Reith, Memorandum to the Crawford Committee on Broadcasting, 1925. On this same theme, see also BBC WAC R4/87/1:

John Reith, Oral evidence before the Ullswater Committee on Broadcasting, 8 May 1935; and John Reith, *Broadcast over Britain* (London, 1924).

38. Reith, *Broadcast over Britain,* 113; Memorandum to the Crawford Committee.

39. House of Commons, 24 April 1923, *Parliamentary Debates,* 5th series, vol. 163, cols. 300–301; BBC WAC R34/137/2: The Broadcasting of Controversial Matters (excluding religious broadcasts): History and Present Practice, undated internal BBC memorandum, item 4.

40. House of Commons, 24 April 1923, *Parliamentary Debates,* 5th series, vol. 163, cols. 300–301; House of Commons, 15 May 1923, *Parliamentary Debates,* 5th series, vol. 164, col. 238.

41. BBC WAC R4/64/2: Sykes Committee: Minutes of Third Meeting, 8 May 1923, Sir William Noble and Mr. A. M. McKinstry of the BBC giving evidence.

42. Asa Briggs, *The History of Broadcasting in the United Kingdom,* vol. 1, *The Birth of Broadcasting* (London, 1961), 175. Morrison testified before the committee in his capacity as leader of the LLP.

43. BBC WAC: Report of the Broadcasting Committee, 1923 (Sykes Committee), Cmd. 1951, 39.

44. House of Commons, 11 July 1924, *Parliamentary Debates,* 5th series, vol. 175, col. 2632.

45. BBC WAC R34/534/1: Westin to Reith, 19 August 1924; Reith to Brown, 3 October 1924.

46. Briggs, *Birth of Broadcasting,* 269.

47. Ibid., 271.

48. John Reith, *Into the Wind* (London, 1949), 96; Briggs, *Birth of Broadcasting,* 271.

49. Sian Nicholas, "The Construction of a National Identity: Stanley Baldwin, 'Englishness' and the Mass Media in Inter-War Britain," in *The Conservatives and British Society* (Cardiff, 1996), 127–146; Philip Williamson, *Stanley Baldwin: Conservative Leadership and National Values* (New York, 1999), chap. 3.

50. John Reith diary, 13 February 1929.

5. The Labour Alternative

1. J. Ramsay MacDonald, *A Policy for the Labour Party* (London, 1920), 75.

2. Ibid., 60.

3. Stuart MacIntyre, "British Labour, Marxism and Working-Class Apathy in the Nineteen Twenties," *Historical Journal* 20, 2 (1977): 479–496; MacDonald, *A Policy for the Labour Party,* chap. 4.

4. Walter Bagehot, *The English Constitution,* 2nd ed. (New York, 1961 [1872]), 20–21.

5. Graham Wallas, *Human Nature in Politics* (London, 1948 [1908]), 173–174.

6. H. C. G. Matthew, R. I. McKibbin, and J. A. Kay, "The Franchise Factor and the Rise of the Labour Party," *English Historical Review* 91 (1976): 748–749.

7. H. C. G. Matthew, "Gladstone, Rhetoric and Politics," in *Politics and Social Change in Britain: Essays Presented to A. F. Thompson,* ed. P. J. Waller (Brighton, 1987), 54, 56.

8. Quoted in Philip Williamson, *Stanley Baldwin: Conservative Leadership and National Values* (New York, 1999), 145, 147.

9. Jon Lawrence, *Speaking for the People* (Cambridge, 1998), 223–225; James Thompson, "'Pictorial Lies?'—Posters and Politics in Britain, c. 1880–1914," *Past and Present* 197 (November 2007): 177–210.

10. E. H. H. Green, "Radical Conservatism: The Electoral Genesis of Tariff Reform," *Historical Journal* 28, 3 (September 1985): 667–692; E. H. H. Green, *Crisis of Conservatism,* esp. 242–265; David Jarvis, "British Conservatism and Class Politics in the 1920s," *English Historical Review* 111 (1996): 58–84; Jon Lawrence, *Speaking for the People: Party, Language and Popular Politics in England, 1867–1914* (Cambridge, 1998); Martin Pugh, *The Tories and the People* (Oxford, 1985); John Ramsden, *The Age of Balfour and Baldwin, 1902–1940* (New York, 1978).

11. Response to the survey, "The Equipment of the Workers," conducted by the St. Philip's Settlement Education and Economics Research Society, Sheffield. Cited in Charles Masterman, *England after War* (London, 1922), 112.

12. Walter Citrine, *Men and Work* (London, 1964), 37.

13. Alan Bullock, *The Life and Times of Ernest Bevin,* vol. 1 (London, 1960), 15–23.

14. Ernest Bevin, *Daily Herald,* 5 December 1919.

15. Sandra Stanley Holton, *Feminism and Democracy: Women's Suffrage and Reform Politics in Britain, 1900–1918* (Cambridge, 1986), chap. 4.

16. Jon Lawrence, "Labour—The Myths It Has Lived By," in *Labour's First Century,* ed. Duncan Tanner, Pat Thane, and Nick Tiratsoo (Cambridge, 2000), 344–347.

17. While it is arguable that the 1884 act did not enfranchise a large enough percentage of the working class to make class politics a viable option in the Edwardian period (Matthew, McKibbin, and Jay, "The Franchise Factor"), the facts of interwar electoral politics do not bear out the argument that 1918 led to the rise of class-conscious voting.

18. Jarvis, "British Conservatism," 64, 80.

19. Bevin, *Daily Herald,* 5 December 1919.

20. Stuart MacIntyre, *A Proletarian Science: Marxism in Britain, 1917–1933* (Cambridge, 1980), 206; Ernest Bevin, *Daily Herald,* 1 December 1919.

21. For a review of this literature, see D. L. LeMahieu, *A Culture for Democracy: Mass Communication and the Cultivated Mind in Britain between the Wars* (Oxford, 1988), 107–109, and Mark Hampton, *Visions of the Press in Britain, 1850–1950* (Urbana, IL, 2004), 136–137.

22. Even skeptics about the power of propaganda such as A. J. Cummings [*The Press and a Changing Civilisation* (London, 1936), 20–32] admitted the power of propaganda in influencing public opinion during the war.

23. MacDonald, *A Policy for the Labour Party,* 67.

24. Ibid., 62, 53.

25. Quoted in Timothy Hollins, "The Politics of Presentation" (PhD thesis, University of Leeds, 1981), 1: 128, 131. For a laundry list of other similar remarks, especially by MacDonald, see MacIntyre, "British Labour," 481–483.

26. MacDonald, *A Policy for the Labour Party*, 36.

27. Norman Angell, "Commercialisation of Demagoguery," *The Nation*, October 20, 1923, quoted in Hampton, *Visions of the Press*, 152.

28. Quoted in MacIntyre, "British Labour," 485.

29. Norman Angell, *The Press and the Organisation of Society* (London, 1922), 68. See also George Orwell, "Boys' Weeklies," in *Essays*, ed. John Carey (New York, 2002), 185–210.

30. NEC, *Annual Report* (1904), 21.

31. MacIntyre, "British Labour," 483.

32. Walter Lippmann, *Public Opinion* (Mineola, NY, 2004 [1922]), 180.

33. Angell, *The Press*, 102, 119–120.

34. LPA LP/DH/248.1: PKTF report, undated, early October 1923; emphasis added.

35. TUC MSS 292/790/4: Allen memorandum to DH board, September 1925.

36. RMD 1/7/2: MacDonald to Allen, 27 November 1925.

37. RMD 1/7/3: MacDonald to Fyfe, 17 December 1924.

38. *Report of the TUC* (1923), 211ff.

39. The party gave up its stake in the paper in early 1926 for financial reasons. By this point, it had contributed £36,000 to the *Herald*. See "The Labour Party," unsigned memo, n.d. (October[?] 1929), filed in NEC minutes.

40. TUC MSS 292/790.1/1: Report of the *Daily Herald* Board of Directors to the General Council of the TUC and the NEC, 22 February 1927.

41. See, e.g., George Lansbury to party conference, *Labour Party Annual Conference (LPAC) Report* (1924), 174.

42. The decline in trade union members in the 1920s and the "contracting-in" clause of the 1927 Trade Union and Trade Disputes Bill combined to weaken the Labour movement financially, particularly the party, which divested itself of its shares in the *Herald* in early 1926. The TUC continued to subsidize the *Herald*, though it was forced to reduce the size of its subvention. See *Report of the TUC* (1928), 494ff.

43. Undated leaflet, John Johnson Collection, Bodleian Library, Oxford.

44. Philip Snowden, "Why Labour Papers Fail," *Sell's World Press* (1919), quoted in Huw Richards, *The Bloody Circus: The Daily Herald and the Left* (London, 1997), 23.

45. LPA LP/DH: Fyfe, "Remarks on the Report of the PKTF Committee," 15 October 1923.

46. Ross McKibbin, *The Evolution of the Labour Party, 1910–1924* (Oxford, 1974), 231–234.

47. Richards, *Bloody Circus*, 76. The Sugar Subsidy Bill was the page 2 story on 19 March 1925.

48. TUC MSS 292/790/4: Ernest Bevin, memorandum on the *Daily Herald*, 15–25 September 1925.

49. McKibbin, *Evolution*, 125.
50. In 1913, Henderson had resigned from the board of the party's earlier, short-lived newspaper, the *Daily Citizen*, when the paper hired a tipster. See NEC minutes, 15 July 1913. For Lansbury's views on horse racing, see Richards, *Bloody Circus*, 43.
51. McKibbin, *Evolution*, 222.
52. Typescript minutes of conference, in TUC MSS 292/790/4.
53. *Daily Mail*, 9 September 1919, 2.
54. Richards, *Bloody Circus*, 30.
55. TUC MSS 292/790/4: Herbert Morrison to Robert Williams, 30 July 1925.
56. *Wipers Times*, 26 February 1919. Reprinted in *The Wipers Times: The Complete Series of the Famous Wartime Trench Newspaper* (London, 2008), 18.
57. TUC MSS 292/790.1/1: Report of the Board of Directors of the VHPC, 22 February 1927.
58. Henry Hamilton Fyfe, *Sixty Years of Fleet Street* (London, 1949), 170.
59. LPA LP/DH: Fyfe, Reply to questionnaire presented by the Editorial Subcommittee, December 1925; TUC MSS 290/790.1/1: Report of the Directors of the VHPC, 22 February 1927.
60. TUC MSS 290/790.1/1: Report of the *Daily Herald* Directors, 22 March 1927.
61. H. Hamilton Fyfe, "A Nice Bit o' Reading," *London Labour Chronicle*, no. 87, January 1923, 7.
62. *LPAC Report* (1927), 211–212.
63. Adrian Bingham, *Gender, Modernity and the Popular Press in Interwar Britain* (Oxford, 2004), 101.
64. Ibid., 43.
65. Ibid., appendix. Bingham's content analysis of women's pages in May 1927 found that 39 percent of the *Mail*, 45 percent of the *Express*, 46 percent of the *News*, 82 percent of the *Mirror*, and only 24 percent of the *Herald* was devoted to fashion.
66. *Report of the TUC* (1927), 399.
67. TUC MSS 292/790/1: J. Atcheson Barrow, *Daily Herald* circulation manager, to Fred Bramley, 31 August 1922; LPA LP/DH/402: Daily Herald circular, January 1925.
68. LPA LP/DH: Henderson et al. circular, 23 November 1923.
69. MacIntyre, "British Labour," 487.
70. TUC MSS 292/790/5: Both cartoons were reproduced in the 1924 *Daily Herald Souvenir Book*.
71. Allen memorandum; LPA LP/DH: Walker memorandum to *Daily Herald* board, 22 September 1925.
72. Duncan Tanner, "Class Voting and Radical Politics: The Liberal and Labour Parties, 1910–1931," in *Party, State and Society: Electoral Behavior in Britain since 1820*, ed. Jon Lawrence and Miles Taylor (Brookfield, VT, 1997), 109.
73. LPA Labour Party leaflets Nos. 15/11/25, 60/11/23, 16/11/23, 194/3/27.

74. Bullock, *Ernest Bevin,* vol. 1, 424.
75. Bevin, *Daily Herald,* 1 December 1919.

6. Battling for Public Opinion

1. Ramsay MacDonald to special conference of trade union executives, 1 May 1926. Quoted in Robert Page Arnot, *The General Strike, May 1926: Its Origins and History* (London, 1926), 138.
2. The Samuel Report, issued in March 1926, was the product of the Royal Commission on the Mining Industry appointed by Baldwin in 1925 and chaired by Sir Herbert Samuel. While the report accepted the need for a cut in wages, it also recommended an enforced reorganization of the industry, though its recommendations fell short of nationalization.
3. Beatrice and Sidney Webb, *The History of Trade Unionism in Britain* (London, 1920), 399–404; James Thompson, "The Idea of 'Public Opinion' in Britain" (PhD thesis, Cambridge University, 1999), 323–335.
4. Eric Wigham, *Strikes and the Government, 1893–1974* (London, 1976), 21.
5. Chris Howell, *Trade Unions and the State: The Construction of Industrial Relations Institutions in Britain, 1890–2000* (Princeton, NJ, 2005), chap. 3; James Thompson, "The Genesis of the 1906 Trades Disputes Act," *Twentieth-Century British History* 9, 2 (1998): 175–200.
6. Georges Sorel, *Reflections on Violence,* ed. Jeremy Jennings (Cambridge, 1999), 161.
7. Quoted in the *British Gazette,* 5 May 1926.
8. *British Worker,* 5 May 1926.
9. Churchill to Geoffrey Dawson, quoted in Martin Gilbert, *Winston S. Churchill,* vol. 5 (London, 1976), 165.
10. In succeeding years, Baldwin continued to refer to the strike as the "tragedy of 1926." See, e.g., party election broadcast, 22 April 1929, reprinted in *The Listener,* 1 May 1929, 614.
11. Stanley Baldwin, BBC broadcast, 8 May 1926. Reported in Arnot, *The General Strike,* 194–195.
12. Philip Williamson, *Stanley Baldwin: Conservative Leadership and National Values* (Cambridge, 1999), 241.
13. Julian Symons, *The General Strike* (London, 1957), 155; Anne Perkins, *A Very British Strike* (London, 2006).
14. Recollection of Cambridge undergraduate, quoted in Symons, *The General Strike,* 68.
15. BBC news bulletin, 13 May 1926, 10 AM. Reprinted in Arnot, *The General Strike,* 232.
16. Laura Beers, "Is This Man an Anarchist? Industrial Action and the Battle for Public Opinion in Interwar Britain," *Journal of Modern History* 82, 1 (forthcoming).
17. It is unclear when the General Council made the decision to call out the printers. The decision was clearly taken before the second meeting of the

publicity committee at 4 PM on 3 May. TUCL General Strike files, TUC Internal Organization: Decisions Taken by Various Committees and General Council since 1 May 1926.

18. *Daily Mail*, 4 May 1926.
19. For an explanation of the incident, see RMD 14/4/37: George Isaacs, Secretary, London Society of Compositors, to Ramsay MacDonald, 3 May 1926.
20. Gilbert, *Churchill*, vol. 5, 150; Symons, *The General Strike*, 59.
21. Patrick Hannan, *When Arthur Met Maggie* (Bridgend, Wales, 2006), 90.
22. Lloyd George, House of Commons, 5 May 1926, *Parliamentary Debates*, 5th series, vol. 195, col. 311.
23. Wadsworth papers A/M7/7a: telegram 3 May 1926, 11:30 AM, C. P. Scott to J. R. MacDonald.
24. *New Statesman*, 8 May 1926.
25. TUCL General Strike files, Milne-Bailey, "Nation on Strike," chap. 13.
26. *Daily Herald*, 24 December 1919.
27. TUCL General Strike files, G.C. 14/3/1925–26: Report of the Publicity Committee to the General Council, re the General Strike, 1926.
28. J. C. C. Davidson, *Memoirs of a Conservative*, ed. R. R. James (London, 1969), 247–248.
29. TUCL General Strike files, G.C. 14/3/1925–26: Report of the Publicity Committee.
30. Ibid.
31. TUC MSS 292/252.62/12: Minutes of the Publicity and Communications Sub-committee, 4 May 1926; TUCL General Strike files, S. R. Marlin to General Council, 5 May 1926.
32. TUC MSS 292/252.62/12: Minutes of TUC Publicity Committee, 7 PM, 4 May 1926.
33. The government arranged to print the British Gazette from the *Morning Post's* offices. See HO 45/12431: J. C. C. Davidson, "Government News Service, Report of the Deputy Chief Civil Commissioner," 24 June 1926. (This document was exempted from the thirty-year rule and remained sealed until 1977.)
34. CPS 336/169: W. Joynson-Hicks to C. P. Scott, 8 May 1926.
35. H. Hamilton Fyfe, *Behind the Scenes of the Great Strike* (London, 1926), 25.
36. TUC MSS 292/252.62/12: Minutes of TUC Publicity Committee, 4 May 1926, 7 PM.
37. Ibid. Emphasis added.
38. RMD/1/4/16: Roy Hopkins to J. R. MacDonald, 7 May 1926.
39. Davidson, "Government News Service, Report of the Deputy Chief Civil Commissioner."
40. *British Gazette*, 5 May 1926.
41. Quoted in Patrick Renshaw, *Nine Days in May* (London, 1975), 194; quoted in Gilbert, *Churchill*, vol. 5, 161; Symons, *The General Strike*, 150.
42. Churchill to House of Commons, 7 July 1926. Quoted in Gilbert, *Churchill*, vol. 5, 174.
43. *British Worker*, 5 May 1926.

44. Kingsley Martin, *The British Public and the General Strike* (London, 1926), 89.

45. On Cabinet opinion on the *Gazette*, see Cuthbert Headlam, *The Headlam Diaries, 1923–1935,* ed. Stuart Ball (London, 1992), 87.

46. The Manchester edition of the paper, established on 10 May, never produced more than 100,000 copies, and other regional editions, printed in South Wales and in Glasgow (as the *Scottish Worker*), showed even smaller print runs. Figures from Gordon Phillips, *The General Strike: The Politics of Industrial Conflict* (London, 1976), 175, 177.

47. CPS 256/24/1: Confidential Memo: *Manchester Evening News* and the General Strike.

48. Martin, *The British Public,* 65; Phillips, *General Strike,* 139.

49. E.g., "Our Duty," *Times,* 6 May 1926.

50. TUC MSS 292/252.62/12: Minutes of TUC Publicity Committee, item 49, 6 May, 11 AM.

51. Margaret Cole, "The Labour Movement between the Wars," in *Ideology and the Labour Movement: Essays Presented to John Saville,* ed. D. E. Martin and D. Rubenstein (London, 1979), 209.

52. TUC MSS 292/252.62/12: Minutes of TUC Publicity Committee, May 6, 11 AM.

53. CPS 256/24/1: Confidential Memo: *Manchester Evening News* and the General Strike; *Times,* 11 May 1926.

54. Fyfe, *Behind the Scenes,* 54.

55. Ibid., 29.

56. BBC WAC CO/34: Reith, "The BBC and the Emergency," 6 May 1926.

57. BBC WAC CO/34: Reith, report to the Board of Directors, 18 May 1926.

58. Davidson, "Government News Service, Report of the Deputy Chief Civil Commissioner."

59. Ibid.

60. LAB/2/1820/CEB449/3/1926: BBC Bulletins during the General Strike.

61. William Bridgeman, *Diaries and Letters,* ed. Philip Williamson (London, 1988), 197.

62. Reith diary, 7 May 1926.

63. Draft broadcast script, included in RMD/1/4/10: MacDonald to Reith, 10 May 1926.

64. Reith diary, 10 May 1926.

65. RMD/1/4/12: Reith to MacDonald, 14 May 1926; RMD1/4/14: MacDonald to Reith, 17 May 1926.

66. Reith diary, 10 May 1926.

67. TUCL General Strike files, G.C. 14/3/1925–26: Report of the Publicity Committee.

68. Reith Diary, 7 May 1926.

69. Asa Briggs, *The Birth of Broadcasting* (London, 1962), 363ff; Symons, *General Strike,* 175; Paddy Scannell and David Cardiff, *A Social History of British Broadcasting,* vol. 1 (London, 1991), 33.

70. Renshaw, *Nine Days,* 207 and passim. On the biases of the interwar BBC more broadly, see Tom Stannage, *Baldwin Thwarts the Opposition* (London, 1980), 182–183; and Jean Seaton and Ben Pimlott, "The Struggle for 'Balance,' " in *The Media in British Politics* (Aldershot, Eng., 1987), 134.

71. "Our Duty," *Times,* 6 May 1926.

72. TUC membership fell significantly in the years after the strike, and did not regain its 1926 level until 1937. For figures, see Henry Pelling, *A History of British Trade Unionism,* 5th ed. (London, 1992), 325.

73. James Cronin, *Industrial Conflict in Modern Britain* (London, 1979), 129.

7. Rapprochement with the Media

1. TUC MSS 292/252.62/4: W. Milne-Bailey, "Chief Criticisms of the General Strike," n.d. (June? 1926).

2. Kingsley Martin, *The British Public and the General Strike* (London, 1926), 89.

3. B. J. Boothroyd, "The How and Why of the Strike," *New Leader,* 12 May 1926, 6.

4. H. N. Brailsford, "The Inner History of the Great Strike: Nine Days That Shook the General Council," *New Leader,* 12 May 1926, 4.

5. TUCL General Strike papers, G.C. 14/3/1925–26.

6. Ibid.

7. Martin, *The British Public,* 65; Beatrice Webb diaries, 4 May 1926; Walter Citrine, *Men and Work* (London, 1964), 267, 269; RMD 1/4/4: MacDonald to Reith, 17 May 1926; Alan Bullock, *Ernest Bevin: Trade Union Leader* (London, 1960), 320; J. C. C. Davidson, *Memoirs of a Conservative,* ed. Robert Rhodes James (London, 1969), 233; Leo Amery, *The Leo Amery Diaries,* vol. 1, *1896–1929,* ed. John Barnes and David Nicholson (London, 1980), 454; BBC WAC Reith diary, 17 May 1926.

8. RMD 1/4/14: MacDonald to Reith, 17 May 1926; BBC WAC CO/28: Ellen Wilkinson, letter published in *Radio Times,* 28 May 1926; Reith diary, 18 May 1926; TUC MSS 292/787.18/2: J. Bromley to J. H. Whitley and John Reith, 7 June 1932. The issue came up again four years later when Citrine and Arthur Greenwood testified before the BBC charter review committee. See BBC WAC R4/87/10, Folio T: Oral Evidence to the Ullswater Committee; R4/77/8: Written Evidence to the Ullswater Committee, National Council of Labour: Precis of Evidence.

9. CPA CCO 4/1/22: Davidson to Baldwin, 24 May 1928.

10. Jean Seaton and Ben Pimlott, "The Struggle for 'Balance,' " in *The Media in British Politics* (Aldershot, Eng., 1987), 134.

11. Sidney Webb, "Stratified Electioneering," *Labour Organiser,* December 1922.

12. TUCL General Strike papers, W. Milne-Bailey, "A Nation on Strike" (unpublished book manuscript, September 1926), chap. 13.

13. George Lansbury to Party Conference, *Labour Party Annual Conference (LPAC) Report* (1924), 174.

14. W. Herron (Chorley DLP) to Party Conference, *LPAC Report* (1926), 209.

15. C. T. Cramp to Party Conference, *LPAC Report* (1927), 211. For his earlier hostility to the "capitalist press" see C. T. Cramp, "Labour and the Press," *Daily Herald,* 10 October 1919.

16. Herbert Morrison, "Labour and the Middle Class, Part VI," *London Labour Chronicle,* no. 95, September 1923.

17. W. J. Brown, "Labour and the Middle Class, Part III," *London Labour Chronicle,* no. 88, February 1923.

18. Advertisements taken out by the mine owners can be found in the *Times,* 3 March, 8 March, and 18 March 1920.

19. NEC, *Annual Report* (1927), 70–71; TUC General Council, *Annual Report* (1927), 256–258.

20. *Daily Mail,* 6 April 1927. The exception was Herbert Morrison's letter to the editor in the *Daily News,* 16 May 1927.

21. "A Warning for the B.B.C. and a Method for Dealing with the Press," *Labour Organiser,* December 1931, 229.

22. *Labour Organiser,* July 1928, 131; October 1935, 195; Harold Croft, *Conduct of Parliamentary Elections* (London, 1945), 32.

23. TUC General Council, *Annual Report* (1934), 186.

24. Hugh Chevins, "The Man Who Couldn't Be a Bore," in *The Great Bohunkus: Tributes to Ian Mackay,* ed. Trevor Evans (London, 1953), 119.

25. NEC, *Annual Report* (1928), 47; *Annual Report* (1929), 51. On the Conservatives, see John Ramsden, *The Age of Balfour and Baldwin, 1902–1940* (London, 1978), 234; Richard Cockett, "The Conservative Party, Press and Publicity," in *Conservative Century,* ed. Anthony Seldon and Stuart Ball (Oxford, 1994), 547–577.

26. E.g., Philip Snowden, *Daily Express,* 2 April 1929. Wilkinson's sketches were later published as *Peeps at Politicians* (London, 1930).

27. Herbert Morrison papers, G. W. Jones interview with James Griffiths, MP, 12 January 1968.

28. Herbert Morrison papers, G. W. Jones interview with David Keir, 24 March 1969.

29. Dalton diary, 29 October 1935; Hugh Cudlipp, *Publish and Be Damned!* (London, 1953), 140.

30. Layton was said to have played a prominent role in the LLPs election campaigns in the 1930s; Herbert Morrison papers, Griffiths interview.

31. Tom Jeffrey, "The Suburban Nation: Politics and Class in Lewisham," in *Metropolis/London,* ed. David Feldman and Gareth Stedman Jones (London, 1989), 189–218.

32. Morrison's impact was also felt on local party organization outside of London. See Duncan Tanner, "Labour and Its Membership," in *Labour's First Century,* ed. Duncan Tanner, Pat Thane, and Nick Tiratsoo (Cambridge, 2000), 251.

33. Duncan Tanner, "Class Voting and Radical Politics: The Liberal and Labour Parties, 1910–1931," in *Party, State and Society: Electoral Behavior in Britain since 1820,* ed. Jon Lawrence and Miles Taylor (Brookfield, VT, 1997), 124.

34. For contemporary Liberal expositions of this view see, e.g., CPS 336/135: Walter Crozier to C. P. Scott, 11 November 1924; *Manchester Guardian,* 10 January 1910; *Daily News,* 5 January 1920. Lord Rothermere, whose papers railed vocally against three-cornered contests in both 1924 and 1929, was a staunch advocate of this view. See, e.g., Rothermere, "Fight the Socialists: Unity Essential to Win," *Daily Mail,* 11 April 1929.

35. Lloyd George, party election broadcast (PEB), 19 April 1929, reprinted in *The Listener,* 24 April 1929, 570.

36. Quoted in Philip Williamson, *National Crisis and National Government: British Politics, the Economy and Empire, 1926–1932* (Cambridge, 1992), 126–127.

37. Snowden, PEB, 3 May 1929, reprinted in *The Listener,* 8 May 1929, 656.

38. Tanner, "Class Voting," 120.

39. Iain Dale, ed., *Labour Party General Election Manifestos, 1900–1997* (London, 2000), 32.

40. Labour Party poster no. 1, 1929 general election, political poster collection, Cambridge University Library.

41. *Daily Mail,* 30 April 1929. For sales figures, see NEC, *Annual Report* (1929), 74.

42. *Daily Express,* 27 May 1929.

43. *Daily Herald,* 13, 14, 17, and 23 May 1929.

44. On benefits to the petty-bourgeoisie: *Daily Herald,* 1, 6, and 21 May 1929; on municipal achievements: *Daily Herald,* 14, 15, and 16 May 1929; on the General Strike: *Daily Herald,* 11, 13, 14, and 15 May 1929; on Baldwin: *Daily Herald,* 9 and 18 May 1929.

45. On Cardinal Bourne: *Daily Herald,* 14, 15, 23, 24, and 25 May 1929; on general "dirty tricks": *Daily Herald,* 18, 23, 24, and 28 May 1929.

46. See, e.g., editorial, *Daily Herald,* 15 and 21 May 1929; Snowden and Henderson, PEBs, reprinted in *The Listener,* 8 May 1929, and 17 April 1929; *Daily Herald,* 9 May 1929.

47. Arthur Henderson, PEB, 11 April 1929, reprinted in *The Listener,* 17 April 1929, 526.

48. Maurice Cowling, *The Impact of Labour* (Cambridge, 1971), chap. 18; John Ramsden, *The Age of Balfour and Baldwin,* 200–203, passim; Stuart Ball, "Democracy and the Rise of Labour," in *Recovering Power: The Conservatives in Opposition since 1867* (London, 2005), 134–168, esp. 141.

49. Tanner, "Class Voting," 122; Philip Snowden, PEB, 3 May 1929, reprinted in *The Listener,* 8 May 1929, 656.

50. J. Ramsay MacDonald, *Daily Mail,* 14 May 1929; Philip Snowden, *Daily Mail,* 16 May 1929; J. H. Thomas, *Daily Mail,* 18 May 1929; *Daily Mail,* 23 May 1929.

51. LPA, LP/DH: *Daily Herald* circular, 21 November 1921.

52. CPA CCO/4/1/22: Reith to JCC Davidson, 9 April 1929.

53. Letter to the editor, *Daily Express,* 6 May 1929; *Daily Express,* 4 May 1929; Asa Briggs, *The History of Broadcasting in the United Kingdom,* vol. 2, *The Golden Age of Wireless* (London, 1965), 135.

54. Adrian Bingham, "Stop the Flapper Vote Folly: Lord Rothermere, the *Daily Mail*, and the Equalization of the Franchise, 1927–28," *Twentieth Century British History* 13, 1 (2002): 17–37.

55. Margaret Bondfield, PEB, reported in *The Listener*, 22 May 1929, 735–736.

56. H. H. Fyfe to Party Conference, *LPAC Report* (1924), 176.

57. LPA LP/DH: Allen memo, September 1925.

58. LPA, LP/DH: Fyfe to subcommittee, December 1925.

59. *Daily Herald*, 8 February 1926.

60. *Daily Herald*, 9 February 1926.

61. Ben Turner, *Report of the Trades Union Congress (TUC)* (1926), 454. Turner edited the *Labour Pioneer*, the journal of the general union of textile workers, from 1919 to 1926. See Chris Wrigley, "Turner, Sir Ben (1863–1942)," *Oxford Dictionary of National Biography*, ed. H. C. G. Matthew and Brian Harrison (Oxford, 2004), CD-ROM edition.

62. Huw Richards, *The Bloody Circus: The Daily Herald and the Left* (London, 1997), 100.

63. H. Eastwood to Party Conference, *LPAC Report* (1926), 210. See also LPA LP/DH: William Mellor to *Daily Herald* board, 31 August 1928.

64. TUC MSS 292/790.1/1: Report of the Board of Directors of the Victoria House Printing Company (VHPC) to the TUC General Council the Labour Party NEC, 26 June 1928.

65. *Newspaper World*, 10 January 1914.

66. TUC MSS 292/790.1/1: Report of the Directors of the VHPC, 18 February 1928.

67. A 1929 *Daily Herald* advertising leaflet quoted MacDonald denouncing the "baits of insurance policies and such like" used by the capitalist press (TUC MSS 292/790/5).

68. Lansbury to Party Conference, *LPAC Report* (1924), 174.

69. Labour Party, *The Speakers' Handbook* (London, 1922), 120, and Lansbury to Party Conference, *LPAC Report* (1924), 174; TUC MSS 292/790/4: Fyfe and Lansbury to Citrine, 8 August 1924.

70. H. H. Fyfe to Party Conference, *LPAC Report* (1924), 177; TUC General Council, *Annual Report* (1932), Item 202.

71. TUC MSS 292/790/1: Report of the Board of Directors of the *Daily Herald*, 1927, for inclusion in the General Council's annual report, 1 August 1927.

72. TUC report (1927), 399.

73. TUC report (1928), 494.

74. Ibid., 497, 501.

75. The Manchester edition was launched on 7 July 1930.

76. TUC MSS 292/790/1: Arthur Pugh and Walter Citrine, *Daily Herald* circular, 13 February 1926.

77. *The Helper*, no. 2, 18 June 1930.

78. With characteristic good form, Beaverbrook wrote to the publisher of Odhams Press, J. S. Elias (later Lord Southwood), to "congratulate you on your triumphant success. There is no stopping your progress" (BBK C/229: Beaverbrook to Elias, 30 November 1933).

79. TUC MSS 292/790/1: The letter was forwarded to Citrine by G. D. Eusden of the Edmonton Trades Council, 20 October 1933.
80. Memo from Mr. Kneeshaw to the annual consultation of organizing staff held in connection with the annual Party Conference, 10 October 1930 (filed in NEC minutes).
81. TUC MSS 292/790/6: "Notes re. Daily Herald," unsigned memo, undated (late 1930); TUC MSS 292/790/1: *Daily Herald* internal survey, July 1938.
82. *Daily Express*, 30 September 1932; emphasis in original.
83. TUC MSS 292/790.6: Undated leaflet, January/February 1931.
84. TUC MSS 292/790.1/3: Pugh to Citrine, 18 January 1934.
85. *Labour Organiser,* April 1932, 60.
86. Bevin to Congress, *Report of the TUC* (1930), 369.
87. The National Government, a coalition of Labour, Liberal, and Conservative MPs with MacDonald still acting as prime minister, was formed in August 1931 as a result of the political deadlock over the destabilization of the economy.

8. Experimenting in the 1930s

1. Forty-six NEC sponsored MPs; three ILPers, and three Independent Labour MPs.
2. Stephen Jones, *The British Labour Movement and Film, 1918–1939* (London, 1987), 47; Lawrence Black, *The Political Culture of the Left in Affluent Britain, 1951–64: Old Labour, New Britain?* (Basingstoke, 2003), 104, 110, 122, passim.
3. F. R. Leavis's *Mass Civilization and Minority Culture* (London, 1930) and Q. D. Leavis's *Fiction and the Reading Public* (London, 1932) served as bibles for a coterie of young Cambridge intellectuals who embraced the couple's critique of commercial culture in the 1930s. D. H. LeMahieu, *A Culture for Democracy: Mass Communication and the Cultivated Mind in Britain between the Wars* (Oxford, 1988), 300ff.
4. J. S. Middleton, circular to local party secretaries re: Special Conference on Film Propaganda at the LPAC in Edinburgh, September 1936 (filed in NEC minutes).
5. Philip Williamson, *National Crisis and National Government: British Politics, the Economy and Empire, 1926–1932* (Cambridge, 1992), 388.
6. Ibid., 451. Andrew Thorpe argues that propaganda was largely immaterial to Labour's electoral defeat, which he attributes to a backlash against a party that had fled the responsibilities of office, and "the decisive rejection of 'socialism' "; *The British General Election of 1931* (Oxford, 1991), 211, 272. Ben Pimlott similarly suggests that "the most plausible explanation is that Labour had manifestly failed to deal with unemployment"; *Labour and the Left in the 1930s* (Cambridge, 1977), 16.
7. Arthur Henderson, "Report on the General Election," submitted to NJC meeting, 10 November 1931 (filed in NEC minutes).
8. Thorpe, *British General Election,* 207.

9. NBKR 3/62: Hugh Dalton to Philip Noel-Baker, 4 September 1931; David Marquand, *Ramsay MacDonald* (London, 1977), 646.

10. Henderson, "Report on the General Election"; "The Post Office Savings Bank Scare," undated draft pamphlet, early 1932 (filed in NEC minutes).

11. Thorpe, *British General Election*, 212–213, 215. NEC minutes: 10 November 1931, re: letter of protest to Sir John Reith. Lloyd George was also allowed one broadcast on 15 October 1931, which effectively made the total six for the government and four against. Henderson, "Report on the General Election." "A Warning for the B.B.C. and a Method for Dealing with the Press," *Labour Organiser*, December 1931, 220.

12. Thorpe, *British General Election*, 216; Ritchie Calder, "We Must Learn to Shoot. . . . The Film as a Powerful Propaganda Medium," *Labour*, October 1936, 35.

13. H. Hamilton Fyfe, "The Poison-Gas Press," *Labour Magazine*, January 1924, 398.

14. For this view, see Henry Pelling, *A Short History of the Labour Party* (London, 1961), chap. 5; also David Marquand, *The Progressive Dilemma* (London, 1991), 46–47. Ralph Miliband's work is still the most prominent exposition of the argument that Labour policy did not change dramatically after 1931, and that the party remained dedicated to a gradualist parliamentarism; *Parliamentary Socialism: A Study in the Politics of Labour* (London, 1961), 193ff.

15. Attlee to Christopher Addison, n.d. (late 1931), quoted in David Howell, *MacDonald's Party* (Oxford, 2002), 410.

16. Richard Toye, *The Labour Party and the Planned Economy, 1931–1951* (Woodbridge, Suffolk, 2003), 50–51, 64, passim; Dan Ritschel, *The Politics of Planning* (Oxford, 1997), 99–101.

17. Pimlott, *Labour and the Left,* 5.

18. Walter Citrine, *Men and Work: An Autobiography* (London, 1964), 300.

19. Cited in Williamson, *National Crisis,* 464; emphasis added.

20. NEC press release, 28 November 1934; emphasis in original (filed in NEC minutes).

21. Dalton diary, 19 January 1934; Pimlott, *Labour and the Left,* 53; *Daily Express,* 16 November 1935. Richard Crossman, *New Statesman,* 22 May 1937, quoted in Pimlott, *Labour and the Left,* 96. Richard Crossman, transcript of conference on "Selling Socialism?" sponsored by the New Fabian Research Bureau, London, 23–24 October 1937, held at the archive of the London School of Economics. I would like to thank Dominic Wring for providing me with the report of this conference. Herbert Morrison, "Can Labour Win London without the Middle Classes?" *Labour Organiser,* October 1923, 19 (reprinted from the *London Labour Chronicle*). Margaret Cole, transcript of "Selling Socialism?"

22. Labour Party, *Labour and the New Social Order* (London, 1918); Labour Party, *Labour and the Nation* (London, 1928), 7–8.

23. Williamson, *National Crisis,* 17.

24. There were, however, several significant exceptions to this trend, particularly in 1929, when Labour captured seventy seats for the first time—including many socially mixed suburban seats. See Duncan Tanner, "Class Voting and Radical Politics," in *Party, State and Society: Electoral Behavior in Britain since 1820,* ed. Jon Lawrence and Miles Taylor (Brookfield, VT, 1997), esp. 120–121; Tom Jeffrey, "The Suburban Nation: Politics and Class in Lewisham," in *Metropolis/London: Histories and Representations since 1800,* ed. David Feldman and Gareth Stedman Jones (London, 1989); John Stevenson and Chris Cook, *Britain in the Depression* (London, 1994), 275–289.

25. Stephen Koss, *The Rise and Fall of the Political Press in Britain,* vol. 2 (London, 1984), 6, 420.

26. Sian Nicholas, "'All the News That's Fit to Broadcast': The Popular Press versus the BBC, 1922–45," in *Northcliffe's Legacy: Aspects of the British Popular Press, 1896–1996* (London, 2000); Paddy Scannell and David Cardiff, *A Social History of British Broadcasting* (London, 1991), 64–69. For discussions between the government and BBC over the India broadcasts, see PREM 1/145; BBC WAC R34/534/2.

27. R. J. Minney, *Viscount Southwood* (London, 1954), 239.

28. J. C. C. Davidson to William Tyrrell, 9 March 1930, in J. C. C. Davidson, *Memoirs of a Conservative,* ed. Robert Rhodes James (London, 1969), 324.

29. *Daily Express,* 26 September 1932, 30 September 1932, 1 October 1932.

30. *Daily Express,* 22 October 1932.

31. Robert Graves and Alan Hodge, *The Long Weekend: A Social History of Great Britain, 1918–1939* (New York, 1963 [1940]), 291.

32. BBK C/299: Aide memoire of conversation with J. S. Elias, 15 March 1935.

33. Ernest Bevin, "Now on to 2,000,000," *Helper* no. 4, 2 July 1930.

34. LPA Labour Party pamphlet 36/41: Hannen Swaffer, "The Power of the Press."

35. Martin Pugh, "The *Daily Mirror* and the Revival of Labour, 1935–1945," *Twentieth Century British History* 9, 3 (1999): 431–432.

36. Francis Williams, *Nothing So Strange* (London, 1970), 130–134, 154–155.

37. TUC MSS 292/790/1: An internal tally by the *Daily Herald* found that in July 1938 the *Herald, Express, Daily Telegraph,* and *News Chronicle* devoted 1091.5, 120, 171.5, and 301.5 column-inches, respectively, to coverage of Labour and trade union news.

38. M-O File Report A11.

39. Huw Richards, *The Bloody Circus* (London, 1997), 157; Ernest Bevin, *Daily Herald,* 1 December 1919.

40. For content analysis of the *Daily Herald*'s women's page, see Adrian Bingham, *Gender, Modernity and the Popular Press in Interwar Britain* (Oxford, 2004), Appendix.

41. *Daily Herald,* 9 October 1935.

42. On the League of Nations Union as a form of non-party political associational culture, see Helen McCarthy, "The League of Nations Union and Democratic Politics in Britain, c. 1919–1939" (PhD thesis, University of London, 2008).

43. *Daily Herald,* 30 October 1935.
44. *Daily Herald,* 11 November 1935.
45. On local government, see articles in *Daily Herald* of 17, 19, 22, and 24 October 1935. On financial probity of Labour's policies, see issues of 31 October and 1 November 1935. On home ownership, see issues of 1, 2, and 12 October, and 11 November 1935.
46. Swaffer, *The Power of the Press.*
47. Institute of Incorporated Practitioners of Advertising (IIPA), *Survey of Press Readership,* vol. 1 (London, 1939), table 2.
48. Tom Jeffrey and Keith McClelland, "A World Fit to Live In: The Daily Mail and the Middle Classes, 1918–39," in *Impacts and Influences: Essays on Media Power in the Twentieth Century,* ed. James Curran, Anthony Smith, and Pauline Wingate (London, 1987), 51.
49. NEC, *Annual Report* (1937), 60.
50. Hugh Dalton diaries, 29 October 1935.
51. *News Chronicle,* 3 March 1937. See also Herbert Morrison, "What Londoners Pay For," *News Chronicle,* 18 February 1937, in which the LLP leader explained the panoply of beneficent services that Londoners received for their rates.
52. *Daily Express,* 24 October 1932; *Daily Express,* 30 October 1931.
53. Bernard Donoughue and G. W. Jones, *Herbert Morrison: Portrait of a Politician* (London, 1973), 269.
54. Pugh, *"Daily Mirror,"* 429, 434.
55. *Daily Mail,* 8 November 1935.
56. Walter Lippman, *Public Opinion* (Mineola, NY, 2004 [1922]), 215.
57. Wilkinson to LPAC, reported in the *Times,* 9 October 1936.
58. Tony Aldgate, "The Newsreels, Public Order and the Projection of Britain," in *Impacts and Influences,* 149; Pathé Gazette, "Jarrow Unemployed March to London," October 1936, http://www.britishpathe.com.
59. For Conservative frustration at the press's fixation with Jarrow as Wilkinson's crusade, see letter from the Chairman of the Jarrow Conservative Association to the *Times,* 4 November 1936.
60. Charles Ammon to House of Commons, 15 November 1926, *Hansard,* 5th series, vol. 199, col. 1605.
61. William Graham and Charles Ammon to House of Commons, 15 November 1926, *Hansard,* 5th series, vol. 199, cols. 1581, 1589, and 1606.
62. For the history of the ban and its repeal, see BBC WAC R34/137/2: The Broadcasting of Controversial Matters (Excluding Religious Broadcasts): History and Present Practice, undated internal BBC memorandum.
63. See BBC WAC R34/599: Lansbury-Reith correspondence over Labour representation on the BBC's Political Advisory Panel, 21 December 1932–8 February 1933.
64. The chasm between Lansbury's personal views and his position as party leader continued to widen, particularly over foreign policy, until he was compelled to resign in 1935 after Ernest Bevin accused him at the party conference of "taking his conscience around from body to body asking

what he should do with it"; reported in the *Daily Express,* 2 October 1935.

65. Though the BBC asserted it was committed to presenting a "balanced" version of political news throughout the interwar period, the specific codification of guidelines for political broadcasting did not take place until after World War II. The ultimate guidelines agreed upon were outlined in a BBC aide memoire, prepared on 6 February 1947, for their 28 February 1947 meeting with the government and the opposition to discuss political broadcasting (CAB 124/408).

66. BBC WAC R34/563/2: Lansbury to Reith, 10 July 1933.

67. BBC WAC R4/77/6: Written Evidence to the Ullswater Committee, Paper 101: National Council of Labour: Precis of Evidence, undated 1935.

68. For a history of Labour's attitude re: budget broadcasts, see BBC WAC R34/559: C. A. Siepmann to Political Advisory Panel, 27 March 1933.

69. Lansbury, NEC minutes, 25 October 1932.

70. *LPAC Report* (1932), 228.

71. See BBC WAC R34/563/2: transcript of 11 July 1933 meeting between Chairman, Vice-Chairman and Director-General of the BBC and representatives of the NCL.

72. See BBC WAC Talks—Herbert Morrison, 1930–1948: correspondence Richard Monachie (of the BBC), Herbert Morrison and Harold Webbe, January 1937.

73. *LPAC Report* (1933), 192.

74. BBC WAC R34/599: Lansbury-Reith correspondence over Labour representation on the BBC's Political Advisory Panel, 21 December 1932–8 February 1933.

75. NEC minutes, 25 March 1936.

76. TUC General Council, *Annual Report* (1930), Item 117, p. 151.

77. For Isaacs's contributions to the Talks Advisory Committee, see TUC MSS 292/787.13/3: Isaacs to Citrine memoranda.

78. TUC General Council, *Annual Report* (1928), Item 186, p. 279.

79. BBC WAC Citrine File/1: Citrine to Sir Stephen Tallents, 19 August 1940.

80. BBC WAC R34/534/2: NJC No. 39, Memo on broadcasting, June 1933.

81. See BBC WAC Citrine File/1: correspondence between Citrine, Reith, Talks department director Charles Siepmann, and assistant director R. A. Rendall, 8 February–25 May 1934 over BBC series "From Tolpuddle to TUC: 100 Years of Trade Union History."

82. Lansbury to party conference, *LPAC Report* (1932), 227; TUC MSS 292/786.3/4: Draft resolution, "Statement of Policy as Regards Broadcasting," International Conference on Workers' Educations, 11–12 July 1936, London.

83. Jean Seaton and Ben Pimlott, "The Struggle for 'Balance,'" in *The Media in British Politics* (London, 1987), 133–153.

84. *LPAC Report* (1933), 146; BBC WAC R4/72/2: Memo by Powell, undated, June 1936. A similar proposal had been mooted in the *Labour Organiser* several years earlier: "A Warning for the BBC," *Labour Organiser,* December 1931, 220.

85. Diana Mosley made four trips to Germany in 1936 during which she discussed with Hitler the possibility of establishing a German-based British Union of Fascists station to broadcast to the British Isles. Mary Lovell, *The Mitford Girls* (New York, 2002), 208–209. The BUF's efforts in this direction continued until the outbreak of the Second World War. See Richard Thurlow, *Fascism in Britain, 1918–1945* (London, 1998), 109–110. On the Communist Party's efforts to establish a radio station in the 1930s, see Andrew Thorpe, *The British Communist Party and Moscow, 1920–1943* (Manchester, 2000), 244.

86. "Mr. Baldwin's Homely Broadcast Speech," *Daily Express*, 23 April 1929; "Premier Is Radio Star of Election," *Daily Express*, 11 November 1935.

87. Susan Pedersen, *Family, Dependence and the Welfare State* (Cambridge, 1993), 193ff.; Pamela Graves, *Labour Women: Women in British Working-Class Politics, 1918–1939* (Cambridge, 1994), 81–107; Stephen Brooke, "'A New World for Women'? Abortion Law Reform in Britain during the 1930s," *American Historical Review* 106 (2001): 431–459; Howell, *MacDonald's Party*, 332–346.

88. Ina Zweiniger-Bargielowsa, "Explaining the Gender Gap: The Conservative Party and the Women's Vote, 1945–1964," in *Conservatives and British Society, 1880–1990*, ed. Ina-Zweiniger-Bargielowska and Martin Francis (Cardiff, 1996), 198.

89. Ina Zweiniger-Bargielowska, *Austerity in Britain: Rationing, Controls and Consumption, 1939–1955* (Oxford, 2000).

90. See, e.g., Stamfordham memo to the King, 2 June 1929, published in *Baldwin Papers*, ed. Philip Williamson (Cambridge, 2004), 220; Bridgeman diary entry, n.d. (October 1931), in *The Modernisation of Conservative Politics: The Diaries and Letters of William Bridgeman, 1904–1935*, ed. Philip Williamson (London, 1988), 250; Andrew Thorpe, *The British General Election of 1931* (Oxford, 1991), 31; David Jarvis, "The Conservative Party and the Politics of Gender, 1900–1939," in *Conservatives and British Society*, 174.

91. Karen Hunt, "Making Politics in Local Communities: Labour Women in Interwar Manchester," and Duncan Tanner, "Gender, Civic Culture and Politics in South Wales: Explaining Labour Municipal Policy, 1918–1939," in *Labour's Grass Roots: Essays on the Activities and Experiences of Local Labour Parties and Members, 1918–1945*, ed. Matthew Worley (Aldershot, Eng., 2005), 79–101, 170–193.

92. U.S. women were perceived to have similar sympathies. See Kristi Andersen, *After Suffrage: Women in Partisan and Electoral Politics before the New Deal* (Chicago, 1996).

93. David Jarvis, "Mrs. Maggs and Betty: The Conservative Appeal to Women Voters in the 1920s," *Twentieth Century British History* 5 (1994): 144–145, 149–151; Bingham, *Gender, Modernity and the Popular Press*, 127–132.

94. Attlee, PEB, reported in *The Listener*, 6 November 1935, 820–821.

95. Bingham, *Gender, Modernity*, 132–134, has noted Labour attempts to use similar imagery in the *Daily Herald*.

96. Greenwood, PEB, reported in *The Listener,* 13 November 1935, 876; Morrison, PEB, reported in *The Listener,* 13 November 1935, 882.

97. Clynes, PEB, reported in *The Listener,* 6 November 1935, 825; Greenwood, PEB.

98. Morrison, PEB.

99. NEC research and publicity subcommittee minutes, 22 February 1934 (filed in NEC minutes). George Bernard Shaw's contribution to the same series was also reproduced, as were broadcasts by Beatrice Webb, Lansbury, Greenwood, and Cripps.

100. BBC WAC N17/1: Attlee to Reith, 14 December 1931; BBC WAC Talks Department index cards: Attlee broadcast on White Paper on Personal Incomes, Home Service, 6 February 1948; BBC WAC Talks Department index cards: Dalton PEB, 15 December 1951; BBC WAC Talks Department index cards: Morrison PEB, 21 October 1951.

101. Sir Stafford Cripps to House of Commons, 22 February 1933, *Parliamentary Debates,* 5th series, vol. 274, col. 1829; BBC WAC Talks Department index cards: Cripps Broadcast Appeal on behalf of the Workers' Educational Assoc., Home Service, 28 October 1945; "How Are We Doing?" Home Service, 28 October 1948; *The Gallup International Public Opinion Polls: Great Britain,* ed. George Gallup (New York, 1976).

102. BBC WAC Citrine File 1: Siepmann to Reith, 24 May 1934, and Rendall to Citrine, 28 June 1934.

103. Koss, *Rise and Fall,* vol. 2, 6.

104. Martin Moore, *The Origins of Modern Spin* (Basingstoke, 2006), 20–22.

105. Dominic Wring, *The Politics of Marketing the Labour Party* (Basingstoke, Eng., 2005), 19.

106. Dominic Wring, "Selling Socialism," *History Today* 55, 5 (2005): 41–43.

107. "The National Campaign and Socialist Crusade Week," undated memorandum, August 1937 (filed in NEC minutes).

108. IIPA, *Survey of Press Readership,* vol. 1, table 4.

109. "Your Britain," *Labour Organiser,* September 1937, 168.

110. *Times,* 6 November 1937.

111. Alan and Isabella Livingston, "Abram Games (1914–1996)," *Oxford Dictionary of National Biography,* ed. H. C. G. Matthew and Brian Harrison (Oxford, 2004), CD-ROM edition.

112. Ibid.

113. NEC, *Annual Report* (1939), 85.

114. Wring, *Politics of Marketing,* 11; Donoughue and Jones, *Herbert Morrison,* 164; advertisement published in *Daily Express,* 4 March 1937; Cuthbert Headlam, *The Headlam Diaries,* vol. 2, ed. Stuart Ball (London, 1992), entry for 5 March 1937.

115. NEC research and publicity subcommittee minutes, 14 December 1937.

116. NEC research and publicity subcommittee minutes, 12 April 1938, 14 June 1938.

117. NEC research and publicity subcommittee minutes, 16 February, 16 March, 14 April 1937.

118. 1935–1939 financial reports. The profit for 1934 was £236; for 1935, £183. The average circulation during 1935 was 14,612 (filed in NEC minutes).

119. "Publicity: The Older Order Changeth and Giveth Place to New," *Labour Organiser,* September 1935, 174; see also series on "Advertisement: An Art We Must Understand and Learn to Apply," *Labour Organiser,* February, April, and June 1936.

120. E.g., "We will have to use more modern methods of publicity in order to sell our goods. . . . I am certain it would be of the greatest possible benefit to all of us . . . to have lectures on the art of modern advertising by a publicity expert." O. A. Emlyn, "Some General Election Problems," *Conservative Agents Journal* (April 1939): 91.

9. Election Victory

1. The Conservatives remained ahead in Gallup polls asking voters whom they would vote for if a general election were held tomorrow through May 1943; *The Gallup International Public Opinion Polls: Great Britain,* ed. George Gallup (New York, 1976).

2. Sonya Rose, *Which People's War? National Identity and Citizenship in Wartime Britain, 1939–1945* (Oxford, 2003), 25; Steve Fielding, Paul Thompson, and Nick Tiratsoo, *"England Arise!": The Labour Party and Popular Politics in 1940s Britain* (Manchester, 1995), 67–68.

3. Kenneth O. Morgan, *Labour in Power, 1945–1951* (Oxford, 1984), 24.

4. Angus Calder, *The People's War: Britain, 1939–45* (London, 1969); Paul Addison, *The Road to 1945: British Politics and the Second World War* (London, 1975).

5. Stephen Brooke, *Labour's War: The Labour Party during the Second World War* (Oxford, 1992); Martin Francis, *Ideas and Policies under Labour: Building a New Britain* (Manchester, 1997); Richard Toye, *The Labour Party and the Planned Economy, 1931–1951* (Woodbridge, Suffolk, 2003).

6. Steven Fielding, "The Second World and Popular Radicalism: The Significance of the 'Movement away from Party,'" *History* 80 (1995): 38–58.

7. Both Wise and White were adopted as official Labour candidates in 1945.

8. BBC WAC R34/53/1: Brooke to Barnes, 10 August 1943.

9. R. A. Butler, *The Art of the Possible* (London, 1971), 129.

10. *Times,* 10 June 1947.

11. M-O File Report 2545, "A Report on Penguin World" (December 1947), 43.

12. Fielding et al., *"England Arise!"* 66; Ronald McCallum and Alison Readman, *The British General Election of 1945* (Oxford, 1947), 269; Henry Pelling, "The 1945 General Election Reconsidered," *Historical Journal* 23, 2 (1980): 410; Addison, *Road to 1945,* 154.

13. For this view, see Steve Fielding, "What Did 'the People' Want? The Meaning of the 1945 General Election," *Historical Journal* 35, 3 (1992): 623–639.

14. Addison, *Road to 1945,* 258–259; Andrew Thorpe, "Conservative Party Agents in Second World War Britain," *Twentieth Century British History* 18, 3 (2007): 334.

15. MSS Attlee 7: Ridley to Shepherd, 10 March 1943.

16. MSS Attlee 7: Ridley to Attlee, 18 March 1943.

17. Brooke, *Labour's War*, 69, 79.

18. CPA CCO 4/2/162: "Political Survey Conducted in October 1941 in London, Home Counties, East Midlands, West Mids, Eastern, Wessex, Western, North Western, Northern regions, Yorkshire and Wales," sent to R. Topping by J. Stuart, 24 November 1941.

19. TUC MSS 292/790/1: H. G. Wells, draft article, 5 February 1940.

20. Labour Party, Statement of Receipts and Payments for Years 1939 to 1943 (filed in NEC minutes).

21. Organization subcommittee minutes, 16 December 1941 (filed in NEC minutes).

22. CPA Whip 2/2: J. Stuart to Col. P. J. Blair, 21 July 1942 (filed in NEC minutes).

23. Brooke, *Labour's War*, 107.

24. The circulation of the major dailies rose from 17.8 to 28.5 million between 1937 and 1947. A. P. Wandsworth, "Newspaper Circulations, 1800–1954," *Report of the Manchester Statistical Society* March (1955): 28.

25. Press and publicity subcommittee minutes, 6 March 1942 (filed in NEC minutes).

26. Harold Croft, *Conduct of Parliamentary Elections* (London, 1945), 32.

27. BBC WAC R51/412: Barnes to Maconachie, 7 April 1942; and Barnes to Laski, 10 April 1942.

28. 22 April 1942; Press and publicity subcommittee minutes, 16 June 1942 (filed in NEC minutes).

29. Morgan, *Labour in Power*, 25.

30. BBC WAC R34/531/1: Fraser's minutes of meeting with 1922 committee, 3 June 1942.

31. CPA Whip 2/2: J. Stuart to Col. P. J. Blair, 21 July 1942.

32. CPA CRD 2/28/2: R. Topping to D. Hacking, 7 October 1941.

33. Cuthbert Headlam, *The Headlam Diaries, 1923–1935,* ed. Stuart Ball (London, 1992), 3 October 1942 entry.

34. BBC WAC R34/531/1: Barnes to Henry Brooke, CCO, 9 August 1943.

35. Jean Seaton and Ben Pimlott, "The Struggle for 'Balance,'" in *The Media in British Politics* (Aldershot, England, 1987), 133–153.

36. BBC WAC R51/600/2: Andrew Stewart to Melville Dinwiddle, 13 December 1943.

37. BBC WAC R51/600/2: Memorandum by Margery Wace, Talks Dept., on her meeting with Walter Citrine, 16 August 1940, and Maconachie to N. Luker, 19 August 1940.

38. BBC WAC R51/412: Minutes of meeting between Labour deputation, the BBC directors-general, and the Chairman, 14 July 1942.

39. Sian Nicholas, "Politics and the Audience: Political Broadcasting and BBC Listener Research c. 1936–1950" (paper presented at the North American Conference on British Studies, Boston, Massachusetts, November 2006).

40. Addison, *Road to 1945,* 169.

41. *Daily Herald,* 2 December 1942.

42. Brooke, *Labour's War,* 71.

43. The *Sketch* article was quoted in the *Daily Herald*'s rebuttal, 23 December 1942.

44. Press and publicity subcommittee minutes, 19 January 1943 (filed in NEC minutes).

45. Pelling, "1945 General Election," 411.

46. Minutes of WFA meeting, 8 February 1943 (filed in NEC minutes).

47. John Bonham, *The Middle Class Vote* (London, 1954), 154, 164.

48. Pelling, "1945 General Election," 407.

49. Herbert Morrison, "Labour Must Capture the East Lewishams," *Labour Organiser,* March 1945, 8–9, quoted in Brooke, *Labour's War,* 309.

50. NEC memorandum, 28 July 1943 (filed in NEC minutes).

51. Butler, *Art of the Possible,* 298.

52. CPA Whip 1/4: Erskine-Hill memo on proposed subcommittees, included in R. Topping to J. Stuart, 5 June 1941.

53. CPA CCO 20/1/1: R. A. Butler to D. Hacking, 20 August 1940; Lady H. Bourne to R. Topping, 30 August 1940.

54. CPA Whip 2/2: R. Topping to T. Dugdale, n.d. [after Skipton by-election, 7 January 1944].

55. Stephen Brooke, "The Labour Party and the 1945 General Election," *Contemporary Record* 9 (1995): 1–21.

56. On constituency activism during the war, see Andrew Thorpe, *Parties at War: Political Organization in Second World War Britain* (Oxford, 2009), 38, 200, 217.

57. Press and publicity subcommittee, 25 October 1943 (filed in NEC minutes).

58. Pelling, "1945 General Election," 411.

59. Mark Franklin and Matthew Lander, "The Undoing of Winston Churchill: Mobilization and Conversion in the 1945 Realignment of British Voters," *British Journal of Political Science* 25, 4 (1995): 429–452.

60. For an example of Labour candidate's discussion of housing, see MSS Castle 223: Barbara Castle, "A Word to the Women: Let's Have Good Housekeeping," *Blackburn's Labour Election Special* (1945).

61. Press and publicity subcommittee, 15 February 1944 (filed in NEC minutes).

62. Addison, *Road to 1945,* 217.

63. "The Labour Party Policy Campaign," NEC memorandum, 28 July 1943 (filed in NEC minutes).

64. MSS Attlee 13: Henderson to Durbin, 8 March 1944.

65. Philip Noel-Baker's papers contain an annotated and heavily scored copy of "Labour and the War Government—Outline Notes for Speakers." See NBKR 2/47.

66. Press and publicity subcommittee minutes, 15 February 1944 (filed in NEC minutes).

67. From 2,673,000 to 3,039,000. Figures from *Labour's First Century,* ed. Duncan Tanner, Pat Thane, and Nick Tiratsoo (Cambridge, 2000), 395.

68. Press and publicity subcommittee minutes, 15 February 1944 (filed in NEC minutes).

69. NEC minutes, 29 November 1935.

70. £13,641 9s 8d in 1935 pounds equated to £21,506 15s 2d in 1944. Conversion from Lawrence H. Officer, "Purchasing Power of British Pounds from 1264 to 2006," online at http://www.MeasuringWorth.com.

71. "Memorandum on Election Services," approved by the full press and publicity subcommittee, 2 May 1944 (filed in NEC minutes).

72. Andrew Thorpe, "Politics or Organization? Labour Party Membership in the Second World War" (paper presented at the European Social Science History Conference, Lisbon, Portugal, March 2008).

73. CPA CCO 4/2/14: Neame to Lloyd, 14 March 1945.

74. Labour's plans were not limited by financial constraints. While total campaign expenditure was only £40,515 10s., this left an unspent balance in the general election fund of £84,953 11s. 7d. See "Statement of Receipts and Payments for the Year Ended December 31st, 1945," in *LPAC Report* (London, 1946), pp. 40–43.

75. Press and Publicity Department, "General Election, July 1945, Report on Campaign Publicity Services," n.d. [July 1945] (filed in NEC minutes).

76. See also general election poster no. 11, "Put Britain's Industry at Britain's Service—Vote Labour"; no. 12, "British Food for British Home and Prosperity for Agriculture—Vote Labour"; and no. 14, "A Non-Stop Drive to Provide a Good Home for Every Family—Vote Labour." Political Poster Collection, CUL.

77. Philip Bell, *John Bull and the Bear: British Public Opinion, Foreign Policy and the Soviet Union, 1941–1945* (London, 1990).

78. Variations in local party colors persisted through the 1950s. See Martin Rosenbaum, *From Soapbox to Soundbyte: Party Political Campaigning in Britain since 1945* (London, 1997), 201–202.

79. Zec produced the entire series in a week, "working night and day." See "Report on Campaign Publicity Services."

80. Herbert Morrison, *Herbert Morrison: An Autobiography* (London, 1960), 237.

81. Ibid.; Bernhard Donoghue and G. W. Jones, *Herbert Morrison: Portrait of a Politician*, 2nd ed. (London, 2001), 335.

82. James Thomas, *Popular Newspapers, the Labour Party and British Politics* (London, 2005), 23.

83. Donoghue and Jones, *Herbert Morrison*, 335. Based on interview with S. Elliott.

84. The total circulation of the three papers in 1945 was 5.8 million. The circulations of the *Daily Express*, the *Daily Mail*, and the tabloids *Daily Sketch* and *Daily Graphic* totaled 5.9 million. Figures quoted from Thomas, *Popular Newspapers*, 15.

85. See especially McCallum and Readman, *General Election of 1945*, 140ff.

86. On Nye Bevan's view that the Churchill cult of personality represented a "degradation to democracy," see Michael Foot, *Aneurin Bevan* (London, 1962), 507.

87. McCallum and Readman, *General Election of 1945*, 149. In his election broadcast, Churchill injudiciously equated the Labour Party with the Gestapo, and depicted Harold Laski as a sinister Gauleiter.

88. "Report on Campaign Publicity Services." In contrast, the party disposed of 1,170,000 of 1,760,000 housing leaflets produced, and 2,050,000 of 2,127,000 leaflets on control of industry.

89. On inflation, see especially Clement Attlee, PEB, 5 June 1945, reported in *The Listener*, 14 June 1945, 657, and Ellen Wilkinson, PEB, 14 June 1945, reported in *The Listener*, 21 June 1945, 688. On housing, see especially Wilkinson, PEB, and Herbert Morrison, PEB, 29 June 1945, in *The Listener*, 5 July 1945, 16. On the nationalization of industry, see especially Attlee, PEB, Morrison, PEB, and Ernest Bevin, PEB, 22 June 1945, in *The Listener*, 28 June 1945, 716. For listener demographics for these broadcasts, see Nicholas, "Politics and the Audience."

90. M-O File Report 2270a: "A Report on the General Election, June–July 1945" (October 1945), 114.

91. Calder, *People's War*, 583.

10. Impacts and Influences

1. Jon Lawrence, *Speaking for the People: Party, Language and Popular Politics in England, 1867–1914* (Cambridge, 1998), 206.

2. Walter Lippmann, *Public Opinion* (Mineola, NY, 2004 [1922]), 186ff. For a survey of the debate over media influence, see James Curran, "Introduction," in *Impacts and Influences: Essays on Media Power in the Twentieth Century*, ed. James Curran, Pauline Wingate, and Anthony Smith (London, 1987), 1–3. Within the field of cultural studies, the seminal British interjection in this debate is Stuart Hall, "Encoding/Decoding," reprinted in *Media Studies: A Reader*, 2nd ed., ed. Paul Marris and Sue Thornham (New York, 2000), 51–61.

3. *Daily Mail*, 7 October 1936.

4. Timothy Hollins, "The Presentation of Politics" (PhD thesis, University of Leeds, 1981), 1, 43, 154; *Report of the Labour Party Annual Conference (LPAC)* (1925), 71; *Daily Express*, 18 October 1924.

5. *Report of the LPAC* (1929), 74. The Conservatives produced 464,614 leaflets in 1929, according to the National Union of Conservative and Unionist Association's records (I would like to thank James Thompson for this figure).

6. James Thompson, "'Pictorial Lies?'—Posters and Politics in Britain, c. 1880–1914," *Past and Present* 197 (2007): 177–210; *Daily Mirror*, 4 November 1935; Graham Wallas, *The Great Society: A Psychological Analysis* (London, 1919), 130; Lisa Tickner, *The Spectacle of Women: Imagery of the Suffrage Campaign, 1907–14* (London, 1987), 152.

7. *Times*, 1 December 1910; Dominic Wring, *The Politics of Marketing the Labour Party* (Basingstoke, 2005), 15; NEC minutes, 24 April 1911, 24 November 1921. The gas mask baby similarly remained in the party's political arsenal

for several years, and was used by Wedgwood Benn in the Gorton by-election in 1937 (*Times,* 8 February 1937).

8. Poster No. 17 sold 20,000 copies, compared to 10,000 apiece for the other twenty-nine posters. Report on General Election Propaganda presented to the Publicity and Research Dept, 19 July 1929 (filed in NEC minutes).

9. Thompson, "'Pictorial Lies'?" 203.

10. Circulation figures from *The Warwick Guide to Labour Periodicals,* ed. R. Harrison (London, 1977); Herbert Drinkwater, "Reverberations," *Labour Organiser,* January 1924; "Running a County Monthly Newspaper: Some Information about Finance," *Labour Organiser,* September 1927, 111. For the difficulties of securing advertisements in gratis dailies more generally, see the "Newspaper Mems." column of the *Labour Organiser,* 1920s–1930s.

11. After 1930, Odhams press often assisted in by-elections by running special local election editions, such as the Wakefield edition run in support of Arthur Greenwood's successful candidacy in April 1932.

12. NEC minutes, 24 January 1938; Hugh Dalton, *The Fateful Years* (London, 1957), 127–128.

13. The prevalence of women reading the *Herald* for this reason was noted by Mass-Observation in September 1942; M-O File Report 1420: "Report on *Daily Herald* Readership."

14. International Institute of Practitioners of Advertising (IIPA), *Survey of Press Readership,* vol. 1 (London, 1939), table 8.

15. Quoted in "The News: Facts about Its Presentation," *Labour Bulletin,* September 1936.

16. For an exposition of this view and a survey of the literature, see D. L. LeMahieu, *A Culture for Democracy: Mass Communication and the Cultivated Mind in Britain between the Wars* (Oxford, 1988), 15.

17. Robert Graves and Alan Hodge, *The Long Weekend: British Society between the Wars* (New York, 1963 [1940]), 291; M-O File Report 1420, "Report of *Daily Herald* Readership."

18. TUC MSS 292/790/1: *Daily Herald* questionnaire, September 1932.

19. TUC MSS 292/790/1: file on *Daily Herald* schemes.

20. TUC MSS 292/790/1: Copy of circular sent by Arthur Hicks to *Daily Herald* editors, 23 September 1932.

21. TUC MSS 292/790/1: *Daily Express* circular from Beverley Baxter to Trade Union leaders, n.d. (November 1932).

22. See, e.g., "No Need to Despair: Strength in Well-paid Labour," *Daily Express,* 24 September 1924; "This Is Our Task," *Daily Express,* 5 August 1931.

23. TUC MSS 292/790/1: Undated draft letter, November 1932. The sentence about the Greeks was excised from the final draft.

24. "The News: Facts about Its Presentation."

25. *Daily Express,* 1 October 1936.

26. "Join Your Union!" *Daily Express,* 14 October 1936.

27. IIPA, *Survey,* vol. 1, table 2. Younger readers are defined as those ages 14 to 24. The *Express* remained the most popular paper in this age demographic,

as well as among readers of all ages, a title which it reclaimed from the *Daily Herald* in 1935; Martin Pugh, "The Rise of the Labour Party and Conservatism," *History* 87, 288 (2002): 518. On the leftward political leanings of Bartholomew and his colleagues William Connor, Hugh Cudlipp, Cecil King, and Richard Jennings, see Maurice Edelman, *The Mirror: A Political History* (London, 1966), 39; and Bill Hagerty, *Read All about It! 100 Sensational Years of the Daily Mirror* (London, 2003).

28. "Fleet St Matters: The Daily Herald," *Newspaper World,* 15 March 1919, 6.

29. LPA LP/DH: Poyser (advertising director) to Barrow (circulation manager), 11 October 1923.

30. James Curran, "Capitalism and Control of the Press, 1800–1975," in *Mass Communication and Society,* ed. James Curran, Michael Gurevitch, and Januaryet Wollacott (London, 1977), 224–225; James Curran, "Advertising as a Patronage System," in *The Sociology of Journalism and the Press,* ed. Harry Christian (Keele, Eng., 1980), 77; emphasis in original.

31. R. J. Minney, *Viscount Southwood* (London, 1954), 226.

32. BBK/H/78: Robertson to A. G. Miller, 2 June 1930.

33. Minney, *Southwood,* 244; TUC MSS 292/790/2: Daily Herald correspondence 1937–57.

34. Edelman, *The Mirror,* 40; Curran, "Capitalism and Control," 225.

35. Martin Pugh, "The *Daily Mirror* and the Revival of Labour, 1935–1945," *Twentieth Century British History* 9, 3 (1998): 431–432.

36. *Daily Herald,* 6 October 1936.

37. The National Government Chief Whip, David Margesson, and Lord Gorell, the Conservative member of the BBC Political Advisory Committee, expended considerable energy in trying to keep Churchill and Lord Lloyd out of a 1934 BBC talks series on India for fear of embarrassing the government. This failure represented a rare victory for the interwar BBC against the government—the BBC held that it was "more or less morally committed" to allow Churchill to broadcast; BBC WAC R34/599: Siepmann to Rankeillour, 8 August 1934. For a full discussion of the controversy over the India broadcasts, see PREM 1/145.

38. Muriel Grant, *Propaganda and the Role of the State in Interwar Britain* (Oxford: 1994); Ian Maclaine, *Ministry of Morale: Home Front Morale and the Ministry of Information in World War II* (London, 1979); Michael Cockerell, Peter Hennessy, and David Walker, *Sources Close to the Prime Minister* (London, 1985); Martin Moore, *The Origins of Modern Spin* (London, 2006), 7–11.

39. *Daily Mirror,* 4 November 1935.

40. *Daily Express,* 9 October 1936.

41. Ian Mackay reply on behalf of the press to vote of thanks from LPAC, October 1952, reprinted in *The Real Mackay: Essays by Ian Mackay,* ed. S. Baron (London, 1953), 203.

42. Characterization of Robert Williams's speech to 1918 Party Conference, *Daily Express,* 15 November 1918.

43. The National Vigilance Association was convinced that many people frequented cinemas for reasons that had very little to do with watching movies.

Matt Houlbrook, *Queer London: Perils and Pleasures in the Sexual Metropolis, 1918–1957* (Chicago, 2005), 57.

44. *Pathé Gazette,* The General Election, October 1935, available online at www
.britishpathe.com; "And a little mouse shall lead them!" Hugh Dalton diary,
26 November 1935.

45. Lawrence Black, *The Political Culture of the Left in Affluent Britain, 1951–
1964: Old Labour, New Britain?* (Basingstoke, 2003), 177–181; Wring, *Marketing the Labour Party,* Part II; Martin Rosenbaum, *From Soapbox to Soundbite: Party Political Campaigning in Britain since 1945* (London, 1997), chaps.
4, 6, and conclusion; Ben Pimlott, *Harold Wilson* (London, 1992), passim.

46. Sian Nicholas, "Politics and the Audience: Political Broadcasting and BBC
Listener Research, c. 1936–1950," North Atlantic Conference on British
Studies, Boston, November 2006; BBC WAC Listener Barometer, 14 July
1940; R9/1/5: Audience Research Bulletins, 3–9 June 1945.

47. Asa Briggs, *The Birth of Broadcasting* (Oxford, 1961), 141; *Daily Express,*
11 November 1935. The *Express* interviewed 2,476 people by phone, and
925 by canvass. According to the category definitions used in marketing analysis, only the wealthiest 5 percent of households—those characterized as AA or
A—were likely to own a telephone in the 1930s; IIPA, *Survey,* vol. 1, appendix C: Definitions of Social Classes.

48. BBC WAC, Listener Barometers, 1940. Morrison's first postscript (in August
1940) rated an audience of 37.9 percent, a figure only topped by Lord
Woolton and Duff Cooper (then Minister of Information), and J. B. Priestley's exceptionally well-attended Postscript of 14 July 1940, which rated an
audience of 44.3 percent of the population. Greenwood's first postscript (19
July 1940) pulled a respectable 33 percent.

49. BBC WAC R51/600/2: Memorandum of interview between N. Luker and V.
Tewson, 25 April 1940; BBC WAC Listener Research Barometers, April–
September 1940.

50. Sian Nicholas, "Politics and the Audience."

51. BBC WAC R9/1/5: Audience Research Bulletins, 3–9 June 1945; *News
Chronicle,* 15 June 1945; Sian Nicholas, "Politics and the Audience."

52. Labour managed to secure an additional speaker in the India round table
discussions, so that the ultimate line-up of political speakers was 2 Government, 2 Labour, 1 Liberal, and one speech apiece by Churchill and Lord
Lloyd; see discussions in PREM 1/145; Sian Nicholas, "Politics and the
Audience."

53. Sian Nicholas, "Politics and the Audience."

Conclusion

1. Paul Addison, *The Road to 1945: British Politics and the Second World War*
(London, 1975), 18, 127–128, 162.

2. David Butler, "Trends in British By-Elections," *Journal of Politics* 11, 2
(1949): 396–407.

3. John Stevenson and Chris Cook, *Britain in the Depression: Society and Politics, 1929–1939* (London, 1994), 131, 139.

4. Duncan Tanner, "Labour and Its Membership," in *Labour's First Century*, ed. Duncan Tanner, Pat Thane, and Nick Tiratsoo (Cambridge, 2000), 252; Matthew Worley, *Labour inside the Gate: A History of the British Labour Party between the Wars* (London, 2005), 38, 60; Tom Jeffrey, "The Suburban Nation: Politics and Class in Lewisham," in *Metropolis/London: Histories and Representations since 1800,* ed. David Feldman and Gareth Stedman Jones (London, 1989), 190.

5. *Times,* 22 June 1934; *Times,* 28 November 1934.

6. On the implication of nondecisive swings in the period between 1945 and 1951, see Ina Zweiniger-Bargielowska, *Austerity in Britain: Rationing Controls and Consumption, 1939–1955* (Oxford, 2000), 248.

7. Sam Davies and Bob Morley, *County Borough Elections in England and Wales, 1919–1938: A Comparative Analysis,* vol. 2: *Bradford-Carlisle* (Aldershot, 2000), 323. The authors attribute the party's remarkable success to the peculiar salience of the housing issue in Burnley in the 1930s. While they thus explain away Burnley as an anomaly, it is suggestive that the Labour Party was seen to be better able to deal with the crisis in municipal housing than the Conservatives.

8. Ibid., 488–489, 497.

9. George Shepherd, "Memorandum on Municipal Elections," n.d., November 1938 (filed in NEC minutes).

10. Kenneth O. Morgan, *Labour in Power, 1945–1951* (Oxford, 1984), 13.

11. On this last, see Clare Griffiths, *Labour and the Countryside: The Politics of Rural Britain, 1918–1939* (Oxford, 2007).

12. Labour Party, *Constitution of the Labour Party* (London, 1918); emphasis added.

13. J. Ramsay MacDonald, *Parliament and Revolution* (Manchester, 1919), 62.

14. See particularly Ben Jackson, *Equality and the British Left: A Study in Progressive Political Thought* (Manchester, 2007).

15. Evan Durbin's *The Politics of Democratic Socialism* (London, 1994 [1940]), 271; emphasis in original.

16. Labour Party, *Labour and the Nation* (London, 1928), 7–8.

17. On such wariness, see Arthur Marwick, "Middle Opinion in the Thirties: Planning, Progress and Political 'Agreement,'" *English Historical Review* 79, 311 (1964): 285–298; Helen McCarthy, "Parties, Voluntary Associations and Democratic Politics in Interwar Britain," *Historical Journal* 50, 4 (December 2007): 891–912.

18. Report of Conference on "Selling Socialism?" sponsored by the New Fabian Research Bureau, London, 23–24 October 1937, held in Fabian Society papers, LSE archives; Martin Moore, *The Origins of Modern Spin: Democratic Government and the Media in Britain, 1945–1951* (London, 2006), 18–20; Ernest Bevin to TUC, Nottingham in *Report of the Trades Union Congress* (1930), 369.

19. Ralph Miliband, *Parliamentary Socialism: A Study in the Politics of Labour* (London, 1961), 348.
20. Raymond Williams, *Culture and Society, 1780–1950* (New York, 1958); Stuart Hall, Charles Critcher, Tony Jefferson, John Clarke, and Brian Robert, *Policing the Crisis: Mugging, the State and Law and Order* (London, 1978). Though Williams was not himself a Gramscian, *Culture and Society* was appropriated by the leaders of the new school of cultural studies; see Geoff Eley, *A Crooked Line: From Cultural History to the History of Society* (Ann Arbor, MI, 2005), 19–24.
21. Lawrence Black, *Redefining British Politics: Culture, Consumerism and Participation, 1954–70* (Basingstoke, 2010); Dominic Wring, *The Politics of Marketing the Labour Party* (Basingstoke, 2005), 72–80.

Index

Advertising, 14, 23, 69–70, 133, 141, 193–194, 203. *See also* Political advertising
Alexander, A. V., 197
Allen, Clifford, 24, 89, 97, 131, 132, 135
Angell, Norman, 9, 24, 71–72, 87–88
Army Bureau of Current Affairs, 159, 162, 166
Asquith, Herbert, 20–21, 23, 37, 81
Attlee, Clement, 140, 156, 157, 163, 178, 186, 195–196, 204

Baldwin, Stanley, 7, 21, 56, 60, 80, 81, 84, 101, 107, 112, 113, 119, 124, 126, 155, 188
Bartholomew, Guy, 181, 193, 194
Baxter, A. Beverley, 145, 191–192
Beaverbrook, Lord (Max Aitken), 21–22, 53, 64, 74, 76–78, 122, 124, 137, 145, 149, 191–192, 202
Belloc, Hilaire, 69–72
Bentham, Dr. Ethel, 131
Beveridge Report, 166, 172–173, 174, 176
Blair, Tony, 28, 204
Bondfield, Margaret, 129, 153
Bourne, Francis Cardinal, 57, 127
Bourne, Lady Hester, 175
British Broadcasting Corporation (BBC), 2, 11, 13, 16–18, 68–69, 77–82, 99, 102, 104–105, 111–115, 117–119, 126, 141, 144, 151–158, 166, 169–172, 175,

196–197. *See also* Party Election Broadcasts
British Gazette, 106–112
British Worker, 106–112, 113, 119
Bromley, John, 42
Butler, R. A., 166, 174–175

Cadbury, George, 23, 53, 76
Capital levy, 50, 54, 56, 57, 59, 127, 193
Chamberlain, Austen, 107
Chamberlain, Joseph, 29
Chamberlain, Neville, 127, 171, 176
"Chinese slavery," 28, 29
Churchill, Winston, 28, 101, 104, 107, 108, 109, 127, 129, 157, 163, 178, 181
Cinema, 13–15. *See also* Newsreels
Citrine, Walter, 85, 108, 118, 135, 137, 142, 153, 158, 171, 192
Clynes, J. R., 31–32, 37, 40, 54, 73, 119
Cole, G. D. H., 35, 39, 44
Common Wealth Party, 166, 175
Communist Party, 6, 56, 58, 110, 154. *See also* Minority Movement; National Unemployed Workers' Movement
Conservative Party, 2, 7, 12, 50–51, 56, 66, 119, 155–156, 165–166, 200, 203; and 1906 general election, 31–32; and 1924 "Red Scare" campaign, 59–64; and 1929 general election, 124–127, 130; and 1931 general election, 141; and 1945 general election, 177, 178, 181, 187, 197; and Lords Beaverbrook and

Conservative Party *(continued)*
  Rothermere, 21–22, 77–78, 124; and
  views of the electorate, 84, 86; and
  World War II party politics, 166–167,
  168, 170–171, 174–175
Cramp, C. T., 94, 120
Cripps, Sir Stafford, 140, 142–143, 157
Croft, Harold, 170
Cudlipp, Hugh, 173

Daily Chronicle, 20, 21, 22–23, 34, 41, 48,
  52, 53, 55, 103, 122, 135, 145
Daily Citizen, 25–26, 38, 107
Daily Express, 15, 19–20, 21–22, 41–42,
  44, 48, 52, 56, 63–64, 68, 73, 76–77,
  95, 109, 121, 122, 123, 124, 125, 129,
  135, 136, 143, 145, 148, 149, 150,
  187, 190–192, 194, 195, 196–197
Daily Herald, 18, 20, 23, 25–26, 41,
  45–46, 48, 55, 68, 74, 75–76, 77,
  82, 88–98, 106, 111, 113, 119, 123,
  126–127, 128, 131–137, 141, 144–148,
  168–169, 172–173, 181, 186–187,
  189–195
Daily Mail, 15, 18, 19, 20–21, 22, 36,
  38–40, 42, 44, 45, 50, 51, 52–53, 54–55,
  56, 57, 58–59, 61–64, 71, 75, 76, 87, 89,
  93–94, 95, 102–103, 108, 109, 111, 112,
  124, 125, 126, 127, 129, 132, 133, 135,
  145, 148, 149, 186, 190, 193, 194
Daily Mirror, 18, 20–21, 87, 108, 109, 123,
  146, 148, 149, 166, 180–181, 188, 190,
  192–194, 195
Daily News, 19, 20, 23, 43, 44, 53, 55, 56,
  68, 76, 89, 92, 93, 122, 132, 145, 193
Daily Sketch, 44, 87, 173
Dalton, Hugh, 140, 143, 171, 189, 195
Dalziel, Henry, 22
Danvers, V. L., 32
Davidson, J. C. C., 22, 106, 111–112, 119,
  137
Dyson, Will, 45–46

Elections, by-, 21, 30, 53, 75, 166, 168,
  175
Elections, general: of 1906, 1, 28; of 1910
  (January and December), 30–31, 188; of
  1918, 21, 27, 32, 37–42, 51, 56, 66, 75;
  of 1922, 20, 21, 52, 53, 56, 57, 65, 66,
  95; of 1923, 56, 57, 65, 66, 68, 75, 76,
  174; of 1924, 56, 58–65, 81, 174; of
  1929, 8, 21, 32, 56, 77, 82, 122, 124–131,
  143–144, 155, 174, 188, 189; of 1931,
  122, 140–141, 151–152, 174; of 1935,
  123, 140, 147–148, 156, 164, 174,
  196–197; of 1945, 1–2, 4, 155, 163,
  165, 172–185, 197; of 1950, 197; of
  1951, 197
Elections, local, 11, 22, 32, 52, 53, 54, 55,
  60, 75, 149, 152, 159, 163, 188, 199,
  200–201
Elias, J. S., 145, 146, 193
Elliott, Sydney, 181
Empire free trade campaign, 21, 124
Evening Standard, 19, 38, 103, 110, 122

Fabians, 5, 18, 24; and Fabian Research
  Department, 35–36
Flappers, 15, 126, 130
"Floating voters," 12–13
Fraser, Sir Ian, 170–171
Fyfe, H. Hamilton, 38, 75, 76, 91–92, 94,
  106, 110–111, 131–132

Gallup Polls, 157, 176, 184–185
Games, Abram, 159–163
General strike (1926), 6, 73, 82, 98,
  99–119, 126, 131, 134, 171, 203
Gould, Barbara Ayerton, 172
Gould, Gerald, 72
Grant, Sir Alexander, 61
Greenwood, Arthur, 39, 114, 172, 207
Grey, Lord Edward, 112

Hardie, Keir, 24, 85, 90
Headlam, Sir Cuthbert, 163
Henderson, Arthur, 25, 26, 27, 34, 37, 38,
  39, 54, 87, 92–93, 95, 103, 129, 141
Henderson, Will, 34, 35, 42, 68, 172, 177,
  178
Hicks, George, 197
Housing, 41, 65–66, 126, 162, 166, 174,
  176, 180, 183–184

Independent Labour Party, 24, 27, 72, 89,
  90, 116

Jarrow Hunger March, 150, 195
J. Walter Thompson Ltd., 194
Joynson-Hicks, William, 112, 129

Labour and the Nation (1928), 137
Labour Leader, 24, 102–103
Labour Organiser, 72, 121, 137
Lansbury, George, 24, 25–26, 70, 91, 92,
  151–154

Laski, Harold, 169, 170, 172, 181
Lawrence, Susan, 39
League of Nations Union peace ballot, 147, 156
Left Book Club, 9, 17, 166
Liberal Party, 2, 12, 21, 23, 29, 31, 41, 55, 98, 139, 149, 152, 188; and Labour's strategy toward in 1920s, 75–76; and 1929 general election, 124, 127–128, 129; and 1931 general election, 141; and 1945 general election, 177, 181, 187; and views of the electorate, 83–84, 86; and World War II party politics, 169, 170
Lippmann, Walter, 70–72, 88, 149–150, 186
Lloyd George, David, 21, 22–23, 37, 45, 47, 48, 52, 53, 55, 75, 100, 103, 108, 124, 127–128, 139
Lloyd George, Gwilym, 22
Lloyd's of London Ltd., 53
London County Council, 11, 32, 53, 54–55, 60, 75, 149, 152, 159, 163, 188
London Labour Party, 37, 53, 54, 55, 76, 148, 156–157
London Press Exchange, 158, 163

MacDonald, J. Ramsay, 6, 20, 22, 27, 28–30, 32, 51, 57, 58, 61, 71, 81, 82, 83, 85, 86–87, 89, 104, 107, 113, 114, 118, 125, 127, 129, 138, 139–140, 140–141, 188
Mackay, Ian, 121–122
Maconachie, Sir Richard, 171
Manchester Guardian, 16, 18, 23, 31, 42, 43, 44, 53, 103–104, 108, 109, 141
Marlowe, Thomas, 22, 43
Martin, Kingsley, 64, 70, 109, 116–119
Masterman, C. F. G., 49
Maxton, James, 73
Mellor, William, 106, 132
Middle classes: and consumerism, 14–16; media preferences of, 16–18, 76; and politics, 1, 11–13, 37, 39–41, 44–45, 49, 57, 60, 64, 83, 97, 101, 116, 118, 120, 125, 127–129, 140, 142, 143, 147–148, 157, 164, 173–174, 180, 184, 197, 199, 202
Minority Movement, 25, 89, 110
Morning Post, 18, 19
Morrison, Herbert, 5, 11–14, 25, 28, 32, 64, 80, 89, 93, 122–123, 134, 143, 147–149, 156–157, 159, 163, 173–175, 180–181, 192, 196–197, 202, 204

National Council of Labour, 138, 153, 171, 201
National Government, 139, 140–142, 149, 150, 152, 156
National Unemployed Workers' Movement, 150
New Leader, 116–117
News Chronicle, 20, 22, 122–123, 136, 141, 148–149, 181, 197
New Statesman, 104, 167–168
Newspaper circulations, 13, 18–20, 93–94, 109, 132, 137, 145–146, 181, 189
Newsreels, 17, 47–48, 77, 141, 150, 195–196
Northcliffe, Lord (Alfred Harmsworth), 13, 20–22, 38–39, 52–53, 71, 73, 133

Odhams Press Ltd., 98, 135, 145, 176, 193–194
Orwell, George, 13, 17, 72–73
Osborne judgment (1909), 24–25

Party Election Broadcasts (PEBs), 2, 6, 11–12, 81–82, 124, 129–131, 140–141, 142, 155–157, 178, 181, 184, 196–197
Pethick-Lawrence, Frederick, 24
Political advertising, 7, 32, 40–41, 44–46, 49, 120–121, 158, 163, 169, 178, 195
Poplar Rates Rebellion, 44–45, 66, 76
Posters, 1–4, 28–33, 44–46, 60–62, 74, 125, 130, 131, 156, 158–164, 177, 179–184, 187–189
Priestley, J. B., 15, 166, 196–197
Printers' Unions (National Society of Operative Printers and Assistants & Printing and Kindred Trades Federation), 43, 88, 92, 99, 102–104, 106, 116–119, 153
Pryse, Gerald Spencer, 30–32, 188
Pugh, Arthur, 114, 137

Railway strike (1919), 37–38, 42–49, 55, 65, 66, 73, 77, 100, 103, 115
"Red Scare," 6, 57, 58–67
Ridley, George, 168
Roberts, F. O., 135
Rothermere, Lord (Harold Harmsworth), 21–22, 52–53, 64, 74, 109, 124, 141

Royal Commission on the Press (1947),
    21, 203
Russia. *See* Soviet Union

Samuel, Herbert, 84, 100, 127, 152
Scott, C. P., 53, 104
Shaw, Ernest, 32
Shaw, George Bernard, 41, 85
Shepherd, George, 177
Simon, Sir John, 75, 127, 197
Snowden, Philip, 85, 86, 90, 122, 125, 127,
    129, 152
Socialist League, 132, 142
Society for Socialist Inquiry and Propa-
    ganda, 142
Soviet Union, 37, 39, 52, 56, 57, 58–63,
    131, 148, 180
Star, 19, 24, 55, 76, 103, 123, 149
"Stratified electioneering," 37, 39, 164
Strube, Sidney, 52, 64, 123
Swaffer, Hannen, 147–148

Thomas, J. H., 26, 42–44, 47–48, 85, 89,
    127–128, 135
Thompson, A. M., 44, 51
Times, 16, 18, 19, 32, 41, 44, 47, 48, 53,
    57, 108, 110, 159, 166, 200
Topping, Sir Robert, 171
Tracey, Herbert, 34–36, 72, 121, 195
Triple Alliance, 37, 45, 54
Turner, Ben, 87, 131, 132, 134

Vallance, Aylmer, 149
Verpilleux, Emile, 32

Walker, R. B., 97, 114
Webb, Beatrice, 35, 56, 68, 118
Webb, Sidney, 5, 27, 30, 35–37, 39, 52,
    85, 158
Webbe, Harold, 152
Wells, H. G., 85, 168–169
Wilkinson, Ellen, 5, 73, 77, 118, 119,
    122–123, 149, 150
Williams, Francis, 146, 147
Williams, Robert, 41, 106
Wipers Times, 93
Women voters, 1, 5, 7–8, 12, 15,
    40–41, 57–58, 61, 64, 87, 95, 97,
    125, 126, 129–131, 140, 155–156,
    180, 201
Workers' Film Association, 168, 173
World War I, 4, 24, 37, 39, 86, 93,
    100
World War II, 2, 149, 158, 164, 165–185,
    195, 196–197, 199
Worthington-Evans, Sir Laming, 127

Your Britain (1937), 159–163, 176, 177,
    186, 189, 197, 202

Zec, Philip, 4, 178–183
Zinoviev letter, 22, 57, 58, 63–64. *See also*
    "Red Scare"